About the Authors

ROSEMARY ROGERS lives in Manhattan under the constant protection of Saint Anthony, Saint Bridget, and Saint John-Baptist-Marie Vianney. She has never written a gothic romance novel. She has, however, lived one.

SEAN KELLY left teaching to edit the *National Lampoon*. Going from bad to worse, he now writes books (e.g., *Boom Baby Moon*) and television shows (e.g., *Shining Time Station*). He lives in Brooklyn, New York, a loyal Canadian exile and practicing ex-Catholic.

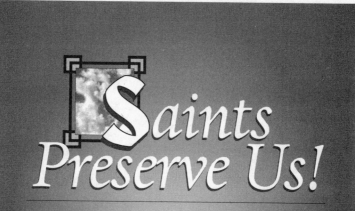

Saints Preserve Us!

Everything You Need to Know
About Every Saint You'll Ever Need

SEAN KELLY
ROSEMARY ROGERS

RANDOM HOUSE
NEW YORK

To the Greater Glory of God

Rory Marchant-Kelly
and
Nell Rogers Michlin

Library of Congress Cataloging-in-Publication Data

Kelly, Sean.
    Saints preserve us! : everything you need to know about every
saint you'll ever need / Sean Kelly and Rosemary Rogers.
      p. cm.
    ISBN 0-679-75038-x
    1. Christian patron saints—Biography—Dictionaries. I. Rogers,
Rosemary. II. Title.
BX4656.5.K45 1993
282'.092'2—dc20
  [B]   93-17367

Design by ROBERT BULL DESIGN

Manufactured in the United States of America on acid-free paper

B987654

Introduction

N O, YOU DON'T HAVE TO be a Catholic—or even Christian—to have Patron Saints. They are like enzymes, gravity, or the CIA—invisible, yes, but eternally present, and hard at work on your behalf, whether or not you know it—or like it. A Holy Host of Heavenly Helpers is at this very moment looking out for you and yours. So take a moment to read about them. You may even end up learning a thing or two about yourself.

Your original Patron Saint is determined, like your astrological sign, by accident of birth. Each and every day of the calendar year is the feast day of several—often many—Saints. (A Saint's designated feast day is almost always the day he or she died, preferably in some unspeakably horrible way, but smiling, and went straight to Heaven.) New Saints are constantly being canonized and old ones deleted, but every Saint who is now or has ever been honored on your birthday has a particular and perpetual interest in your personal welfare.

By Church Law, every child at baptism is "christened," that is, given a Saint's name, a "Christian name" or what we now call a first or given name. This practice long inspired the infants of Christendom to follow the virtuous example of the Saints as they grew up, and it assured at least one Saint's lifelong protection of each new member of the Faith. Even today, unless you were tagged "La Toya" or "Skip," chances are there is someone in Heaven who shares your name, or a variant of it, and by virtue of this, he or she is another of your Patrons. (See Appendix I for a list of today's most popular given names and the feast day of their Name Saints.)

There are Patron Saints who watch over you simply because you are—as all of us proudly or otherwise are—ethnic. The racial or national origin of your ancestors entitles you to the Supernatural Protection of your homeland's designated Patron.

As does your job. Whatever your occupation or profession—housewife, astronaut, student, hairdresser, arms dealer, beggar, or beekeeper—there is an official, Vatican-approved (or unofficial, but tradition-sanctioned) Patron Saint assigned to it.

Almost every physical illness has a Patron Saint—someone who, while on earth, suffered from it, was miraculously cured of it, or died from it (smiling, of course). There are also Saints specializing in every human dilemma, from lost keys to lonely hearts to real estate. You'll find Saints associated with everything from recreational activities to personal crises, from environmental concerns to the family pet.

This book is organized into three sections. The first and most edifying is the alphabetical, biographical list of the Saints themselves. When looking up your original Patron Saint you may be surprised at how similar his, or her, virtuous character—not to mention thrilling life story—is to your own.

Part II is a calendar of Saints assigned to each day of the year. Look up your birthday to locate your original Patron Saint. Not all Saints are Patrons. We have been unable to establish Vatican-confirmed or tradition-sanctioned responsibilities for the Holy Souls commemorated on precisely fifty-two calendar days. We have nevertheless included biographies of these as yet "clientless" (so to speak) Saints. Feel free to implore their powerful intercession in any good cause.

Part III is a group of lists based on ecology, ethnicity, illness, life-style, occupation, personal problems, recreational activity, and much more. Here you may discover the entire Pantheon (so to speak) of Saints who have a particular interest in your well-being.

For the most part, this book consists of unblushing hagiography—the Lives of the Saints. The editors have consulted no end of ancient tomes and pious pamphlets for the facts, as well as ransacking their respective parochial school memories for titillating embellishments. Not all the details of the lives of these Saints—beautiful blonde Italian first-century Virgin Martyrs, astonishingly self-abusive desert anchorites, levitating medieval monks, courageous Crusaders, meek miracle workers, hammers of heretics, visionary spinsters, and learned doctors—can be verified. Some of the details might not be strictly historical, or even . . . believable. But isn't that where *faith* comes in? (And isn't it likely that to the folks who first told and heard these tales, they were no more "realistic"—and no less—than our own formulaic, moralistic, happy-ending television dramas are to us today?)

But *we* haven't made anything up. So help us, Saint Christina the Astonishing.

PART I

Lives
of the
Saints

Abdon—July 30
PATRON OF BARREL MAKERS

He was a Persian cooper, or barrel maker, who, together with his friend Saint Sennen, testified in the year 250 or so his faith in Christ by spitting publicly on pagan idols. They were thrown to the lions and tigers and bears, but the savage creatures declined to harm them, whereupon gladiators hacked them to bits—but "the more their bodies were mangled with wounds, the more were their souls made beautiful by Divine grace."

Acacius—June 22
PATRON INVOKED AGAINST HEADACHES

This utterly fictitious Roman officer was one of 10,000 utterly fictitious soldiers who, after their simultaneous and utterly fictitious conversion en masse to Christianity, were all crucified on the slopes of Mount Ararat in Armenia (which actually exists). Their example of military valor was a particular source of spiritual strength to the Crusaders, but their heavenly help in all medical and spiritual emergencies is still depended upon. Because Acacius was crowned with thorns, he is especially important to those suffering from headache. His crown, and many other relics, are venerated in Cologne, Germany, and Prague, Czechoslovakia.

Adalbert of Prague—April 23
PATRON OF PRUSSIA

Christened Voytech, he assumed the name of an earlier missionary Saint, his mentor Adalbert, and in the 990s entered Prague barefoot in an attempt to Christianize the Czechs. When a spot of trouble arose over a noble adulteress to whom he granted sanctuary—the locals stormed the church and slew her at the altar—he returned to Rome. He eventually managed to achieve martyrdom, being killed as a "Polish spy" in pagan Prussia in 997.

Adam—December 24
PATRON OF GARDENERS

The first man, Adam, lived, of course, in a garden—and when expelled from it was obliged to "earn his bread in the sweat of his face"—hence his Patronage. Because he (and his wife, Eve) repented their sin, both were presumed to be among the Old Testament Saints released from Hell by Christ in the time between His death and Resurrection. Adam's feast day (in the Eastern Church) was celebrated on Christmas Eve. So (in the West) was the feast of any Saint named "Adam"—including the thirteenth-century British bishop who raised the tithes so high (one handful of butter for every ten cows) that his flock burned down his house, with him in it.

Addai and Mari—August 5
PATRONS OF SYRIA AND IRAN

King Abgar the Black of Persia and Jesus Christ were pen pals; in one of his letters, Abgar made mention to Our Lord of an excruciating disease from which he was suffering, and inquired (tactfully) about a possible cure. The compassionate Savior immediately assigned the case to the Apostle Saint Thomas (*whom* SEE), who passed it along to a disciple named Addai. Addai set out at once for Abgar's capital city of Edessa, carrying with him the miraculous (but not, alas, autographed) portrait of Jesus, known today as "The Mandalyion." Upon his arrival, Addai not only cured the king, but converted him and all his subjects to the Faith. Addai then dispatched *his* disciple Mari on a mission down the Tigris River to Nineveh, where he succeeded in destroying numerous pagan temples and erecting monasteries. Like the Nestorian Christians of old, present-day Catholic Chaldeans venerate both these Saints highly.

Adelaide—December 16
EMPRESS

The daughter of King Rudolph of Burgundy, Adelaide was forced by the shockingly degenerate Italian King Hugh to marry his loathsome son, Lothair, at the same ceremony in which he (Hugh) married *her* own widowed mother. This incestuous union happily ended with the death of Lothair (he died raving mad), leaving Adelaide free to marry the recently widowed Otto the Great of Germany. In 962 they were crowned Holy Roman Emperor and Empress by Pope John XII (arguably the worst of all the "Bad Popes"—he bragged of worshipping Satan at the altar and having sexual relations with his own mother). Upon Otto's demise in 973, Adelaide quarreled bitterly with her stepchildren, with her own son, Otto II, with her Greek daughter-in-law, Theophano, and eventually with her grandson, Otto III. Nevertheless, many clergymen spoke highly of her, as she was exceedingly generous to the Church, and even founded a convent.

Adelard—January 2
PATRON OF GARDENERS

Like his cousin Charlemagne, Adelard (aka Adalhard) was a grandson of Charles "Hammer of God" Martel—that is, a member of proto-French royalty. A monk renowned for his learning (he wrote in Latin, French, and German), he was often summoned to court for his advice, and then exiled for the advice he gave. His final exile was to Corbie, in far-off Normandy, where he enthusiastically took up gardening.

Adelelm—January 30
PATRON OF MENSERVANTS

This twelfth-century French nobleman abandoned a distinguished military career for the priesthood. One night on the road to Lyons he was surprised by a sudden tempest. Father Adelelm instructed his manservant to light a candle—and despite the wind and the rain, it remained alight until they found shelter. British hagiographer Sabine Baring-Gould erroneously attributes the origin of the nautical term "Saint Elmo's fire" to this miraculous illumination (SEE Elmo).

Adjutor—April 30
PATRON OF SWIMMERS AND YACHTSMEN; INVOKED BY THOSE IN
DANGER OF DROWNING

In 1095, this noble Norman youth set off for the Holy Land with the First Crusade. Adjutor was captured by the Muslims and imprisoned, but one night Saint Mary Magdalene (*whom* SEE) appeared in his cell, struck off his chains, and transported him home. Back in France, he sprinkled a dangerous whirlpool in the Seine with holy water, rendering it incapable of drowning boaters.

Adrian—September 8
PATRON OF ARMS DEALERS, BUTCHERS, AND PRISON GUARDS

A Roman officer in fourth-century Nicodemia, Adrian was so impressed by the bravery of his Christian captives that he asked to be jailed with them. His wife, Natalia, was delighted, and shaved her head in order to disguise her sex and be able to visit him in prison, where she kissed his chains and urged him to endure martyrdom. When his legs were cut off, she prayed that his hands might be removed as well, as befitted a true Saint. After his death, a miraculous rainstorm extinguished the flames to which his body had been consigned, and Natalia got away with at least one hand—a precious relic. Adrian's sword is still venerated in Walbech, Germany.

Aedh Mac Breic—November 10
PATRON OF HEADACHE SUFFERERS

An illiterate farmer, Aedh was bilked of his inheritance by his brothers. Seeking revenge, the future Saint abducted their maid and headed south. A local bishop, after convincing him to return the girl, said he had learned in a vision that the not-particularly-religious Aedh should start his own monastery. From that time on, many miracles have been attributed to him, including the ability to fly and the restoring of slit throats; but his signature feat was assuming Saint Brigid's chronic headache as his own. When he knew it was time to die, Aedh asked one of his monks to join him, but the selfish man refused. A convenient peasant volunteered instead, and the two lay down on the Saint's bed and died together.

Afra—August 5
PATRONESS OF FALLEN WOMEN

In the early fourth century, at Augsburg, this daughter of Saint Hilaria became a prostitute and a brothel-keeper. During a time of persecution, Saint Narcissus, a fugitive bishop, sought shelter in her establishment. She and all her employees were soon converted to the True Faith, and arrested along with their holy guest. At the trial, Afra cleverly debated the judge (who had once, ironically enough, purchased her favors), but in the end she was burned to death.

Agabus—February 13
PATRON OF FORTUNE-TELLERS

Every trade and craft once had a Patron Saint, including the theologically dubious profession of foretelling the future. According to the Acts of the Apostles (11: 28–29), Agabus was a Jewish convert to Christianity who predicted that a dreadful famine would befall the Roman empire—as it did, in the year 49. He also correctly foretold Saint Paul's capture and imprisonment, and his own martyrdom. Medieval seers and soothsayers invoked Saint Agabus against their inevitable persecution by religious and civil authorities—distress which they (who better?) could foresee.

Agapitus—August 18
PATRON INVOKED AGAINST COLIC

This fifteen-year-old Christian lad was martyred at the Palestrina in 275. He was beaten, jailed, starved, had hot coals dropped on his head, was hung upside down over smoke, and then had boiling water poured on his abdomen (which accounts for the colic connection). When he continued not only to live, but to praise the Lord, the governor, Antiochus, fell off his throne in a fit and died. Emperor Aurelian himself then ordered the faithful and courageous boy decapitated. No fewer than five complete skeletons of this Saint are venerated throughout Italy.

Agatha—February 5
PATRONESS OF MALTA, NURSES, BELL FOUNDERS, BELL RINGERS,
JEWELERS, AND WET NURSES; INVOKED AGAINST BREAST DISEASES,
FIRES, AND VOLCANIC ERUPTIONS

In the year 251, this noble Sicilian virgin rejected the advances of a Roman senator, Quintianus. He spitefully accused her of following Christianity, and ordered her breasts cut off, but through the intercession of Saint Peter, who appeared in her prison cell and applied a "celestial ointment," they were restored. (Agatha is traditionally depicted carrying her severed mammaries on a plate. In the Middle Ages, the faithful mistook these mysterious pictured objects for bells, and named her the patroness of bell founders; or for buns, for which reason loaves are blessed in churches on her feast day.) She next survived, *intacta,* a period of time spent in a house of shame, along with the bawd Aphrodesia and her six shameless daughters. An attempt by the authorities to burn this beautiful maiden at the stake failed (hence she is invoked against fire) when it was interrupted by a volcanic eruption (against which she is similarly petitioned). So they cut off her head.

Agatho—January 10

A married Sicilian and a successful businessman, he became a monk at Palermo and, in 678, the seventy-ninth pope. Elected at the age of 101, this pontiff was the first to propose his own infallibility.

Agnes—January 21

PATRONESS OF VIRGINS AND GIRL SCOUTS

In 304, when she was thirteen years old (says Saint Augustine of Hippo), this beautiful maiden rejected all her ardent Roman suitors, among them Eutropius, the governor's son. Spurning his costly love gifts she declared, "I have chosen a Spouse who cannot be seen with mortal eyes, whose mouth drips with milk and honey." Understandably jealous, her mortal swain waxed ill for love, and his father summoned the maiden before him, offering her honors and estates if she would marry his heathen son, then threatening her knavishly. Agnes was unmoved when exposed to the sight of cruel instruments of torture. "You will soon learn that my God is a God of purity. He will bring your wicked purpose to naught," said she. The governor ordered her stripped naked and led through the streets to be placed in a den of iniquity. Miraculously, her rich golden hair suddenly grew in great profusion and entirely concealed her shame. An angel appeared to her in the brothel, and clothed her in a shining white garment. The only customer bold enough to approach her lewdly was Eutropius himself. He was immediately struck blind or dead (accounts differ), but out of the goodness of her heart, Agnes cured him. This kind deed led her to be charged with witchcraft, and she was sentenced to be burned, stabbed, or beheaded (accounts differ). Says Saint Ambrose (*whom* SEE), who wasn't there, "She went to the place of execution more cheerfully than others go to their weddings." Legend has it that unmarried girls dream of their future husbands on the eve of her feast day if they fast for twenty-four hours and then eat an egg with salt just before bedtime. On the day itself, the pope blesses two lambs in Rome, and sends their wool to his archbishops. ("Agnes" sounds like *"agnus,"* Latin for "lamb," so a lamb is her symbol.)

Agnes of Bohemia—March 2

This nobly born virgin refused two offers of marriage before taking the veil. She was declared a Saint in 1989, a mere 707 years after her death, but just in time to be invoked by Roman Catholics in the nationalist revolt against the godless Communist government of Czechoslovakia.

Agricola of Avignon—September 2

PATRON OF AVIGNON; INVOKED AGAINST RAINSTORMS AND PLAGUES OF STORKS

Agricola's father was Magnus, a senator of Gaul who, upon the death of his wife, became bishop of Avignon. In the year 660 (when he himself was only thirty years of age), Agricola was summoned from a nearby abbey and elected co-bishop of the see; together, they formed one of the few father-and-son team-bishoprics in Church history. Agricola's most celebrated miracle was banishing, by the power of his blessing, an infestation of storks, and since his name means "farmer" in Latin, he takes an ongoing interest in crops and weather.

Agrippina—June 23

PATRONESS INVOKED AGAINST DEMONS, LEPROSY, AND STORMS

This Roman maiden who, in the year 262, was publicly stripped, scourged, and executed by order of the Emperor Valerian, is venerated in both Eastern and Western churches. Her entire body lies in state at Mineo, Sicily, as well as in Constantinople, and works wonders physical, spiritual, and meteorological.

Ailbe—September 12

PATRON OF WOLVES

Ailbe's natural mother was a serving girl and his father an Irish chieftain who was so disgusted by the child's birth that he threw the infant to the wolves. A she-wolf suckled Ailbe until a hunter discovered him in the wolves' den and adopted him. Many years later, after he had become a disciple of Saint Patrick and been made a bishop, Ailbe was tearfully reconciled with his aged foster-parent. Promising "I will protect thee, Old Mother," Ailbe had the wolf spend her last years in his hall. A magnanimous Saint, Ailbe prayed for 100 horses as a gift for King Munster. A cloud arose, from which 100 steeds burst forth. Ailbe persuaded the same king to give the Aran Islands (which the monarch did not know he possessed until he saw them in a dream) to Saint Enda (*whom* SEE).

Alban—June 21
PATRON OF REFUGEES

Britain's first martyr, Alban was a Roman soldier beheaded in 305 for harboring—and then impersonating—a fugitive priest. At his execution, he asked for water, and, when refused, caused a miraculous fountain to appear. Upon his death, the headsman's eyes popped out. The Anglican Church celebrates his feast five days early, due to a mistaken reading of the Roman numerals on his tomb, at the Roman town of Verulam, which became the English cathedral city of St. Albans. He is traditionally depicted with his head in a holly bush.

Albert of Trapani—August 7
PATRON INVOKED AGAINST EARTHQUAKES, JAUNDICE, AND STIFF NECKS

Like most Saints venerated in earthquake-prone Sicily, Albert is invoked for protection against such disasters; his selfless nursing of plague victims also entitles him to be appealed to by sufferers from many physical ailments. He was a Carmelite friar at Messina, famous for his knack of refuting Jews in debate, as well as for the excessive severity of his self-discipline. It was widely believed that, through his prayers, a blockade of the city by the warlike king of Naples was miraculously lifted in 1305.

Albert the Great—November 14
PATRON OF MEDICAL TECHNOLOGISTS, SCIENCE STUDENTS, AND
SCIENTISTS

After he entered the Dominican Order, Albert's German military family tried to have him kidnapped, but he prevailed and soon distinguished himself as a scientist. He resigned his post as bishop, disliking administration, and devoted himself to teaching and studying the natural sciences—as well as philosophy and metaphysics. Although his volumes on astronomy, chemistry, and geography (tracing the mountain ranges of Europe) were centuries ahead of his time, he failed to grasp some of the basics of biology. He maintained that frequent intercourse (an act, he pointed out, man "shared with beasts") could lead to sickness, body odor, baldness, and could cause one's brain to shrink to the size of a pomegranate. Along with his pupil Thomas Aquinas (*whom* SEE), Albert held the controversial notion that the teachings of Aristotle could be integrated into Christian theology. He carried out experiments in his lab and collected plants, insects, and chemical compounds; he was even called upon to design the new cathedral in Cologne. He was scientific in his misogyny as well, calling women "misbegotten men" and explaining that the females of the species are less moral, since they "contain more liquid," and liquid will "take things up easily and hold on to them poorly." His liquid theory may explain his supposition that women ejaculated semen during intercourse. He traveled all over Europe wearing clogs—thus was called "clodhopper." His memory failed him when he was giving a lecture (a prediction that the Blessed Virgin had made when She visited him years earlier) and he died soon after. Albert was suspect in many Church quarters—some viewed him as a wizard and magician—but evaded the Inquisition because he was a Dominican, and the Dominicans themselves headed the Inquisition. But he wasn't canonized or made a Doctor of the Church until 1931, almost 700 years after his death; in 1941, Pope Pius XII declared "Albertus Magnus" to be the Patron of scientists.

Albinus of Mainz—June 21
PATRON INVOKED AGAINST GALLSTONES, KIDNEY DISEASE, AND SORE THROATS

An orthodox priest in fifth-century Albania, Albinus fled to Milan when his homeland was overrun by Arian heretics. Saint Ambrose (*whom* SEE) liked the cut of his jib, made him a bishop, and sent him into the wilds of Gaul to preach to the barbarians. He was beheaded by Vandals at Mogontiacum on the Rhine, which later became the city of Mainz.

Aldegund—January 30
PATRON INVOKED AGAINST CANCER, CHILDHOOD ILLNESSES, EYE DISEASE, FEVER, WOUNDS, AND SUDDEN DEATH

The tale of this daughter of Frankish nobility, who was born in 630 in Hainaut, reads like a miraculous version of "Snow White." Her parents, Walbert and Bertilia, were Saints, as was her sister Waudru, but Aldegund's wicked stepmother wanted this dedicated virgin to marry. The maiden escaped to the woods (crossing a raging river dry-shod), where she was granted the gift of invisibility whenever her stepmother or jilted fiancé came to harm her. In true Disney style, her pet, a fish, was once attacked by a naughty raven—but defended by a fierce lamb. Aldegund settled in a hermitage at Maubeuge, in the wilds of Flanders, which afterward became a Benedictine convent. She died there in 684, of a slow and painful cancer.

Aldric—January 7
PATRON INVOKED AGAINST ASTHMA

This Saint (sometimes known as Elric) was, in his youth, a member of Charlemagne's imperial court, and, being a diplomatic and skilled statesman, attained the bishopric of Le Mans. He served as "guide of conscience" to Charlemagne's successor Louis the Pious, and in 853 upheld the imperial claims of Charles the Bald. The documents supporting some of Aldric's personal territorial claims proved, even in his lifetime, to be forgeries; and Our Saint has lately been accused of having concocted that scandalously fraudulent document, "The Donation of Constantine." The connection, if any, between his counterfeiting career and his heavenly concern for asthma sufferers is unknown.

Alena—June 18
PATRONESS INVOKED AGAINST EYE DISEASE AND TOOTHACHE

The daughter of pagan parents, this maid of Vorst, Brussels (*circa* 640) heard her father tell of a Christian priest he had seen in a rude chapel in the neighboring woods. Little Alena secretly sought out this man of God, and was baptized by him. Thereafter, it was her wont to daily steal away from home to attend Matins, Mass, and Vespers. Her father, suspecting the worst, had the child followed by a band of ruffians, who, in their attempt to detain the girl, slew her. The priest heard the Virgin Martyr's cries but arrived too late to save her mortal life. A large and locally venerated nut tree grew from the spot in which he buried her.

Alexander the Charcoal Burner—August 11
PATRON OF CHARCOAL BURNERS

When Saint Gregory the Wonderworker (*whom* SEE) was in Asia Minor, searching at length and in vain for a candidate worthy to serve as bishop, some wag sarcastically suggested appointing Alexander, a grimy and ragged local character who turned out to be both holy and wise. Alexander was martyred in the year 275, dying—ironically enough—by fire.

Alexis—July 17
PATRON OF BEGGARS

A rich but chaste fifth-century Roman, Alexis married, but on his wedding night escaped to a distant country disguised as a beggar. Years later, on the advice of a talking statue of the Blessed Virgin, he returned, still in disguise, and suffered many indignities from his parents and their servants. Just before he died he revealed all, and enjoyed a splendid funeral.

Alice—June 15

This maid of Brussels joyfully joined a Cistercian nunnery when very young, but was soon afflicted with leprosy. Segregated from her companions, she met, in her solitary cell, Jesus Himself. Her greatest sorrow was that she could not, perforce, drink from the communal Communion chalice, although "she craved the blood with a burning desire," as her biographer, another nun, put it. Although her disease first blinded and later paralyzed her, she was consoled by visits from her Guardian Angel, and offered up her sufferings for the souls in Purgatory. She died in the year 1250.

Alkelda—March 27
PATRON INVOKED AGAINST EYE TROUBLES

In or about the year 800, this Anglo-Saxon princess was martyred—strangled by a pair of Danish women. A church dedicated to her memory still stands in the quaint English village in the Midlands that revels in the euphonious name of Giggleswick. Near the church is a holy well, in whose waters the Faithful bathe their aching eyes.

Allan—January 12

Allan, aka Elian, a Cornish or English monk of the early sixth century, is sometimes (quite improperly) confused with Saint Hilary of Tours. "Allan's Well" can be found in western England, in Denbighshire, where (for a price) the Faithful write their enemies' names on pebbles and drop the stones into the water. The Saint then visits these unfortunates with cramps or ague. This well is the opposite of a wishing well—it is a cursing well.

All Souls—November 2

All Souls is the Day of the Dead, when Catholics the world over remember and pray for the Souls of Faithful Departed who are neither in Heaven or in Hell, but atoning for their sins in the fires of Purgatory. For instance, the departed sister of Saint Peter Damian (*whom* SEE) was once beheld in a vision suffering unspeakable agonies for the "venial sin" of having enjoyed listening to a ribald song. A tenth-century French pilgrim to the Holy Land chanced upon an opening in the earth through which the howls and moans of Souls could be heard. He told Abbot Odo of Cluny (*whom* SEE) about it, and that good man immediately instituted (in the year 998) the Feast of All Souls.

Aloysius Gonzaga—June 21
PATRON OF YOUTH

A noble lad of Venice, his father wished Aloysius to be a soldier, but the boy had a tendency to faint when he heard vulgar talk. Sent to serve in the luxurious court of Philip II of Spain, he put chunks of wood in his bed at night to ward off temptations of the flesh. He was especially wary of females, and would never be alone in a room with one—not even his mother. (He claimed never to have looked a woman in the face.) He enjoyed mortifications of all sorts, including carrying out the slops of total strangers. When climbing or descending stairs, he said a "Hail Mary" at every step, which slowed him down somewhat. When his father caught his seventeen-year-old son and heir flogging himself in his room, he permitted the boy to join the newly founded Jesuit Order. But Aloysius died before his priestly ordination, of a plague he contracted while nursing the sick. Aloysius is one of the pathologically priggish "Boy Saints" held up as role models by generations of Jesuits to their adolescent students. The fey teddy bear featured in Waugh's *Brideshead Revisited* was doubtless named in his honor.

Alphonsus Mary de' Liguori—August 1
PATRON OF CONFESSORS AND MORAL THEOLOGIANS

Born in Naples in 1696, Alphonsus became a successful lawyer at the age of sixteen, but, upon losing his first case, became a priest, and in 1732 founded the missionary Redemptorist Order. His life's work, *Theologae moralis* (reissued seventy times), firmly "established sexual ethics as a specialized science for celibate experts," as Uta Ranke-

Heinemann nicely puts it in her book *Eunuchs for the Kingdom of Heaven*. In his extremely detailed handbooks for confessors, Alphonsus took a moderate position between the extremes of "all sex is evil" and "some sex is good." He concluded that *almost* all sex is evil. He considered marital intercourse and unmarried hand-holding to be only venial sins, provided no pleasure was taken or given.

Amalburga—January 8
PATRONESS INVOKED AGAINST BRUISES

Charles the Great (Charlemagne), the Holy Roman Emperor (742–814), although he was a married man, took a shine to this virtuous and beautiful German maiden. Amalburga naturally spurned his untoward advances and, when he persisted, cut off her magnificent locks and left town. The lust-crazed tyrant followed her, found her in a church, and brutally laid hands upon her, causing the bruises against which she is now invoked. Once more she escaped, crossing the river Scheld on the back of a large and accommodating sturgeon. She died a maiden. Among her domestic skills was the ability to carry water in a sieve.

Amand of Maastricht—February 6
PATRON OF BEER AND WINE SELLERS AND OF HOTEL WORKERS

A wandering bishop, Amand preached the Gospel with great zeal but mixed success to the Danubian Slavs, the Franks, and the people of Flanders. He founded a religious house at Ghent, where he died, aged ninety, in 679. His Patronage of bartenders and innkeepers is traditional; perhaps it reflects his mortal reputation for hospitality.

Ambrose—December 7
PATRON OF BEEKEEPERS, GEESE, AND ORATORS

A swarm of bees settled in Ambrose's mouth when he was in his cradle, foreshadowing his oratorical gifts. Ambrose was a lawyer in

Milan who had not yet been baptized when, inspired by the miraculous shouts of a child in the crowd, the people of the city made him their bishop in the year 270. He insisted that the Church take precedence over the State, declaring, "An Emperor is within the Church; he is not above it," and strongly rebuked the Emperor Theodosius for being insufficiently anti-Semitic in judging a case of synagogue-burning. His many "bewitching" sermons are filled with theologically dubious Neoplatonism, yet he preached mightily and successfully against the Arian heresy. Having been raised by his mother and his aunt (a nun), Ambrose was a fierce advocate of celibacy—he is frequently depicted wielding the scourge with which he had his rival Jovian flogged for daring to suggest that marriage was no less pleasing to God than virginity.

Americus—November 4
PATRON OF AMERICA

Americus was groomed by family and clergy to take over the crown from his father and fellow Saint, King Stephen of Hungary (*whom* SEE). The finishing touches had just been made to Americus's coronation robes when news reached King Stephen that his son had been killed in a hunting accident. The father never recovered from his son's death; the two were buried together and, soon after, canonized together. Miracles are said to occur at their tomb. The navigator and mapmaker Amerigo Vespucci was named after this Saint, as, in turn, was the New World.

Andeol—October 15
PATRON OF SWITZERLAND

In the year 318, Saint Justus, bishop of Lyons, fled France (then known as Gaul) for Egypt, where he became a desert monk. His deacon, Andeol, was sent to fetch back the beloved bishop, but found him unshakable in his resolve, and was obliged to return without him; whereupon Andeol was made bishop in Justus's stead. What this all has to do with Switzerland is anybody's guess.

Andrew—November 30

PATRON OF FISHERMEN, GREECE, RUSSIA, SCOTLAND, SAILORS, AND
SPINSTERS; INVOKED AGAINST GOUT AND NECK PROBLEMS

Andrew was a fisherman who followed John the Baptist. When he met Jesus, Andrew left John to become His disciple. He enlisted his brother Peter, and Jesus soon offered to make them both "fishers of men." Andrew was present at the wedding in Cana, and in Jerusalem for the Passion and the Crucifixion. He is mistakenly believed to have founded the Greek Orthodox Church, and is a Patron Saint of Russia—a country he never visited. Andrew did, however, spend time in a kingdom ruled over and inhabited by cannibals, where he freed prisoners intended for the king's supper. He once came to the defense of a man whose lecherous mother had unjustly accused him of incest; Andrew produced claps of thunder, which caused the earth to shake and the evil mother to drop dead.

Andrew was put to death for baptizing Maximilla, the wife of Egaes (the Roman governor of Patras in Achaia); the heathen administrator blamed the Apostle for the fact that his now-Christian wife would no longer sleep with him. (Curiously, Andrew became the object of a spinster cult. Luther describes certain German maidens stripping naked on Andrew's feast day, a performance guaranteed to provide them with visions of their future husbands; in Poland even

today, on Saint Andrew's Eve, girls still hold black cats over fires in hopes that this bizarre rite will give them magical glimpses of their future swains.)

Long after Andrew's death at Patras—he was crucified on an X-shaped cross—an angel told Saint Rule to take some of Andrew's relics "to the ends of the earth." Rule, accompanied by Saint Theneva (*whom* SEE), traveled to Scotland, where they were joined by (a miraculously revived) Andrew and together built St. Andrew's Church. This marked the beginning of the Saint's flourishing cult in the West: he became the subject of several early poems and even had a golf course named after him. His bones (in Amalfi, Italy) have for fourteen centuries been producing that mysterious oil known as manna (not the desert food that appeared in the Bible), which at times is so abundant that it trickles from his tomb down the aisle of the church (unless it is in powder form, which it sometimes is). This remarkable phenomenon usually occurs on January 26, 28, and on the Saint's feast day, November 30.

Crusaders stole Andrew's head from Constantinople, where it had been brought by Constantine, and gave it to the pope. It wasn't returned until Pope Paul VI sent it back to its hometown in 1972. Saint Andrew's symbol is the X-shaped cross on which he met his death: it is depicted on the flag of Scotland.

Andrew Avellino—November 10

PATRON OF SICILY; INVOKED AGAINST APOPLEXY AND SUDDEN DEATH

Andrew Avellino's mother called her handsome son Lancelot ("Lancellotto"), and like his namesake, he fought to remain pure despite numerous female advances. On vacation from school, he recoiled from the effusive welcome of his former nanny and rushed to become a priest, practicing ecclesiastical law on the side. His first assignment in the clergy was to close a convent its nuns had turned into a brothel. His efforts upset the busy ex-nuns as well as their clients, one of whom attacked Andrew with a sword. The Saint abandoned the practice of law when, after telling a fib in court, his Bible ominously fell open to the words "The lying mouth kills the soul." He joined Saint Charles Borromeo (*whom* SEE) in reforming Milan, even inducing ladies of the nobility to enter a convent. Andrew is the Patron Saint invoked against sudden death because he himself was struck down by apoplexy in the middle of saying Mass. Even as it lay in state, his body remained healthy and rosy-cheeked. His followers, snipping off locks of hair as relics, eventually became more impassioned and made nicks in his flesh, which started to bleed spontaneously—the kind of "blood miracle" that flourished in the region. Certain latter-day historians believe that Andrew, supposedly dead and lying in state, was actually catatonic and was in fact buried alive.

Andrew Bobola—May 21

A young Polish Jesuit, Andrew Bobola was tortured to death by savage Cossacks near Pinsk in 1657. When he continued to cry out the names of Jesus and Mary, they extracted his tongue through the back of his head.

Andrew Corsini—February 4

PATRON INVOKED AGAINST SUDDEN DEATH AND QUARRELS

Before *this* Andrew was born, in Florence in 1302, his mother dreamed she gave birth to a wolf that turned into a lamb when it entered a Carmelite church. Sure enough, after a violent, dissolute youth, Andrew joined the peaceful Carmelites and even became a bishop. He is depicted in art with a wolf and a lamb at his feet.

Andronicus—October 9

PATRON OF SILVERSMITHS

Andronicus's traditional Patronage of the craft derives, reasonably enough, from the fact that this Saint was himself a silversmith, who practiced his trade in Antioch. He was for many years happily married to a woman named Athanasia, but, devastated by the sudden deaths of their two beloved children, the couple resolved to separate and become desert hermits. Years later, Andronicus happened to meet upon the road a beardless monk called Athanasius. The two became fast friends, and lived contentedly in neighboring hovels, fasting and praying together, until Athanasius died, leaving behind a note for Andronicus, revealing in it a secret which you, dear reader, surely have already guessed.

Angela Merici—January 27

Certain traditional aspects of Catholic life, assumed to be universal and eternal, are, in fact, recent innovations. Bingo was not invented until 1778. And there was not a single order of schoolteaching nuns until 1535. On November 25 of that year, in Brescia, Italy—in the church of St. Afra (*whom* SEE)—Angela Merici gathered twenty-eight stereotypically strict-but-fair women together, and named the company "the Ursulines," in honor of the great Saint Ursula (*whom* SEE). The rest is not only history, but quite a lot of catechism, as well.

Anne—July 26

PATRONESS OF CANADA, HOUSEWIVES, GRANDMOTHERS, AND
CABINETMAKERS

The mother of Mary and the
grandmother of Jesus, Anne somehow contrived to conceive her
daughter "immaculately," that is,
without the "original sin" nor-
mally transmitted by the act of sexual intercourse. In the fifteenth
century, she appeared to Saint Co-
lette in a vision, and confirmed the
old rumors that she had been married three times. In Brittany, it is
widely believed that Anne was a
princess of that country who emi-
grated (in a "ship of light" piloted
by an Angel) to Judaea. In her old
age, she returned to France with
her Grandson, where He person-
ally created the fountain at Sainte-Anne-de-la-Palude. Saint Anne's
entire head, a precious relic, is displayed and venerated (simultaneously) at Lyons, Apt, Aix-la-Chapelle, and Chartres in France; in
Bologna; in Sicily; and in Duren, Germany. Martin Luther's decision
to become a priest was triggered by a thunderstorm during which he
prayed to Saint Anne for protection.

Anskar—February 3

PATRON OF DENMARK, ICELAND, AND NORWAY

"The Apostle of the North" was continually dispatched (over a
thirty-year period, 826–54) by Pope Gregory IV, King Louis the Pious
of the Franks, and King Louis the German to baptize and civilize the
savage Scandinavians, whose Viking raids were an ongoing irritant to
Christendom. He eventually succeeded in converting the kings of
Sweden and Denmark, but upon his death Sweden immediately
relapsed into its barbaric heathen condition.

Ansovinus—March 13

PATRON OF HARVESTS

This ninth-century Italian bishop worked many wonders—in

times of famine, for instance, the granaries he opened to the poor supernaturally refilled themselves (which accounts for his traditional patronage of harvests). But Ansovinus performed his most celebrated miracle in a tavern. While on the road from their native Camerino, Umbria, to Rome, he and his companions stopped at an inn at Narni, and ordered some wine. The surly innkeeper served them a bottle of the local vintage that had obviously been watered down to a criminal degree. Nor would he provide the company with cups to drink it from, saying his customers were expected to bring their own. The wily bishop removed his cloak and instructed the insolent publican to pour the wine into the garment's hood. When he did, the water drained out, leaving pure wine for the merry company to consume with undiluted pleasure.

Anthony Claret—October 24

PATRON OF SAVINGS BANKS AND WEAVERS

Anthony was the son of a weaver, who followed his father's trade before becoming a priest and founder of the Spanish missionary Claretian Order. A man of considerable energy and learning, he

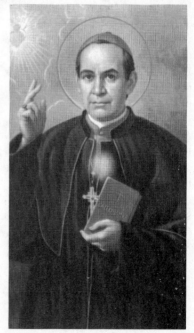

preached 25,000 sermons and published 200 books. In 1850 he was appointed archbishop of Santiago, Cuba. Among his tireless labors for the poor of Santiago was the founding of savings banks for their use. In 1856, Claret reformed the mistress of a local thug, for which he was nearly assassinated. Upon his return to Spain he became rector of the Escorial, where he encouraged the study of natural science. Nevertheless, astonishing supernatural powers were attributed to this sensible man, so that he was popularly identified with reaction and royalism, and as a result was sent into exile during the Spanish revolution of 1868.

Anthony the Great—January 17

PATRON OF BASKET WEAVERS, BRUSH MAKERS, BUTCHERS, DOMESTIC
ANIMALS, GRAVE DIGGERS, SWINE; INVOKED AGAINST ECZEMA AND
"SAINT ANTHONY'S FIRE," *I.E.*, ERGOTISM

Despite a life of relentless privation, starvation, and exposure to
the elements, Anthony was 105 years old when he died in 356. Cer-

tain that the world was about to end, young Anthony left Memphis, Egypt, for the desert, determined to lead a life of unbridled sanctity. He spent twenty years living in a tomb, doing loud and constant battle with the Devil, who assaulted him in terrifying forms that included a beautiful naked woman and a Negro. He emerged convinced that there was someone out there in the desert even holier than he, and sought out the amazingly holy Paul the Hermit (*whom* SEE). Anthony's disciple and biographer Athanasius writes of Our Saint, "He always fasted, his outer garment was a sackcloth and his inner garment a hair shirt. He never washed his body or his feet. . . ." Naturally, he attracted a crowd of admirers who wanted to be just like him—they became the first Christian monks. They sat in caves and lean-tos in the desert, and tried not to eat, sleep, or entertain impure thoughts. At Anthony's recommendation, they all took up mat-weaving and brush-making—he, if anyone, knew what kind of work the Devil finds for idle hands. In Christian iconography, Anthony is portrayed with a bell and a pig. The smallest pig of the litter and the smallest bell in a carillon are called "tantony" in his honor.

Antony of Padua—June 13
PATRON OF HARVESTS, PORTUGAL, THE POOR, SPINSTERS; INVOKED
AGAINST INFERTILITY AND BY THOSE LOOKING FOR LOST OBJECTS

We are told that "severe temptations against purity afflicted Antony during his teens" (when his name was Ferdinand and he lived in Lisbon), but he overcame them with prayer and joined the Augustinian Order. In 1219, he changed habits, becoming a Franciscan in order to travel to Africa and be martyred by savage Moors. He adopted the name of Antony, but ill health forced him to abandon his mission to the Muslims. When he attempted to sail home, a providential storm blew his ship off course, landing him in Sicily. There he met with Saint Francis of Assisi himself, who commanded him to go forth and preach against the heretics. Antony was some preacher. In Rimini, when the unbelievers refused to hear him, he went to the riverbank and preached to the fishes, who stood on their tails in the water and listened. (When his remains were unearthed in Padua long after his death, the flesh had decomposed, except for the tongue, which was "fresh and red.") A novice who borrowed Antony's prayer book without permission hastily returned it after suffering "a fearful apparition"—hence the Saint's association with the recovery of lost articles. Like all Franciscans, Antony was devoted to those in need. On his feast day, charitable donations are left before images of the Saint, folding money is often pinned to stoles draped around his statues' necks, and loaves of "Saint Antony's bread" are distributed to the poor. Although he was nicknamed in his lifetime "the hammer of heretics," his emblem is a lily.

Apollonia—February 9
PATRONESS OF DENTISTS; INVOKED AGAINST TOOTHACHE

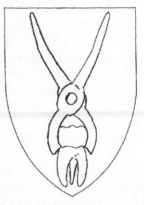

A spinster in third-century Alexandria, Apollonia's home was a refuge for Christians. She was attacked by a pagan mob, and, in the course of her martyrdom, broke—or extracted—her teeth. Her emblem is a tooth gripped by forceps. Rather than deny her faith, she leapt into a fire—Saint Augustine goes to considerable lengths to prove that this was not a suicide. The teeth and/or jaws of this holy woman can be found in Antwerp, Brussels, Naples, Liège, and Cologne.

Armel—August 16
PATRON INVOKED AGAINST FEVER, HEADACHE, GOUT, AND
RHEUMATISM

The northeast coast of France is, to this day, called Brittany because of the many saintly Celtic-British monks who migrated there at the time of the Anglo-Saxon invasion of their homeland. Armel, a cousin of Samson of Dol (*whom* SEE), was among them; he was famous as a dragon-tamer and worker of miraculous cures, for which

reason many French hospitals are named in his honor. In 1485 (933 years after Armel's death), Henry Tudor (soon to be King Henry VII) launched an invasion of England *from* Brittany, and claimed to have been saved from shipwreck through this Saint's Divine intercession.

Arnulf of Metz—July 18

PATRON OF MUSIC AND MILLERS; INVOKED FOR HELP IN FINDING LOST
ARTICLES

Arnulf (in English, Arnold) was a Frankish soldier and statesman, a
friend and advisor to King Dagobert. One day, on a whim, he threw a
ring into a river. On the day he was proclaimed bishop of Metz; a fish
was served to him—and inside it was that very ring! He had two sons,
one of whom succeeded him as bishop of Metz; the other became the
grandfather of Charlemagne. A drunken lout named Noddo once
publicly called into doubt Our Saint's chastity, slandering him as "full
lusty and ready to all delices." That night in bed, Noddo's pants
caught fire.

Arnulph of Soissons—August 15

PATRON OF BAKERS

This later Arnulf, who died in 1087, was likewise a French soldier
turned clergyman. He unwillingly accepted the position of abbot of
his monastery, and even more reluctantly became the bishop of Soissons. Driven from his episcopate by invaders, he moved to Flanders.
In art, Our Saint is always depicted holding what
appears to be a long-handled, flat baker's
shovel, which accounts for his traditional Patronage of bakers.

Athanasius the Athonite—July 5

Founder of the famous Greek monastary on Mount Athos, he died
in 963 in the collapse of a building he was dedicating.

Athanasius the Fuller—September 6

PATRON OF FULLERS

Fullers were craftsmen who soaked and pressed newly woven and
bulky wool into fine cloth. Athanasius, a nobleman of first- or second-
century Aquila, took literally Saint Paul's epistolary admonition to
the Thessalonians to "work with your own hands" and journeyed to
Dalmatia to labor at the fullers' trade. In a time of persecution, he

boldly inscribed a cross on his front door and was cast into the sea with a millstone around his neck.

Audrey—June 23
PATRONESS INVOKED AGAINST NECK AND THROAT DISEASES

Once upon a time (*circa* 640) there was an English princess named Ethelreda, but everyone knew her as Audrey. Because she was as chaste as she was beautiful, she was (understandably) ever so slightly vain. Although she had sworn a vow of perpetual virginity, she consented, for reasons of state, to marry a (fifteen-year-old) neighboring prince. In time, her husband began pestering Audrey; he even attempted to bribe the holy local bishop, Saint Wilfrid of York (*whom* SEE), to release his wife from her sacred vows. But Wilfrid would have none of that, and with his aid, Audrey fled the palace of her lustful consort. The passionate prince pursued her south, to the sea, as far as a promontory now known as Colbert's Head, where a heaven-sent seven-day high tide intervened between the frustrated husband and unwilling wife. (Saint Audrey's footprints may be seen there to this day, pressed adamantly into the rock.) In the end, the prince gave up, returned home, and remarried. Audrey took the veil, and founded the great abbey of Ely, where she lived a life of unbridled austerity until she died of an enormous and unsightly tumor on her neck— which she gratefully accepted as Divine retribution for the jeweled necklaces she had worn in her youth. (Seventeen years after her burial, Saint Wilfrid exhumed her body. It had not decayed, but the tumor on her throat had disappeared.) Throughout the Middle Ages, a festival, "Saint Audrey's Fair," was held at Ely on her feast day, at which the exceptional shoddiness of the merchandise—especially the neckerchiefs—contributed to the English language the word "tawdry," a corruption of "Saint Audrey."

Augustine (or Austin) of Canterbury—May 27
PATRON OF ENGLAND

A Benedictine bishop sent from Rome in 597 by Gregory the Great (*whom* SEE) to convert and civilize the Anglo-Saxons of England, this tedious prig is sometimes confused with his more famous namesake below. When he preached in Dorset, the local fisherfolk mocked him by pinning fishtails to the back of his robe—which explains why the people of Dorset are, to this day, born with tails.

Augustine of Hippo—August 28
PATRON OF BREWERS AND PRINTERS

It would be difficult to overstate Augustine of Hippo's role in shaping our Christian way of life; it is to his wisdom that every pope still defers when making pronouncements about birth control, and it was from his philosophy that John Calvin learned the awful truth of predestination. Augustine was born rather far inland in North Africa—his race remains a subject of speculation. In his famous *Confessions* he claims to have been a naughty young man. "Like water I boiled over, heated by my fornications" is the picturesque way he put it. With his mistress and their son, he joined a local mumbo-jumbo sect, the Manichaeans, much to the dismay of his relentlessly pious mother, Saint Monica (*whom* SEE). After moving to Milan, he was converted to the True Faith by her tearful entreaties and the sermons of Saint Ambrose (*whom* SEE). He returned to Africa as bishop of Hippo, and devoted the rest of his life to writing hundreds of books proving that all the unbaptized—including infants—go straight to Hell for eternity, and that, furthermore, the God of Love had, for all eternity, planned that they do so. He was also the first to make the all-important connection between the "original sin" of Adam and Eve, and sexual pleasure, which, he argued, was how it was passed along. Like herpes. Among his important notions was that before "the fall," in Paradise, the sexual organs were completely subject to their owners' willpower. He cites, as examples of this sort of "mind over matter" control, some people's ability to wiggle their ears, or to fart musically. The city of Saint Augustine, Florida (the oldest city in America), was named in his honor, for it was on his feast day that the Spanish first landed there, in 1565.

Ava—May 6
PATRONESS OF CHILDREN LEARNING TO WALK

In Brittany, the home of her cult, Ava (or Avoy) is held to have been the only maiden spared of all the 11,000 companions of Saint Ursula (*whom* SEE). Imprisoned by the savage Huns, she was daily fed dainty buns (through the bars of her cell) by the Virgin Mary in person. Exposed to several lions (the Huns traveled with them as mascots) she remained unscathed, so the heathens put her to the sword. Her horribly mutilated body sailed to sea in a stone boat, which washed ashore near the town of Avray; today, toddlers are dipped in this boat to help them develop strong little legs.

Avertin—May 5

PATRON INVOKED AGAINST DIZZINESS

Avertin is an utterly mythical, totally fictitious character. A church is dedicated to him in Tours, France.

Aya—April 18

PATRONESS OF LAWSUITS

This wealthy Belgian widow of the seventh century, before her demise, bequeathed all her wealth and property to a convent at Mons. When her heirs contested the will, Aya testified against them "in a hollow voice" from her tomb. Case dismissed.

Balbina—March 31
PATRONESS INVOKED AGAINST SCROFULA

According to the totally bogus *Acts* of Pope Alexander, Balbina was a noble Roman virgin baptized by His Holiness and soon thereafter martyred. There is a Balbina cemetery in Rome, on the Appian Way, which perhaps accounts for her invention.

Baldus—October 29
PATRON OF CATTLE AND OF PEACE IN THE FAMILY; INVOKED AGAINST COLIC AND GOUT

As a youth, this Spaniard, known to the English as "Saint Bond," murdered his parents by accident. Striken with guilt, he took to the roads, wandering as far as Jerusalem and Rome before arriving in Sens, France. There he confessed his sin to Bishop (and Saint) Artemis, who planted his staff in the ground and commanded Baldus to water it daily. After many years, the staff burst into bloom, signifying the parricide's forgiveness. A similar tale concerning the German folk-hero Tannhäuser provided Wagner with the climactic scene of a long, loud opera.

Balthazar, Caspar, and Melchior—January 6
PATRONS OF TRAVELERS

On the day variously called the Epiphany, Little Christmas, and Twelfth Night, we honor this trio of travelers from the East, variously known as the Three Kings, the Wise Men, and the Magi, who followed the Star to Bethlehem.

Barbara—December 4
PATRONESS OF ARCHITECTS, ARTILLERY, FIRE FIGHTERS, FIREWORKS MAKERS, MINERS, SAILORS; INVOKED AGAINST EXPLOSIONS, FIRE, LIGHTNING, AND SUDDEN DEATH

Dioscurus of Heliopolis was a jealous father. He hid his beautiful daughter Barbara away in a tower, so that no man should see her great beauty. But a Christian, disguised as a physician, gained access to her, and instructed her in the Faith. While Dioscorus was away on business, he commanded that an elaborate bathroom (or swimming pool) be constructed in, or near, his daughter's tower. Because of Barbara's holiness, its waters instantly acquired miraculous curative powers. The maiden then asked the reluctant construction workers to add a third window to her tower, in honor of the Blessed Trinity—which they did. At the sight of this third window, the newly returned Dioscurus suspected the worst. He drew his sword to slay his child, but she leapt out the new window and flew away to a cave in the mountains. An evil shepherd disclosed her refuge to Dioscurus (Our Saint cursed the shepherd, turning his sheep to locusts and him to stone), and the criminal parent dragged his daughter by the hair into the custody of civil authorities. She would not renounce her Faith, although she was stripped and flogged, then hung between trees "that they should break her reins with staves and burn her sides with burning lamps . . . and hurted her head with a mallet . . . and cut off her paps." Finally Dioscurus took matters into his own hands, led his difficult daughter up a mountain, and there cut off her head. A mighty clap of thunder was then heard, and a "fire from Heaven" struck Dioscurus, reducing him to ashes. All who handle explosives—miners and gunners and so on—are in Saint Barbara's care. (The French call a powder magazine *"une Sainte-Barbe."*) Her Patronage of sailors inspired Spanish mariners to name the difficult straits off the California coast Santa Barbara.

Barnabus—June 11
PATRON OF CYPRUS AND HARVESTS

Before the calendar was reformed, June 11, the feast of Saint Barnabus, was the year's longest, sunniest day—hence the folk expression for good weather, "Barnaby bright." The Saint is sometimes pictured holding a hay rake. The historical (that is to say, scriptural) Barnabus was a Cypriot Jew, the disciple who introduced the newly converted Saint Paul (*whom* SEE) to the Apostles. He invariably took Paul's side in his quarrels with Peter—the thanks he got was Paul's turning bitterly against *him*. He was stoned to death in Salamis. Holy relics (in the form of pieces of his skull) are venerated in churches in Prague and Cremona. Possession of his entire head is claimed by Genoa, Toulouse, Naples, Bergamo, and Bavaria.

Bartholomew—August 24
PATRON OF ARMENIA, CHEESE MERCHANTS, TANNERS, PLASTERERS;
INVOKED AGAINST NERVOUS TICS

Bartholomew was one of the twelve original Apostles, known in John's Gospel, for some reason, as Nathanael. (This is one reason it is even harder to name the twelve Apostles than it is to name the Seven Dwarfs.) It is believed Bartholomew-Nathanael traveled as far as India and Turkey before being martyred in Armenia, where he was skinned alive by heathens; thus he is usually pictured holding a tanner's knife, with his own hide draped over his arm. This arm has been venerated at England's Canterbury Cathedral since the eleventh century. The curved knife accounts for his Patronage of medieval cheese merchants, who apparently took it for a cheese-cutter.

Basildes—June 28
PATRON OF PRISON GUARDS

In Alexandria, early in the second century, Saint Potemania, a Christian maiden as beautiful as she was chaste, was condemned to be stripped and dipped in boiling oil. Basildes, the guard escorting her from her cell to the place of public execution, was touched, and, acting on his own authority, consented to her pleas that she be allowed to keep her clothes on. Later that day, the Virgin Martyr Potemania appeared to Basildes in *his* prison cell, and showed him the heavenly crown awaiting him after his beheading.

Basilissa—January 9
PATRONESS INVOKED AGAINST BREAST-FEEDING PROBLEMS AND
CHILBLAINS

There are four Saints by this name, all exceedingly lovely; this one married a man named Julian, and on their wedding night persuaded him to join her in a vow of perpetual chastity. As they prayed together to "overcome the wiles of the old serpent," as their biographer puts it, their nuptial chamber was filled with unearthly light and the odor of lilies, and they lived thereafter as brother and sister in perfect chastity; which accounts for the chilblains, but hardly the breast-feeding.

Basil the Great—January 2
PATRON OF RUSSIA AND HOSPITAL ADMINISTRATORS

Basil was born in 329 in Caesarea, the capital city of the Roman province of Cappadocia—present-day Turkey—into a highly religious family. His grandmother (Macrina), both his parents (Basil the Elder and Emmelia), two of his brothers (Gregory of Nyssa and Peter of Sebaste), and his sister (Macrina the Younger) are officially canonized Catholic Saints, with their own feast days. As a bishop, Basil strove mightily to combat the politically popular Arian heresy. The Emperor Valens, himself an Arian, determined to write Our Saint a rude and threatening letter, but when his pen miraculously broke three times into three pieces, he realized Basil was correct about the nature of the Trinity, and gave it up. The rules Basil established for monastic living prevail to this day in the Eastern (Greek and Russian Orthodox) churches, and he has always been much revered in Russia. Perhaps something of his personality—his generosity, eloquence, shrewdness, and pigheadedness—appeals to the Russian spirit.

Bathild—January 30
PATRONESS OF CHILDREN

An English girl (born 630), Bathild was carried off by pirates and sold as a slave to the mayor of the palace of King Clovis II of the Western Franks. She worked in the kitchen. The mayor took a fancy to her, but Bathild smeared her pretty face with soot and clad her lovely body in rags to escape his unseemly attentions. By all accounts a model servant, she rose quickly in the ranks, waiting at table on her fellow servants and eventually upon King Clovis himself. At first glance, His Majesty—a bit of a rogue, if the truth be known—fell passionately in love with the little serving girl, and soon made her his queen. She bore him three sons in as many years, whereupon he died; for the next eight years this Anglo-Saxon ex-slave ruled as regent for her son, Prince Chlotar III. Rumors that during her reign she arranged for the assassinations of ten difficult bishops are doubtless exaggerated. In 665 she was ousted by the nobles in a palace coup, and retired to live out her days in an abbey she had founded. Her emblem in art, as befits such an "upstairs/downstairs" story, is a ladder.

Bede—May 25
PATRON OF SCHOLARS

This Northumbrian monk (673–735) was the author of the justly famous *History of the English Church and People*. A student of Saint Benedict (later Benet) Biscop and disciple of Saint John of Beverley (*both of whom* SEE), his chronicle of Britain from Roman times to his own was meticulously researched, concisely and fluently written (in Latin), and remarkably fair—even to the Celts, with whom Bede, a Saxon, had his differences. The only Englishman named in Dante's *Divina commedia* (in "Paradiso," naturally), Bede's sanctity was recognized even in his lifetime, yet he was not formally canonized until 1899. For a thousand years he was known by the title bestowed upon prospective Saints, "Venerable."

Bega (Bee)—September 6
PATRONESS OF LABORERS

Bega was a beautiful Irish princess who was betrothed to Christ from infancy. She received, via some Angels, an engagement bracelet marked with the Sign of the Cross, and this enabled her to escape her arranged marriage to a prince of Norway. On the eve of her wedding she slipped out from the drunken revels and sailed from Ireland on a piece of sod, wearing nothing but the bracelet. She washed up on the coast of Cumberland, where she was sustained by food delivered by sea gulls and gannets. Bega eventually became a nun, and laundered and mended the clothes of the workers who built her monastery. A strong cult continues to exist around Bega in the northwest of England, whose residents are still in possession of her miraculous bracelet. They take solemn oaths on it, and use it to threaten revenge on foreign enemies.

Benedict—July 11

PATRON OF ARCHITECTS, COPPERSMITHS, THE DYING, EUROPE, FARM WORKERS, MONKS, SERVANTS, SPELUNKERS; INVOKED AGAINST GALLSTONES, POISON, AND WITCHCRAFT

Benedict, the founder of Western monasticism, had an immense influence on the Christianization of post–Roman Empire Europe. His "how-to" book for monks, the *Rule of Saint Benedict,* is one of the basic documents of the Middle Ages, those centuries during which monasteries were Europe's only surviving centers of art, learning, law, science—in a word, civilization. He was born in Norcia, Italy, early in the fifth century, of noble parents. His twin sister was Saint Scholastica (*whom* SEE). As a student in Rome, he feared spiritual contamination from his godless peers, and after his first miracle (he repaired, by prayer, a dish a servant had broken by accident) he retreated to an underground cave at Subiaco, where he lived for three years dressed in animal skins, fed either by a fellow hermit named Romulus or a magic raven. During this period, the Devil tormented him constantly. At one point the Tempter assumed the form of a black bird and flew into the Saint's face, reminding him of a beautiful girl he had seen in Rome. Thinking fast, Benedict tore off his garments and threw himself into a thorn bush. He was never again troubled by sexual desire. He was soon joined by disciples and students, and together they formed a religious order, the one still known as "Benedictine." It was dedicated to the principle "To work is to pray"—thereby opposing the foolish prejudice of those unenlightened days against manual labor. Benedict could read the minds of his fellow monks, and follow them in his own mind on their distant journeys. He was obliged to leave Subiaco when a wayward priest named Florentius dropped by and tried to poison Our Saint (by putting a toad in his drinking cup), as well as turning loose a troupe of naked hussies among the monks. Benedict made his way to Monte Cassino, a malarial swamp, where he transformed ruined temples of Jupiter and Apollo into oratories to John the Baptist and Martin of Tours, thereby laying the foundation for the greatest monastery in all Christendom. His miracles continued. He healed the sick and raised the dead, and caused the pitiless barbarian Galea to faint with fright by unbinding a prisoner with a glance. He foretold, accurately, the imminent death of Totila the Barbarian, but could, alas, also foresee the destruction of Monte Cassino by the Lombards. After Benedict's death, his great monastery was indeed razed to the ground, restored, sacked by the Saracens, rebuilt, and destroyed a final time by the Allies in World War II, who incorrectly thought it to be a German headquarters. Pope Pius XII declared Benedict Patron of cave explorers and architects. John XXIII made him Patron of farm workers, and Paul VI proclaimed him Patron of all Europe.

Benedict Labre—April 16
PATRON OF BEGGARS AND THE HOMELESS

Born in France in 1748—at the dawn of the "Age of Reason"—Benedict Joseph Labre decided to take the words of the Gospel seriously. This eccentricity rendered him as unfit for membership in any religious order as he would have been for a place in the court of Louis XV. He was rejected, in short order, by the Trappists, Carthusians, and Cistercians, so he embarked, on foot, on a four-year-long pilgrimage to all the shrines of Christendom. Wandering across Europe, this holy hobo was careful to practice absolute poverty, which rendered him emaciated and somewhat unkempt in appearance, not to mention verminous. Upon his arrival in Rome, he spent seven years camped out in the ruins of the Colosseum by night, and praying fervently in one church or another by day. The citizens took to calling him "the beggar of Rome" and "the new Saint Francis," among other things.

Benedict the Black—April 4
PATRON OF AFRICAN AMERICANS

Born on a farm near Sicily in 1526, this son of African slaves was granted his freedom by his kindly master at eighteen. Benedict first displayed an entrepreneurial spirit, purchasing a team of oxen and laboring as a plowman. He endured many racist taunts like "Big Black Ben," but his piety and charity soon earned him another nickname, "Il Santo Moro," that is, "The Holy Negro." At the urging of a passing hermit, Benedict sold his team and retired to the woods, where he dressed only in palm leaves. When Pope Pius IV commanded that all solitary hermits join organized religious communities, Benedict entered a Franciscan monastery, where he was employed as a cook. Although he could neither read nor write, he was eventually elected Superior, and then gladly returned to the kitchen. His culinary skills were remarkable—enhanced by his extraordinary notion that eating was a sinless pleasure, as well as his miraculous ability to multiply food. Despite his cloistered humility, he acquired a popular reputation for sanctity, in part owing to the heavenly light that surrounded him when he prayed. On his sickbed he was visited by Saint Ursula (*whom* SEE), as well as by the Blessed Virgin Herself, Who permitted him to hold the Christ Child in his arms.

Benen—November 9
PATRON INVOKED AGAINST WORMS

Benen, the son of an Irish chieftain, was a mere child when he fell in love with the visiting Saint Patrick. He sprinkled flowers on Patrick while the Saint was sleeping, and clung to his feet when he tried to leave. Relenting, Patrick took Benen from his family, explaining that "the child shall inherit my kingdom," which he did, captivating everyone with his gentle disposition and lilting voice. Patrick wrote a hymn—"The Deer's Cry"—about how he and his disciples once escaped being ambushed by Druids: they transformed themselves into deer, and Benen into a fawn. Benen succeeded Patrick as bishop of Armagh, and in time went to join his mentor in retirement as a hermit. Before his death, Patrick instructed Benen to build a cell wherever his staff burst into leaves. The staff blossomed in the middle of a swamp, and a spring gushed forth. It was there that Benen stayed until his death. At his tomb, people miraculously vomit the intestinal worms that have been plaguing them.

Benet Biscop—January 12

PATRON OF ARCHITECTS, ARTISTS, GLAZIERS, AND MUSICIANS

This Saint was born Biscop Baducing in seventh-century Northumbria. Upon becoming a Benedictine monk, he changed his name to Benedict—which was anglicized to Benet. A scholar, a founder of abbeys and builder of churches, he traveled frequently to the Continent, bringing back to his primitive native land whole collections of paintings and whole libraries of manuscripts. He imported sophisticated builders—French masons and glaziers—and introduced Roman-style chanting to his abbey choirs. In another age, he might have been a museum curator, or host of a cultural talk show on the BBC—or PBS, as it is known in America.

Benno—June 16

PATRON OF WEAVERS

When Benno was formally canonized, in 1523, Martin Luther threw a fit, calling this "New Idol" an "Old Devil." Devil or Idol, Benno was, for the first eighty-seven years of his life, politically unwise. He supported the Saxons in their doomed uprising against the Emperor Henry IV. He took the losing side of Pope Gregory in his quarrel with Henry, and then upheld the failed papal claims of antipope Guibert. Although in life he was bishop of (now Protestant) Meissen, in Heaven he is the official Patron of (forever Catholic) Munich, and of its cloth-making industry. In German folklore, Benno is renowned for successfully commanding frogs to stop croaking, and for recovering from the gills of a cooked fish the cathedral keys that he had previously tossed into the river Elbe.

Bernadette—April 16

PATRONESS OF SHEPHERDS

Outside the mountain town of Lourdes in southwest France, in February 1858, the Mother of God appeared to a fourteen-year-old asthmatic, undersized, backward shepherdess named Bernadette Soubirous, while she was gathering firewood by the river. Our Lady was praying the rosary at the time—saying, presumably, "Hail Me, full of grace, the Lord is with Me, blessed am I among women," etc. . . . Thereafter, on seventeen occasions over the next six months, Our Lady reappeared to Our Saint, pointing out the hidden source of a spring, asking Bernadette to eat grass in penance for the sins of mankind, and identifying herself as "the Immaculate Conception." Today, 27,000 gallons of miraculous curative waters flow from that spring every week. Three million pilgrims a year visit Lourdes, where an underground concrete church seats 20,000. Bernadette herself became a simple nun. She died in 1879, having worked hard at her earthly task, which she once described as "being ill." Her visions and tribulations were the subject of a big fat pious bestselling book and a two-and-a-half-hour-long Hollywood movie, *The Song of Bernadette*.

Bernardino of Feltre—September 28

PATRON OF BANKERS AND PAWNBROKERS

This Saint changed his name from Martin Tomitani when Bernardino of Siena *(below)* foretold his coming: "After me will come another Bernardino." Around the same time he gave up music, maintaining that "chants are not pleasing to the Lord." He overcame his stage fright and self-consciousness about his *piccolino* (minuscule) height to become a firebrand preacher, once breaking a blood vessel during a zealous sermon from the pulpit. Ber-

nardino, unsparing of either clergy or nobility, railed against fast living and its trappings—finery, hairpieces, dice—and ended his missions with a "bonfire of the vanities." He directed his wrath at Jewish moneylenders, and established his own *mons pietatis* (church-sponsored pawnshops). Shortly before his death in Pavia, he predicted the invasion of Italy, saying he could "hear the French shoeing their horses."

Bernardino of Siena—May 20

PATRON OF ADVERTISING AND PUBLIC RELATIONS; INVOKED AGAINST
HOARSENESS AND LUNG DISEASE

Even as a child, Bernardino was famously
handsome; there exists an edifying tale of his
gathering his little playmates together to help
him beat up an older fellow who had made
improper advances toward him. He became a
Franciscan friar at the age of twenty, but not
until 1417, when he was thirty-seven, did he
set out upon his evangelical mission as a traveling preacher. He visited, on foot, every
town and city in Italy. His open-air sermons would last for hours, and
he delivered several every day. His voice, once weak and raspy, became loud and resonant when he denounced sorcery (i.e., heretics),
corruption (i.e., gamblers), and usury (i.e., Jews). Bernardino employed as a "visual aid" a placard on which were blazoned the letters
IHS—a "corporate logo" as it were for the firm of Jesus & Co. A
printer of playing cards, bankrupted by Bernardino's condemnation
of gambling, made a fortune peddling a line of IHS cards. Competing
preachers, jealous of his popularity, complained (to no avail) to the
Office of the Holy Inquisition that Bernardino's methods encouraged
superstition, if not outright idolatry. Our Saint's miracles were many,
and included raising from the dead a member of the audience who
was gored by a bull during one of Bernardino's sermons. After his
own death (in 1444) a street brawl broke out in front of the church
where he lay in state, but a river of his venerable blood, pouring out
the church doors, soon put an end to *that*.

Bernard of Clairvaux—August 20

PATRON OF GIBRALTAR, BEES, BEEKEEPERS, CANDLE MAKERS, AND WAX
MELTERS

French poetry first flourished in the twelfth century, when the
epic *Song of Roland* was composed, and the troubadours of Provence
created their immortal verse. Bernard, born in 1090, the scion of
Burgundian nobility, showed early promise as a poet. A proto-Ro-
mantic, he declared that "we can learn more from the woods, from
stones and trees, than from teachers and books." But when his
mother died—he had been her favorite—Bernard changed. He

began flinging himself into icy ponds at the sight of young women, and before long joined the austere Cistercians, an order of "primitive" Benedictine monks. Afflicted with anemia, migraine, gastritis, hypertension, and an atrophied sense of taste, Bernard had obvious monastic leadership potential; he soon founded his own monastery. His poetic urges poured into voluminous writing and preaching, his "honey-sweet" style earning him the title of *Doctor Mellifluus,* from which derived his emblem, a beehive, and his patronage of the beeswax and honey trades. Our Saint often wrote commentaries at length about the biblical Song of Songs, to prove it was not about sex. Certain as he was that "original sin" was passed on through the sexual act, he argued publicly and vehemently against the then popular notion of Mary's Immaculate Conception. Nevertheless, his personal devotion to the Virgin was most intense. (Once, when he was afflicted with writer's block, Our Lady appeared in his cell, and nursed him from Her very own breast.) Neither was Bernard impressed with the new, rational "Scholastic Philosophy" being practiced in Paris. He dismissed it as "scandalous curiosity" and prevailed upon the pope to excommunicate such dangerous intellectuals as Peter Abelard. In fact, for a sickly, cloistered mystic, Bernard involved himself considerably with the politics of his day, supporting the (quite unjustified but ultimately victorious) cause of Pope Innocent II against his rival Anacletus II, and devoted considerable time and energy to preaching the Divinely Guaranteed Success of the perfectly catastrophic Second Crusade.

Bernard of Montjoux—May 28
PATRON OF SKIERS AND MOUNTAIN CLIMBERS

For centuries, pilgrims on the path to Rome from France and Germany felt obliged to cross the Alps on foot in winter. In the eleventh century, Bernard, a tireless Augustinian missionary in those regions, established two hospices for travelers at the top of the two mountain passes that still bear his name. There, too (although considerably later), his successors bred the large hairy dogs that are, very properly, also named after him.

Bernard Tolomei—August 21
PATRON OF OLIVE GROWERS

Born in Siena in 1272, Bernard became both a wealthy attorney and a successful politician—some accounts say he was mayor of his

city. A partisan speech he was giving one
day turned, much to his surprise, into a sermon on the vanity of vanities, and he resigned to found a religious order. They
were known as "the Oliventines" because
their abbey was located on the slopes of
Monte Oliveto.

Bernward—November 20
PATRON OF ARCHITECTS, ARTISTS, GOLDSMITHS, AND SCULPTORS

Bernward, who was born *circa* 960 in Hildesheim, was orphaned at
six and raised by his uncle, the bishop of Utrecht. Ordained as a priest
by his future adversary Saint Willigis, Bernward's avocation was ecclesiastical art, especially metalworking: he created the sixteen-foot
bronze gates of the cathedral of Hildesheim. When the Princess Sofia
decided to enter the nunnery of Gandersheim, she insisted that Saint
Willigis perform the initiation ceremony, even though the nunnery
was out of his jurisdiction. An old bishop was shoved aside, a noisy
quarrel broke out in the cathedral, and Bernward alone stood in opposition to Willigis *and* the throne. This relatively minor issue es-
calated, and the conflict over the diocese to which Sofia's nunnery
belonged went on for years, involving the emperor and even the
pope. In the meantime, Sofia shuttled back and forth from convent to
castle, inciting nuns and nobility alike against Bernward. (She was living with Willigis on what has been described as "most familiar
terms.") A synod eventually decided in Bernward's favor, and Willigis openly repented and went on to Sainthood. Bernward became
bishop of Utrecht—a post that has produced an unusually high number of Saints.

Besse—August 10
PATRON OF DRAFT DODGERS

In the villages of the Italian Alps on the tenth day of August, the
people—young men in particular—honor Saint Besse with joyous
festivities and invoke his heavenly assistance in staying out of the
army. Besse himself was a Roman soldier, a member of the famous
Theban Legion commanded by Saint Maurice (*whom* SEE). Near Lake
Geneva, in the year 290, all 6,660—or 600, accounts vary—of these
brave Christian warriors refused to honor the Emperor Maximian as
a god, and were "decimated" (one man in ten was beheaded). As they

persisted in their Faith, the process was repeated until everyone was slain, except Besse, who somehow escaped, and made his way to the mountains of the Soana valley, where he preached the Gospel to the natives. Ironically, Besse achieved the martyr's crown anyway—he was stabbed and/or thrown from a cliff by unreconstructed pagans— but for his example of resistance to military service he is still venerated by the fiercely independent denizens of the area.

Bibiana—December 2
PATRONESS INVOKED AGAINST HANGOVERS

Because the Spanish pronounce the letter *V* as the Romans did the letter *B*, this Saint, whose name means "full of life" (Latin—*vivo*) was thought by them to be "full of drink" (Latin—*bibo*). Consequently, the Spanish invoked her protection against the morning-after ravages of alcoholic indulgence. An ancient church in Rome is dedicated to the Virgin Martyr Viviana, who was scourged to death for her Faith in the year 363, during the persecutions undertaken by the Emperor Julian the Apostate.

Blaise—February 3
PATRON OF SICK CATTLE AND WOOL COMBERS; INVOKED AGAINST
THROAT DISEASE AND ATTACKS FROM WILD ANIMALS

Blaise was both a physician and a bishop in Armenia at the turn of the fourth century. Fleeing persecution, he lived in a cave in the woods, to which many wild beasts would repair for sanctuary and medical assistance. He was reported to the authorities by irate hunters. On his way to prison, he encountered a woman whose pig had just been carried off by a wolf. Blaise reasoned with the savage beast, who contritely returned the porker, and in gratitude the woman brought candles to Our Saint in jail. Among his other miracles was the removal of a fish bone from the throat of a choking child. Blaise was tortured with the steel combs used in carding wool before being beheaded. To this day, on his feast (which occurs at the height of 'flu season) crossed candles are applied, in Catholic churches, to the throats of the faithful. And water blessed on that day works wonders with ailing livestock.

Blandina—June 2
PATRONESS OF YOUNG GIRLS

In Lyons, in the second century, it was widely believed that the Christians practiced incest ("Brothers and sisters, love one another") and cannibalism ("Take, eat, this is my body"). One group of these "perverts" who were arrested and tortured in the local arena included the slave girl Blandina, as well as her mistress, a local bishop, and a teenage boy named Ponticus. When they were exposed in the arena to wild beasts, Our Saint "strove to comfort them like a mother," according to eyewitness accounts. The bears and lions devoured the others, but spared Blandina. She was then tied in a net and gored to death by a bull.

Bona—May 29
PATRONESS OF FLIGHT ATTENDANTS

In 1962, Pope John XXIII, in what one can only hope was a fit of his characteristic whimsy, placed air hostesses and flight stewards under the Patronage of this Saint.  Her father sailed away from Pisa to the Crusades in 1159, when Bona was only three. When the child was seven, she had her first vision: Jesus appeared to her and told her to stop sleeping with her mother. Deeply impressed, the pious Bona began sleeping in a manger, without blankets. When she was ten, Our Lord reappeared, and gave her money with which to buy a scratchy hair shirt, in order that she might do proper penance. Bona's religious zeal seemed to affect her mother, who soon had a vision of her own: by Divine command, her thirteen-year-old daughter was to leave home in search of her father in the Holy Land. But Papa turned out to be a bit of a scoundrel, with a second wife and three grown sons. On her return journey, Bona met up with a holy hermit, and they attempted to convert a passing party of Saracen pirates. They were imprisoned for their pains. Bona escaped, through the supernatural intervention of Saint James the Greater (*whom* SEE), and upon her return to Pisa immediately organized a pilgrimage to his shrine at Santiago del Compostela in Spain, a thousand miles away. This indefatigable traveler led nine more guided tours before peacefully dying, in her little room at home, in 1207.

Bonaventure of Potenza—October 26
PATRON INVOKED AGAINST DISEASES OF THE BOWELS

A Franciscan monk of Amalfi famous for his humility and unquestioning obedience to authority, Bonaventure died (aged sixty) of acute intestinal distress—but also in a state of ecstasy induced by relentless psalm-singing. His religious Superior ordered, for reasons of his own, the corpse of Bonaventure to bleed from the arm—which it immediately did.

Boniface of Mainz—June 5
PATRON OF GERMANY, PRUSSIA, AND BREWERS

In the Dark Ages, the centuries between the fall of the (pagan) Roman empire and the rise of the Holy Roman Empire, barbaric German tribes overran (not for the last time) Europe. The pope of Rome called to Catholic England for missionaries to convert these hordes. Saints Willibrord and Swithbert (*both of whom* SEE) went to labor among the pagan Frisians in Holland. Boniface (who had been born in England and baptized Wynfrith, but changed his name, sensibly enough) set out for Hesse, in the very heart of Germany. He was pleased to discover that the native "German Franks" were really Saxons like the English, "blood of our blood, bone of our bone," as he wrote in a letter home. He knew how to appeal to their practical nature. *His* God was more powerful than *their* gods, he said—and proved it by chopping down an ancient oak tree sacred to Odin. Thereafter, Boniface had little difficulty convincing the Germans to join his efficient, hierarchically structured, Rome-centralized organization. Most of his problems were with the few surviving Gaulish priests (one of whom was distributing his own fingernail parings as holy relics), and with a gaggle of competing Irish missionaries, who tended toward the misty-mystical school of theology. Boniface prevailed. He was made bishop of Mainz, primate of Germany, apostolic legate to Germany and Gaul. Twenty-five years after his departure from England, he personally crowned Pepin as Most Catholic Emperor of All the Franks. Full of years and honors, he was on his way home to Devon when, passing through Holland, he was brutally martyred by a band of Frisian pagans Willibrord must have missed.

Boniface of Querfurt—June 19
PATRON OF PRUSSIA

Boniface, the name of an early martyr, was long a popular pseudonym assumed by popes and missionaries, such as Boniface of Mainz *(above)* and Boniface *(né* Bruno) of Querfurt. A German monk, Bruno had some success evangelizing the Magyars of Hungary and the Pechenegs of Kiev, but he and eighteen companions were massacred for attempting the conversion of the Prussians in 1009.

Boris—July 24
PATRON OF MOSCOW, RUSSIA

Boris was a Russian prince, the son of the saintly Tsar Vladimir of Kiev *(whom* SEE), and a victim of palace intrigue. His elder brother, Syvatopolk, contrived his murder, as well as the assassination of their younger brother, Gleb, who was stabbed in the throat by his cook. Boris and Gleb met their violent ends with Christ-like meekness, typical of the Eastern Saints known as *"strastoterptites,"* meaning "passion-bearers"—innocents accepting death with resignation. When a fourth brother, Yaroslav, opposed and overthrew the dreadful Syvatopolk, the incorrupt bodies of both Saints were enshrined in the cathedral of St. Basil, where their tombs became places of pilgrimage and miracles.

Brendan—May 16
PATRON OF SAILORS; INVOKED AGAINST ULCERS

It is certain that Brendan founded many important monasteries, and was abbot over 3,000 holy monks; there is no doubt that this seafaring Irish monk of the sixth century sailed to Scotland, Wales, and

Brittany (where he is invoked by those suffering from ulcers). But to this day no one knows
whether to classify the published saga of his
voyage to North America, *The Navigation of
Saint Brendan,* as fiction or fact. The Promised
Land of the Saints, as he named the tropical island he discovered somewhere in the Atlantic
Ocean, may have been one of the Canaries or
the Azores, or the Florida Keys . . . or it could

have been a mirage. Could he and his crew have sailed the seas for
seven years in a curragh or coracle—a round hide boat like a glorified
canoe? Were the lovely mermaids he encountered and baptized fig-
ments of a Celtic-celibate imagination, or were they actually seals?
Did he really sight Christ's betrayer Judas Iscariot taking a brief "vacation from Hell" by cooling himself on an iceberg? In 1976, author
Tim Severin built a boat to Brendan's specifications, and sailed it
from Ireland to America.

Bridget—July 23
PATRONESS OF SWEDEN AND SCHOLARS

This Swedish mystic, born *circa* 1303, lady-in-waiting to the wife of
King Magnus, was married at thirteen to Ulf Gudmarsson. One of her
first visions inspired her to tell that wicked king to mend his ways,
and the repentant monarch gave Bridget the money to start up an
order of monks and nuns after her husband's death. The layout of her
monastery—dictated by another vision—segregated the sexes except
for the shared church—which was designed, however, so that the
men and women couldn't see one another. Bridget's visions com-
pelled her to distribute advice worldwide—to several kings and even
to the pope, then at Avignon. She embarked on a series of pilgrimages, the last being to the Holy Land (where she saw all the scenes of
the Passion reenacted), and never returned to Sweden. In the Holy
Land, on a less sanctified note, her married son became romantically
entangled with Queen Joanna of Spain, causing Bridget considerable
despair. On this same pilgrimage, Bridget was almost shipwrecked off
the coast of Jaffa, which may explain why she is depicted in religious
art with seashells pinned on her cloak. Bridget was canonized a record three times, and her daughter went on to become Saint Catherine of Sweden (*whom* SEE). Today only a handful of the order she
founded, the Bridgettines, remain.

Brigid—February 1
PATRONESS OF IRELAND, NEW ZEALAND, MILKMAIDS, FUGITIVES,
NEWBORNS, NUNS, AND POULTRY RAISERS

The illegitimate daughter of a (pagan) Celtic chieftain and a (Christian) slave girl, Brigid—Patroness of milkmaids, who throughout her life was able to magically multiply the household supply of butter— was born while her mother was on her way from the dairy. After her mother's early death, the girl-child was claimed and raised by her father, and grew to be outstandingly beautiful. She hated her own beauty, for it attracted numerous lusty suitors, despite her well-known vow of perpetual chastity. Finally, her constant prayers to become ugly were answered—miraculously, one of her eyes became grotesquely huge, while the other disappeared—so her father consented to her becoming a nun. It is said that, during the ceremony, Angels shoved aside the attending priest and presented her with the veil, the wooden steps of the altar burst into leaf, and her good looks were instantly restored. Known as "the Mary of Ireland," Brigid was a powerful force in early Gaelic Christianity, founding numerous churches, convents, and monasteries. Since she was born sixty-six years after the death of Saint Patrick (*whom* SEE), reports of their intimate friendship are doubtless exaggerated. Nor is it necessarily true that the holy but drunken Saint Mel consecrated her a full-fledged bishop. Some facts we may be sure of, though. Her bath water was sometimes transformed into beer for the sake of thirsty clerics; she would often hang her damp cloak on a sunbeam to dry (obliging the sunbeam to remain all night); she taught a fox to dance; and she made armies invisible to each other. It is the merest coincidence that her feast day falls on that of a Celtic goddess named Bridget. Her tomb at Downpatrick was looted by English troops during the reign of Henry VIII, but her cloak survives as a relic in Belgium, and her head remains in Lisbon.

Brioc—May 1
PATRON OF PURSE MAKERS

Like many other sixth-century Celtic monks, Brioc commuted frequently across the English Channel, between the towns later named after him, Saint Breock in Cornwall and Saint-Brieuc in Brittany. Because he was famous for his charity, Our Saint was often painted and sculpted holding his (open) purse—for which reason the guild of purse makers took him as their Patron.

Bruno—October 6

PATRON INVOKED AGAINST DEMONIC POSSESSION

The founder of the Carthusians, Bruno was born in Cologne in 1030. He became a scholar and teacher at Rheims, where he ran afoul of the scandalously corrupt and worldly archbishop Manassas. When a dead man whose funeral Our Saint was conducting sat up and spoke emotionally about God's strict Judgment, Bruno resolved to become an old-fashioned desert-style hermit, and, with six companions, set out for the mountain wilderness of the Grande Chartreuse, near Grenoble. There they were welcomed by Saint Hugh, the local bishop, who had recently received a vision of "seven stars"—clearly prophesying their arrival. Bruno and his fellows lived with extreme frugality, in mud huts. They slept little, prayed, fasted, and copied manuscripts. Bishop Hugh once heard that an order of beef had been delivered to them, and arrived to find the holy hermits in their dining hall, sitting at table in a trance before the offending carnal joint. Hugh made the Sign of the Cross over it, transformed it into a turtle, and awakened the monks, who ate sinlessly.

Bueno—April 12

PATRON OF HEALTHY CATTLE

Bueno's birth was announced to his aged parents by an Angel. His boyhood friend, the powerful Welsh leader Iddon ap Ynyr Gwent, gave Bueno a land grant that the Saint immediately abandoned, traumatized after hearing a neighboring Saxon calling to his hounds. The sound of the English tongue was so odious to Bueno that he retreated deeper into Welsh territory: "The nation of that man," as he put it, "has a language which is abominable." The most famous miracle attributed to Bueno involves a bridegroom who cut off his sleeping bride's head and ran off with her gold and horses. Bueno found the bride and restored her head, causing a fountain to spring up where she had lain. Later, the bride's brother found the runaway bridegroom and cut off *his* head—but Bueno restored that, too, although without producing a fountain. A variation on this story has the wicked Welsh King Caradoc attempting to seduce Saint Winifred, who rebuffs him. The king cuts off her head, Bueno restores it, and curses the king, who dissolves into a puddle. These stories fail to explain why he is the Patron of healthy cattle, but centuries after his death the Saint's earthly representatives collected money in Bueno's name as a means of ensuring the health of farm animals.

Cadoc—September 25

PATRON INVOKED AGAINST CRAMPS, DEAFNESS, AND GLANDULAR DISORDERS

Cadoc's dashing father, a Welsh king, abducted the daughter of a rival, and after a fierce battle escaped with the princess. The Saint was born soon afterward. On the night of Cadoc's birth, an Irish monk came to retrieve a stolen cow and the king saw this as a sign to entrust his newborn son to the old monk. Animals continued to figure prominently in the Saint's life, even after he became a monk himself. A white mouse once led him to a stash of corn (after he had tied a spool of thread to its leg) that enabled him to feed the starving monks in his monastery. And a white boar cut a swath in the fields, showing Cadoc what would be the site of his future monastery and church, the Church of the Stags. When an armed chieftain came to retrieve his son from Cadoc's monastery, the Saint greeted him bathed in sunshine, while the chieftain and his men groped in total darkness. Cadoc, an avid reader of Virgil, once wept all night because he realized that the pagan poet wasn't in Heaven—but he was relieved when a voice called to him, saying, "Pray for me, pray for me . . . I shall yet sing eternally." Cadoc's macabre sense of humor once led him to order his monks to shave half the heads of some sleeping robbers, and to cut off the ears and lips of their horses as well. He was transported on a white cloud to meet his martyrdom at the hands of the Saxons, and continued to miraculously cure many diseases after his death, so that access to his grave was forbidden for centuries for fear that pilgrims would steal his relics.

Caedmon—February 11

PATRON OF POETS

A Saxon cowherd or stableboy, Caedmon lived, in the year 680, on lands belonging to the abbess Saint Hilda. Illiterate and tone deaf (he departed from feasts when the singing began, and fled the very sight of a harp), he was awakened one night by a Voice urging him to sing, which he commenced to do perfectly. His verses were, understandably, of a religious nature. The holy abbess became his Patroness—and since Caedmon was the first native English poet, Hilda is often considered the founder of English Literature. Before dying, Caedmon asked if anyone had any grudges against him. They all said no. His original hymn was preserved by Saint Bede (*whom* SEE) in his *History of the English Church and People,* although Bede apologizes for the inadequacy of his translation from Anglo-Saxon to Latin.

Callistus I—October 14

Callistus was born in second-century Rome, the Christian slave of a Christian master. Placed in charge of a Christian bank, he lost or misplaced all the Christian money. He skipped town, but was caught and sentenced (by a civil court) to the treadmill. Released by his merciful Christian creditors, Callistus started a brawl in a synagogue, blaming the Jews for his financial embarrassment. For this offense, he was condemned to the dreadful salt mines of Sardinia. Released by claiming (falsely) that his name had been inadvertently omitted from an amnesty list, he returned to Rome and was hired by Pope Zephyrinus to supervise the papal cemetery. Eighteen years later, Callistus succeeded Zephyrinus as pontiff. A man who knew something about guilt and rehabilitation, Callistus ruled that penitent sinners, even murderers, fornicators, and adulterers, were welcome in church. He also formally recognized the many shocking liaisons between Christian widows and their Christian slaves as legal marriages. This led to schism, and riot, in the course of which the forgiving slave-convict-pope was thrown down a well to his heavenly reward.

Camillus de Lellis—July 14

PATRON OF HOSPITALS, NURSES, AND THE SICK; INVOKED AGAINST GAMBLING

Born in Abruzzi in 1550, when his mother was close to sixty—she died soon after his birth—Camillus, who was six feet six inches tall, was a giant by the standards of his day. He led a dissolute youth, and after a stint in his father's regiment became a soldier of fortune. He was a compulsive gambler who, at the age of twenty-five, having literally lost the shirt off his back, began his life as a penitent. Rejected by a monastery because of an ulcerated sore on his leg, he went to work in a hospital serving incurables. Sometimes, unable to walk because of his rotting extremity, Camillus would crawl from sickbed to sickbed. In 1585, along with Saint Philip Neri (*whom* SEE), he founded a congregation of male nurses, the Servants of the Sick. He was a pioneer in hospital hygiene and diet, and successfully opposed the prevailing practice of burying patients alive. His order was sent to the battlefields of Hungary and Croatia, and formed the first military field ambulance. Camillus often saw his Guardian Angel by his side, and the two are represented together in art.

Canute IV—January 19
PATRON OF DENMARK

Canute (or Cnut, sometimes Kanute) is remembered bitterly by the English for his rape and pillage of Yorkshire in 1075. But his subjects, the Danes, admired him greatly in life, and soon after his death (at his brother Olaf's hand) they reported many miracles at or near his grave, thus persuading Pope Paschal II to number King Canute among the Blessed.

Casilda—April 9
PATRONESS INVOKED AGAINST BAD LUCK AND STERILITY

Casilda was a Moorish princess, whose father, the king of Toledo, persecuted Christians and kept them captive in his castle. Casilda visited the prisoners, bringing them food and wine, and in due time they converted her. When she was on one of her missions of mercy, her father confronted her, demanding to know what she carried in her cloak. Casilda answered, "Roses," and in the tradition of Saints Zita and Elizabeth of Hungary (*both of whom* SEE), the food she was carrying was transformed into flowers. She lived as a solitary by the Lake of Saint Vincent, died at the age of 100, and is still revered in Toledo.

Casimir—March 4
PATRON OF POLAND AND LITHUANIA; INVOKED AGAINST PLAGUE

This Polish prince proved a terrible disappointment to his father, King Casimir IV. The lad simply refused to lead an army into Hungary, preferring to remain at home clad in a hair shirt and repeat aloud the extremely long Latin prayer "Daily, daily, sing to Mary" (now known as "Saint Casimir's Hymn"). Neither would he marry the daughter of the German Emperor Frederick III, having sworn

himself to perpetual celibacy. In 1484, on a visit to neighboring Lithuania, Our Saint died of tuberculosis at age twenty-six. Miracles occur
frequently at his tomb in Vilna.

Cassian of Imola—August 13
PATRON OF TEACHERS

In 1952, the devout Catholic stenographers of Naples petitioned
Pope Pius XII to assign them a Patron Saint appropriate to their vocation, and on December 23 of that year His Holiness informed them
by Apostolic Letter that Saint Cassian was now and henceforth to be
their Heavenly Example and Protector. Imagine their chagrin when
they consulted *Lives of the Saints* and discovered that Cassian was a
martyr who had been stabbed to death with *pens*! He had been an unpopular schoolteacher, convicted of Christianity and condemned to
death, which sentence was carried out by his own pupils, who happily carved, slashed, and punctured him with the sharp steel writing
implements of the time. It seemed that Pope Pius XII was playing a
cruel joke on those Neapolitan takers of dictation, when, in fact, the
Holy Father had actually recommended *another* Cassian, who had
been a court stenographer in Tangier, and whose feast day is December 3.

Cassian of Tangier—December 3
PATRON OF SHORTHAND WRITERS AND STENOGRAPHERS

Cassian was a court stenographer in north Africa in the year 298,
when Saint Marcellus the Centurion was tried, convicted of Christianity, and sentenced to death. Cassian took exception to this injus-
tice, and threw down his pen and tablets, causing the judge to leap
from the bench in anger. This unseemly scene is alleged to have
moved Saint Marcellus to laughter; Cassian was executed with him.

Cathal—May 10
PATRON INVOKED AGAINST HERNIA, DROUGHT, AND STORMS

This Irish-born missionary priest of the seventh century has been
the subject of a cult in southern Italy since his relics, including a
bishop's staff, were discovered at Taranto in 1071. He is especially
adept at curing ruptures, and is apparently also influential in the
weather department.

Catherine Labouré—November 28

Catherine (*neé* Zoé), an illiterate farm girl, moved to Paris, worked briefly as a waitress, then entered the convent in 1830. Not long after, in the middle of the night, Catherine's Guardian Angel, "a shining child," appeared and led her to the chapel. Here she found the Blessed Virgin waiting for her, sitting in the Mother Superior's chair. The two women chatted for a couple of hours, and Catherine was able to place her hands on the Virgin's knees. Light poured from Mary's hands and writing surrounded her as she ordered Catherine, "Have a medal struck!" The vision turned its back on Catherine, indicating to her the way She wished the design on the reverse of the medal to look. Catherine's apparition was judged authentic, and the medals struck—now known everywhere as "miraculous medals"— became immensely popular. They were considered miraculous more because of their origin than for any intrinsic wonder-working property. After her vision, Catherine went back to working with poultry and the infirm, retreating into obscurity. Her superiors, knowing nothing of her true identity, described her as "cold, almost apathetic." She predicted she would never see the year 1877, and died on December 31, 1876. Her body reposes under glass, and her clear blue eyes remain open. Her incorrupt hands have been amputated and may be found in her old convent, along with the chair on which the Virgin sat. Visitors leave slips of paper bearing their secret wishes and intentions on it.

Catherine of Alexandria—November 25

PATRONESS OF LAWYERS, LIBRARIANS, MILLERS, NURSES, PHILOSOPHERS, ROPE MAKERS, SECRETARIES, SCHOOLGIRLS, SPINSTERS, STUDENTS, WHEELWRIGHTS, AND UNIVERSITIES; INVOKED AGAINST DISEASES OF THE TONGUE

One of the most popular Saints in Christendom, Catherine of Alexandria was an Egyptian queen who, despite her great beauty, preferred the study of philosophy to the prospect of marriage to the Roman Emperor Maxentius. Inspired by a visit by the Blessed Virgin, a desert hermit sought her out, and showed Catherine a picture of the Madonna and Child. Immediately she not only became a Christian but "mystically married" the Christ Child (He's said to have given her a ring). Appalled, Maxentius summoned a team of fifty pagan phi-

losophers to debate religion with her. She not
only confounded them in argument, but converted them to the Faith. The emperor had
them all slaughtered, but spared Catherine,
after whom he continued to lust. Rebuffed
once more, he ordered her chaste body
stretched out on a spiked wheel, the infamous
"catherine wheel." Before her torture could
begin, lightning-wielding Angels appeared and shattered the device,
causing its blades to hack up bystanders. She was then beheaded, but
milk, not blood, flowed from her holy neck. The Angels transported
her body to the monastery of Saint Catherine below Mount Sinai.
Catherine's feast falls immediately before the beginning of Advent,
during which no weddings can take place. November 25 was, therefore, a sort of deadline for the unmarried women of the Middle Ages,
who prayed to her thus:

> A husband, Saint Catherine,
> A good one, Saint Catherine,
> A handsome one, Saint Catherine,
> A rich one, Saint Catherine—
> And *soon*, Saint Catherine!

Catherine of Bologna—March 9
PATRONESS OF ARTISTS

Born Catherine de' Vigri in 1413, this pious virgin was tormented
with diabolic visions that caused her to doubt the "Real Presence" of
Christ in the Eucharist. She got over it, and joined the Order of the
Poor Clares. One Christmas Eve, after reciting a thousand decades of
the Rosary, she was visited by Our Lady, who briefly permitted her
to baby-sit the Christ Child. Some years after her death in 1463, her
body was disentombed, and found to be sweet-smelling and uncor-
rupted. It was placed in a glass case in the convent chapel, where it
remains on display to this day, somewhat (alas) worse for wear. Also
exhibited is a breviary she illustrated with considerable artistic skill.

Catherine of Genoa—September 15
PATRONESS OF NURSES

Catherine of Genoa was married at sixteen to the son of a rival family, in the hopes of patching up a blood feud. During the first five years of their marriage, her husband, Julian, behaved badly—he was unfaithful, bad-tempered, and an ostentatious dresser. Catherine took to her room and alternated between depression and hysteria, acerbating the long-standing feud. Then, after seeing a vision of Christ crucified, blood spouting from His wounds and covering the walls of the house, she underwent a spiritual transformation. Following this, she kept her eyes downcast, put thistles in her bed and wormwood in her food, and rubbed her tongue along the ground to punish herself if she spoke unnecessarily. She eventually converted the now-bankrupt Julian, and they moved to a small house, living in chastity. They administered to the poor and the sick, especially during the plague of 1493, tending sores and delousing garments. After kissing a plague-tormented patient, Catherine suffered lifelong sickness. When Julian died, she cared for his former mistress and his illegitimate daughter. Catherine spent her final years writing (actually dictating) her long and psychedelic *Treatise on Purgatory,* and undergoing visionary experiences.

Catherine of Palma—April 1

Orphaned at age seven, Catherine was exploited as a household drudge by her wicked uncle, until she was rescued by Saints Catherine of Alexandria and Antony of Padua (*both of whom* SEE). They appeared to the poor child in a vision, urging her to enter the religious life. Despite the lack of a dowry, she was admitted to a convent, where she soon began to exhibit unusual behavior. After receiving Holy Communion, she would enter a trancelike state, shuffling about with her eyes closed, deep in conversation with invisible spirits. Every year she spent the fifteen days preceding the feast of her great namesake Catherine in catatonic ecstasy. She was also often tormented by a naughty demon, who subjected her to lewd remarks and physical abuse—her holy shrieks of protest frequently disturbed the tranquil meditation of the other nuns.

Catherine of Siena—April 29

PATRONESS OF ITALY, NURSES, PHILOSOPHY, AND SPINSTERS; INVOKED AGAINST FIRE

Catherine had her first vision of Christ at the age of six, when He appeared to her dressed in papal vestments and flanked by the Saints

Paul and John. In her teens, refusing to marry, she cut off her hair and lived in a cramped space over her parents' kitchen. She eventually attracted a following, and quickly became an influential leader in the Church and State, forcing advice on kings and dukes. During the Avignonese captivity—the Great Schism that rent the Western Church—Catherine convinced Pope Gregory XI to leave Avignon, effectively returning the papacy to Rome after sixty-eight years. She worked toward the recognition of his successor, Urban VI, as well as toward the unification of Italy and a new Crusade against the Turks. Highly energetic, Catherine dug graves for lepers and plague victims and, despite her illiteracy, dictated several treatises, including her most famous, *The Dialogue*. Once, when she was chanting the Song of Solomon, Christ appeared to her and kissed her on the mouth. Finally, during the carnival celebrations on the eve of Ash Wednesday, in a marriage ceremony presided over by the Blessed Virgin, Christ put a ring set with precious stones on her finger. She received the Stigmata when staring at a crucifix—five blood-red rays pierced her hands and feet. She was frequently visited by a host of Saints, including Dominic, Mary Magdalene, and John the Divine (*all of whom* SEE). She fasted for long periods, subsisting only on Holy Communion wafers, and wore a hair shirt day and night, changing it only when, for sanitary reasons, she switched to iron chains. The twenty-fourth of twenty-five children, she was vehemently opposed to birth control and, in fact, once had a vision of Hell in which she saw a large group of sinners who "had sinned in the married state," that is, practiced contraception. She died in agony at the age of thirty-three, convinced she was wrestling with demons. Her body parts—arms, shoulder blades, various ribs, hands, fingers, feet, bones, and ashes—are found in churches all over Europe. Catherine is a Doctor of the Church and one of only four laywomen canonized in the fourteenth and fifteenth centuries.

Catherine of Sweden—March 24
PATRONESS INVOKED AGAINST ABORTION

The fourth of eight children born to Saint Bridget of Sweden (*whom* SEE), Katherine Ulfsdotter demonstrated her devotion to Holy Chastity early in life. As an infant, she would refuse her mother's breast "as if it were absinthe" after those occasions when Bridget had been obliged to endure carnal relations with her husband. Katherine herself was married at fourteen, but persuaded *her* husband to respect (however reluctantly—she was famously attractive) her treasured virginity. After five years, she left, over his objections, to join her mother on a pilgrimage to the Vatican and remained in the Holy City. Once in Rome, many noble suitors attempted, without success, to woo or even rape her. They later testified at her canonization hearings (which took place three years after her death, in 1381) that their wicked stratagems were invariably foiled by the sudden and distracting appearance at her side of a shining white doe.

Cecilia—November 22
PATRONESS OF COMPOSERS,
MUSIC, AND MUSICIANS

Full of despair, Cecilia played the organ on her wedding night, asking God to help her in her hour of need. "While the musicians played and sang at her nuptials, she sang in her heart to God only." (She could play any musical instrument, sing any song, hear the Angelic harmonies—and may have invented the organ.) When the dreaded moment arrived, Cecilia confessed to her husband, Valerian, that she had consecrated her virginity to God and that, furthermore, she had a very strict Guardian Angel: "If you touch me in the way of marriage, he will be angry." After Valerian had agreed to be baptized, the Angel appeared and crowned

the chaste couple with roses and lilies. Valerian was soon executed, his last words slandering the gods. (Jupiter, he swore, was "a libertine.") Cecilia was condemned to die in her own steam bath. She survived the boiling steam, but was struck three times in the neck with a sword. She lived for three more days, lying by her bathtub with her head severed, making the Trinity sign with her fingers. Cecilia was buried in gold robes (with her customary hair shirt beneath them). Twelve hundred years later, when her body was exhumed, the sculptor Maderna, who was present, depicted her in the languorous pose in which she had met her death. Unfortunately the corpse disintegrated shortly after being exposed to the air. Cecilia's emblem is the organ, and she is frequently shown in art with white and red roses and with the three wounds in her throat.

Celestine V—May 19
PATRON OF BOOKBINDERS

In the Year of Our Lord 1294, in a cave in the hills of Abruzzi, there lived a holy—if malodorous—eighty-year-old hermit named Peter. He spent his days praying and binding books. Then one day a party of cardinals arrived, knelt before him, and told him he had been elected pope. Peter took the name Celestine, rode to his coronation on a donkey, moved into a small wooden cell built in a corner of the splendid papal palace, ate nothing but bread and water, and commenced to give away the treasures of the Church to the poor. After nearly four months of this, Cardinal Benedetto Caetani boldly acted to save Christendom. He bored a hole in the wall of Celestine's cell, and inserted a speaking tube. For several nights, identifying himself as the Holy Ghost, he urged the old man to abdicate—which he did, on December 19, full of tears and apologies. Caetani became Pope Boniface VIII. Peter longed to return to his hermitage, but Boniface, fearing competition, had his predecessor imprisoned in the castle of Fumone, where after two years he died of hunger and neglect. Three popes later, in 1313, Celestine was canonized.

Chaeremon—December 22

Not even the Faithful of faraway Egypt were spared during the cruel persecutions of the Roman Emperor Decius, *circa* 250. Chaeremon was a very ancient Christian citizen of Nilopolis, who, with several companions, escaped into the barren mountains of Arabia, where it is reasonable to assume he died.

Charles Borromeo—November 4

PATRON OF APPLE ORCHARDS, CATECHISTS, SEMINARIANS, AND STARCH
MAKERS; INVOKED AGAINST STOMACHACHES AND ULCERS

Charles, who was born with the proverbial silver spoon in his mouth—his mother was a Medici—turned to a life serving God after the death of his brother. His uncle, Pope Pius IV (who wrote the landmark bull on anti-Semitism), made young Charles a cardinal even before he joined the priesthood. He continued his studies, overcame a speech defect, and assumed the role thrust on him by his uncle. Charles used his immense power and considerable fortune to build hospitals and schools and to pioneer sweeping reforms of the clergy, but he still found time to discover rich husbands for his sisters. As papal secretary of state, he authored the final decrees at the Council of Trent in 1562, eventually bringing it to a close after twenty years. His pastoral renewal had a lasting effect on the Christian world—children today still attend the religious classes he inaugurated. Charles was an avid chess player—asked what he would do if the world ended, he responded, "Keep on playing chess." He made enemies (even Saint Philip Neri [*whom* SEE] called him a thief) because of his icy demeanor and zeal for reform. One disgruntled friar of the Order of the Humiliati, whose lucrative dealings in the wool trade were aborted by Charles, made an attempt on his life in exchange for forty gold pieces. Charles fought the Protestant theology in Switzerland, as well as the witchcraft and sorcery prevalent there. His finest hour was during the plague of 1576—he remained in Milan to treat the sick and dying after the government deserted, calling the governor a coward. He ruined his health and exhausted the remainder of his fortune in paying for plague relief, was brought home to Arona on a stretcher, and died in the night. His followers donated jewelry and valuable gems to his shrine, and a large statue, affectionately called "Big Charles," was erected in his honor.

Charles Lwanga—June 3

PATRON OF AFRICAN YOUTH

Not all of Uganda's rulers have been as statesmanlike and humanitarian as Idi Amin. Mwanga (ruled 1884–97), for example, maintained a stable of teenage boys in his palace, ostensibly as "royal pages," but in truth to serve as the objects of his ravenous and unnatural lust. One of these poor lads was Our Saint, Charles Lwanga, a recently baptized Catholic who ceaselessly endeavored to convert his fellows to the One True Faith—one in which participation in such goings-on is quite expressly forbidden. Outraged, Mwanga ordered Charles and twenty-two Christian companions transported to Namugongo, where they "cheerfully chattered" (according to a witness) while they were wrapped in reed mats. They were then burned alive. Two years later, Mwanga was overthrown and exiled; he was restored to his throne only through the tireless efforts of Christian missionaries.

Christina the Astonishing—July 24

PATRONESS OF PSYCHIATRISTS

Christina, the youngest of three sisters, was born in Belgium and orphaned at fifteen. She was assumed to be dead after suffering from a cataleptic fit, but at her funeral Mass she flew out of her coffin and took refuge in the rafters of the church. The mourners fled in horror, leaving only one of her sisters and the priest, who finally persuaded her to come down. She had been offended, she explained, by the garlicky breath of the congregation. Christina then related the story of her "death" and out-of-body experiences: she had visited Hell and Purgatory, saw friends in both places, and, when she finally arrived in Heaven, heard the priest at her funeral Mass intoning the Agnus Dei. She thereupon decided not to pass on but to return to earth and liberate the souls she had seen in Purgatory. She was tormented throughout her life by her acute sense of smell (she found men particularly offensive), and to avoid noxious odors was forced to sit in baptismal fonts, perch on towers, balance herself on weathervanes, and crawl into ovens and other remote places. Many people became convinced she was "full of devils," and attempts, usually unsuccessful, were made to confine her. She even once escaped after being chained to a pillar—and she was suffering from a broken leg at the time. Later in life, however, she achieved respectability and many notable people sought her inevitably wise advice.

Christopher—July 25

PATRON OF BACHELORS, BUS DRIVERS, FERRYBOAT MEN, HORSEMEN, POLICE OFFICERS, SKIERS, TRAVELERS, TRUCK DRIVERS; INVOKED AGAINST NIGHTMARES, PERIL FROM WATER, PLAGUE, SUDDEN DEATH, AND TEMPESTS

Christopher was a twenty-four-foot-tall giant from Palestine, a blacksmith's son obsessed with the desire to serve the most powerful

king in the world. He first joined the mercenary army of a fierce tribal chieftain, but after he witnessed his master tremble before a wicked necromancer, Christopher resolved to follow the mighty Satan. But the Devil cowered and fled from the crucifix worn by an ancient hermit; so Christopher bound himself in service to that holy old man, whose task it was to ferry travelers across a river. One stormy night a child (usually pictured as a baby) appeared, and asked Christopher to carry him on his shoulders across the raging flood. During the crossing, the child grew increasingly heavy, so that the giant barely reached the far shore—where the child revealed himself as Christ, and told Christopher (Greek for "Christ-bearer") that he had just born the weight of the world on his shoulders. Christopher planted his staff by the side of the river, where it instantly became a palm tree, and set out on a career of preaching and brothel-closing. Some historians maintain that Christopher had the head of a dog; others say he opposed the wicked King Dagon, whose archers tried to slay the Saint, but whose arrows were suspended in midair. Christopher's cult was strong throughout the Middle Ages, for it was believed that anyone who looked upon his image would not die that day. His popularity declined during the so-called Enlightenment, but has flourished in our own age of dangerous road and air travel; a Saint Christopher medal dangles from the rearview mirror of many an agnostic's automobile. In 1969, the doubtlessly mythical Christopher's feast was expunged from the official Roman Catholic liturgical calendar, but he remains the best-known and probably most-loved of all the Patron Saints.

Clare of Assisi—August 11
PATRONESS OF EMBROIDERERS AND TELEVISION; INVOKED AGAINST SORE EYES

Beautiful and kindly, lively and rich, the eldest daughter of the Offreducio family had many noble suitors; but on the night of Palm Sunday, 1212, Clare of Assisi eloped. Clad in her best gown, wearing all her jewels, she slipped away from her father's house to become a bride. Awaiting her at a small church was Saint Francis of Assisi (*whom* SEE). Clare removed all her finery, and put on a sackcloth robe. Francis himself cut off her flowing hair, and married her . . . to Christ. Her father was not pleased; and when her sister Agnes left to join Clare in her cloister, he sent a band of ruffians to fetch the younger girl back. They burst into the convent, seizing Agnes by the hair. Clare prayed for a miracle. Suddenly, tiny, slender Agnes became heavy—so heavy the assembled hooligans could neither lift her up nor drag her away! And off they slunk. In the rules for the order she founded (now called the Poor Clares), Our Saint was a stickler for strict Franciscan details. Her followers wore no shoes, ate no meat, slept on the ground, and lived in absolute poverty—that is, on alms alone. As individuals and as a community, they were to own *nothing*. This policy in particular scandalized wealthy churchmen—several popes tried to persuade her of its folly—but Clare had her way. Because she and her sisters stitched vestments and altar cloths, Clare was adopted by embroiderers as their Patroness. Her name, which means "light," accounts for her traditional invocation by those with sore eyes. And Pope Pius XII, in 1958, declared her Patroness of Television. It seems that one Christmas Eve, when she was old and sick (she died in 1253), she could not leave her bed to partake in the midnight services. But in her cell she heard the singing, and on its wall saw clearly, as if by television, the manger at Bethlehem.

Clarus—January 1

PATRON OF THE SHORTSIGHTED;
INVOKED AGAINST SORE EYES AND MYOPIA

A French monk of the seventh century, Clarus was so holy he was appointed spiritual director of the convent in which his own widowed mother was a nun. For the sole reason that his name, in Latin, means "clear," his aid is traditionally invoked by persons whose vision isn't.

Claude—June 6

PATRON OF LINSEED GROWERS, TOY MAKERS, AND WHISTLE MAKERS;
INVOKED AGAINST BAD LUCK, LAMENESS, AND TWITCHING

The abbey of Saint-Claude in the Jura mountains of eastern France is named in memory of this Benedictine abbot, a bishop of Besançon who died in 699. In religious art Claude is shown either (like Saint Elmo, *whom* SEE) with his intestines being torn out—although there is no evidence he was martyred—or raising a child from the dead, although there is no reference to such a miracle in his official (skimpy) biography. Somewhere there must be a legend involving linseed, whistles, twitches, lameness, resurrections, and mutilations, but we can't track it down.

Clement—November 23
PATRON OF BLACKSMITHS, FARRIERS, STONECUTTERS, AND SHOE
TANNERS, AND OF TRINITY HOUSE, WHICH OVERSEES BRITAIN'S
LIGHTHOUSES

The third pope and a Jew by birth, Clement was converted by Paul and baptized by Peter. His family history prior to his conversion was troubled: his mother left home to avoid her lecherous brother-in-law and was lost in a shipwreck. It wasn't until twenty years later that Peter reunited Clement's family with the poor mother, who had become  a beggar. Clement witnessed Peter's martyrdom and later was himself banished to the marble quarries in Russia by the Emperor Trajan. The exiled pope made many converts in Russia, especially after he miraculously created a spring for the thirsty marble workers. Refusing to sacrifice to idols, Clement was thrown into the Black Sea with an anchor around his neck. Angels made him a tomb in the ocean, which was revealed yearly at low tide on the anniversary of his death. The Saints Cyril and Methodius (*whom* SEE) discovered his body 700 years later and delivered it to the church of San Clemente in Rome. Documents asserting the power of the papacy and general misogyny ("only men may be with men") were attributed to Clement, but later revealed to have been written 300 years after his death. Saint Clement's Day festivities usually involve a procession of blacksmiths.

Cloud—September 7
PATRON OF NAIL MAKERS; INVOKED AGAINST CARBUNCLES

The grandson of Clovis, the first Christian king of the Franks,

Cloud was raised with his two brothers by his holy grandmother, Saint Clothilde. Greedy for the throne, Cloud's two uncles, Childebert and Clotaire, tricked the old lady into sending the boys to them, with the promise they would one day assume power. Instead, the uncles stabbed Cloud's two brothers in the armpits; but Cloud, then only eight, managed to escape to Provence. As an adult, Cloud made no attempt to recover his kingdom and instead hid himself in a hermit's cell, venturing out to do some occasional preaching. Once a beggar came to his cell and Cloud gave him his only worldly possession, his hood. Later, when the beggar was walking in the dark, the hood gave off a heavenly light, indicating to the neighborhood that there was a Saint in their midst. Sometime shortly before his death at the age of thirty-six, Cloud returned to Paris to confront his uncles. No longer afraid of him and possibly feeling some guilt, the uncles endowed him with his own monastery. He is the Patron Saint of nail makers because of a crude pun on his name, *"clou"* being French for "nail."

Colman—October 13
PATRON OF AUSTRIA, HANGED MEN, AND LIVESTOCK

It appears that Colman was once a popular Irish given name, for there are over 300 official Saints Colman—for the most part holy monks, with a bard or two tossed in for variety. *This* Colman attempted, in the year 1012, to pass through Austria on his pilgrim's progress to the Holy Land. The Austrians, at war (as usual) with the Moravians, arrested the stranger as a spy. At his trial, he could not speak German, which proved his guilt, and he was summarily hanged. The resignation with which he went to his death—and the fact that his body would not decompose—convinced his hosts of his sanctity, and they concocted a bogus royal (Scottish) lineage for him. Horses and cattle are blessed in Austria on his feast day.

Colman of Cloyne—November 24

Another of the 300 Saints bearing this name, *this* Colman is the poet laureate of Ireland, the "sun-bright bard" who introduced Latin rhythms into Celtic verse. Colman was fifty years old when, after having assisted Saint Brendan (*whom* SEE) in transferring the remains of the "Wolf Saint" Ailbe (*whom* SEE), Brendan informed Colman that the hands touching hallowed relics should not remain pagan, so our Saint converted. During the Yellow Plague in 580, he took his poetry students to an island "nine waves from the shore," where the pestilence could not reach them. It was here he was inspired to write his most famous poem, the "Hymn Against Pestilence," which invokes numerous important figures from the Old Testament.

Columba—June 9
PATRON OF IRELAND AND POETS

One of Ireland's most beloved Saints (he was buried at Down with Patrick and Brigid [*both of whom* SEE]), this sixth-century poet-prince-warrior-exile was, as the saying goes, "typical Irish." Columba was born in Donegal, of the royal clan O'Neill, and given the name "Columcille" (pronounced KAW-lum KILL), meaning "Dove of the Church." An excellent student, he became, in the natural course of things, a priest. He was famous in youth as a writer—both as a scribe, turning out hundreds of copies of sacred texts in his fine calligraphy, and as a creator of original verse. He copied one manuscript without its jealous owner's permission, which led to history's first copyright lawsuit and trial. The High King of Ireland, no friend of the O'Neills, decided the case against Columba, and all Hell (quite literally) broke loose—a war, "the Battle of the Book," fought in Sligo. Because of Columba's pride and bad temper, 3,000 warriors were slain. Our Saint, naturally, repented, and his penance was this: he must leave Ireland forever ("Never again gaze on the face of a man or woman on Irish ground"), and bring to Christ as many souls as he had sent untimely to Heaven in battle. With a few choice companions, Columba sailed to pagan Scotland, establishing a monastery on the small, barren island of Iona, from which, on a (rare) clear day, you can see the hills of Ireland. From there he set out on his mission to the savage natives of North Britain, the heathen Picts. By his eloquent preaching and many miracles (such as banishing a monster from the river Ness out into the loch), he brought many more than 3,000 souls to salvation. Despite his vow, Columba did come back once to Ireland. The High King had taken it into his head to outlaw the Guild of Poets, and the bards appealed to Our Saint to come and plead their cause. He arrived blindfolded, and so gazed on 'no face; his passionate and lyrical plea in defense of poetry's power and honor prevailed; and he returned to exile. For centuries, the O'Neills carried the book Columcille copied into victorious battle; it is now on display at the Royal Irish Academy. A standing stone in Donegal marks the place of his birth, and generations of his countrymen have visited it before going into their well-known worldwide exile.

Columban (Columbanus)—November 23
PATRON INVOKED AGAINST DEPRESSION AND FLOODS

Although sins of the flesh are generally not a problem for Irish monks, Columban once found himself taunted by immodest local girls and ran to a female hermit for advice. The hermit reminded him of Adam and Eve, Samson and Delilah, etc., and suggested he leave Ireland for points south, where the women were less beautiful. Columban literally stepped over his pleading mother's body and headed for the Continent. By the end of the sixth century he had single-handedly revitalized the Faith, which had been placed in such chaos by the barbarian hordes. He was known to everyone, and cut a distinctive figure—he shaved the front of his shoulder-length hair into a half-tonsure, squirrels nested in his cowl, and he wandered around brandishing his staff and downing oak trees with his fist. While in France, Columban and his monks followed the Irish tradition, often criticized by many as being too severe: a monk who cut his finger badly while reaping had the wound cleaned by Our Saint's saliva and was ordered back to work. The Saint's stubborn orthodoxy, characteristic of the Celts, put him in conflict with the French Church, with whom he argued, among other things, about the correct date of Easter. He refused to bless the illegitimate sons of King Thierry II, calling them a bad breed, "the fruit of adultery, children of shame," thus earning the hatred of the king and his wicked mother, Brunhild. Brunhild, with the consent of the French clergy, ordered Columban and his monks deported. Their route across Europe—through France, Germany, Switzerland, and Italy—can be traced by the monasteries they founded on the way, centers of learning in the Dark Ages. Columban met up with his greatest frustration in the Rhine Valley, where, having set a vat of beer on fire with his breath, Columban damned to Hell everyone in the area. Once when

he was alone in the woods, talking to himself, Columban debated
which was worse: the savagery of beasts or the cruelty of man. Just
when he had decided on the cruelty of man (they lost their immortal
souls), twelve ravenous wolves surrounded him. He stood his
ground, reciting *"Deus in adjutorium"* until the wolves dispersed.
Columban finally settled in Italy, where he founded a monastery and
library in Bobbio, building them with his own hands even though he
was well into his seventies. Still outspoken at the end of his life,
Columban warned the pope of the potential abuse of the papacy,
speaking, as he put it, with "the native liberty of my race." He wrote
poems, and even a rowing song with the rousing chorus "Heave,
lads, and let the echoes ring."

Concordia—August 13
PATRONESS OF NANNIES

The story of the martyrdom of Saint Lawrence (*whom* SEE) was
endlessly embellished with gruesome details and secondary charac-
ters, including Hippolytus (*whom* SEE)—the jailor Lawrence converted and baptized—and Concordia, the old lady who had long ago
been Hippolytus's childhood nurse. She, too, subscribed to the Faith
and suffered for it, being scourged to death with leaden whips.

Conrad—February 19
PATRON INVOKED AGAINST FAMINE AND HERNIAS

Conrad was a married nobleman, inadvertently responsible for a
fire. At first he let a local thug take the blame, but eventually confessed and was subjected to a severe fine. He and his wife lost all their
possessions (including her dowry), and entered the Franciscans and
the Poor Clares respectively. Conrad became famous for his piety,
and for certain miracles: once during a famine the bishop came to his
cell and asked him if he had anything that could help relieve the people's hunger. Miraculously, Conrad produced freshly baked cakes.
Whenever Conrad made his confession, he was surrounded by birds.
He is invoked against hernias because, since his death in 1351, such
ailments have been cured in those praying at his tomb.

Contard Ferrini—October 20
PATRON OF UNIVERSITIES

This modern-day Italian scholar, who died in 1902, is held up to
the Faithful as an example of academic holiness—all too rare in

these days of secular humanism. During his college days in Milan, Contard had a reputation for being something of a nerd—but a pious one, it was agreed. He mastered a dozen languages, and earned a Ph.D. In 1880, he (reluctantly) left home for the first time to pursue his studies at the University of Berlin. Shocked by the morals of his fellow students, and indeed of that whole Protestant city, he made a secret—and possibly quite unnecessary—vow of perpetual virginity. Back in Milan, he became a professor of Roman law, concentrating on the Byzantine period. Allegedly, students crowded his lectures, "amazed to discover a professor who believes in God." His wit, it is said, was dry. An active member of the Saint Vincent de Paul Society, his hobby, curiously enough for a double-dome—was rock climbing.

Cornelius—September 16

PATRON OF CATTLE; INVOKED AGAINST EARACHES AND TWITCHING

When Cornelius was elected pope in 251, he beat out several rivals, including the controversial Novatian. Even though his checkered past included a bout of demonic possession, Novatian believed himself the better candidate for the papacy, being the superior theologian and ascetic. Novatian enlisted some bishops, "heated them up with wine," and succeeded in having them declare him the first formal antipope. Occurring simultaneously was a parallel feud between Saint Cyprian (*whom* SEE), backer of Cornelius, and the troublemaker Novatus, a backer of the antipope. The foursome fought over the issue of penance for lapsed Christians, with Cornelius and Cyprian for and Novatus and Novatian against. Pope Cornelius and Cyprian prevailed on the theological issue, overthrew the antipope, and excommunicated their rivals. The two Saints had some fallings out (Cornelius thought Cyprian too slow to recognize his election) but are joined together in the liturgy of the Mass; in their letters they addressed each other as "My dear priest." In the persecutions that followed, Cornelius was banished, his sufferings in exile earning him the title of martyr. His relics were later transferred to France by Charles the Bald; a mosaic of Cornelius, along with Saint Hippolyta, is in the church of St. Apollinaire (Nuevo) in Ravenna, Italy. Cornelius is generally depicted in art wearing papal robes and with a cow's horn, *"cornus"* being Latin for "horn".

Cosmas and Damian—September 26

PATRONS OF BARBERS/MEN'S HAIRDRESSERS, DOCTORS, SURGEONS, DENTISTS, DRUGGISTS, AND CHEMICAL WORKERS

Twin brothers born in Arabia, Cosmas and Damian were doctors who never charged a fee, and subsequently became known as "the moneyless ones." When a grateful patient forced three eggs on Damian as payment, a disgusted Cosmas announced that he refused to be buried with his twin. After their martyrdom, their followers, complying with Cosmas's request, started to bury the twins separately. A camel (the Saints were veterinarians as well) trotted over and begged the mourners, in the name of all cattle, to bury the twins together. The brothers' primary contribution to medical research was the practice of "incubation," whereby a patient would sleep in a church in the hope of a dream cure. The Saints' most famous feat was grafting a healthy white leg onto a diseased black patient (or vice versa). At their martyrdom, Cosmas and Damian caused arrows and stones to boomerang back to the executioners until they succumbed to the usually fail-safe method of beheading. Some heretical historians maintain they are merely an extension of the twins of Greek mythology, Castor and Pollux. However, centuries after their death, they answered the prayers of the Emperor Justinian, curing him of a serious illness, and he restored the city of Cyrus in their honor. In Rome, the Medicis (whose name means "doctors" in Italian) were likewise devoted, and named a number of their offspring Cosmo. Damian, on his own, cures bladder problems.

Crispin and Crispinian—October 25

PATRONS OF SHOEMAKERS

So traditional is their patronage of the cobbler's trade that "crispin" was long a synonym for "shoemaker," and Monday, the cobblers' day off, was called "Saint Crispin's Day." They were Roman brothers who ac-

companied Saint Quentin (*whom* SEE) on his
mission to the Gaulish pagans of Soissons,
France. There they supported themselves by
practicing their craft; they shod the poor for
free, night-visiting Angels (not elves) provid-
ing them with leather. They were martyred for their Faith in the
year 290; their beheaded bodies floated across the Channel to Faver-
sham, England, where the two shoemaker-Saints are still much revered.

Cunegund—March 3
PATRONESS OF LUXEMBOURG AND LITHUANIA

A princess of Luxembourg, Cunegund was wooed and won by the
Bavarian prince (later emperor, and, still later, Saint) Henry II. They
lived sinlessly, respecting each other's vows of perpetual chastity—so
that when Cunegund was accused of depraved and scandalous con-
duct, her consort was delighted to see her prove her innocence by
walking barefoot upon a bed of red-hot plowshares. After Henry's
death in 1024, the empress happily took the veil, eventually becoming an abbess. According to an edifying legend, she once slapped an
unruly novice in the face, leaving the marks of her fingers on the
gratefully corrected nun's cheek until that young woman's dying day.
In 1715, Pope Clement XI named Cunegund Patroness of Lithuania, a
nation that did not exist during her lifetime, but is, geographically
speaking, territory her husband once stole.

Cury—December 12
PATRON INVOKED AGAINST BLINDNESS, DEAFNESS, LAMENESS,
MUTENESS, AND DEMONIC POSSESSION

Corentin, or Cury, was a sixth-century hermit whose chapel at
Plomodiern in Brittany is still visited by the Faithful. In the nearby
stream lived a wonderful fish. For his dinner each day, Saint Cury
would cut a bit off the obliging creature and return it to the water,
where it would by the grace of God reconstitute itself overnight. On
one occasion Good King Gradlon and his attendants dropped by
unexpectedly, and Cury's fish fed the entire company. But one
wretch returned to steal the miraculous creature, and in his greed
killed it, forcing Cury to restore it to life and grant it its freedom. The
people of the neighborhood begged Cury to become their bishop,

and he reluctantly agreed. The Gothic cathedral of St. Corentin remains the pride of the city of Quimper; below the base of its spires is a statue of the Saint's friend, King Gradlon.

Cuthbert—March 20
PATRON OF SAILORS

A strapping shepherd lad from the north of England, Cuthbert became a monk (reports the historian Bede) in response to a vision. It was Cuthbert's custom to pray naked, winter and summer, immersed in the icy North Sea. Witnesses said that local seals (or otters—accounts vary) would snuggle up to him for warmth. He preferred a life of solitude on a barren island, but served as bishop of Lindisfarne from 685 to 687. Of his episcopal zeal, Baring-Gould writes, "No saint of his time or country had more frequent or affectionate intercourse than Cuthbert with the nuns." Included among his miracles were instances of restoring dead children to life, and verbal communication with sea fowl.

Cyprian—September 16
PATRON OF ALGERIA AND NORTH AFRICA

Cyprian was an orator and advocate who led such a dissolute life that when he converted at the age of fifty and took a vow of chastity, an onlooker exclaimed, "Whoever saw such a miracle!" He then devoted himself to Christian studies, preceding Saint Augustine of Hippo as a great teacher in North Africa. He became a priest and then bishop of Carthage, using his oratorical skills to preach of Heaven and Hell. Borrowing from Greek mythology, he vividly described the horrors of Hell, the "murmuring and groaning of souls bewailing, and with flames belching forth through the horrid darkness of the thick night." He went into hiding during the Decian persecution, causing many people to call him a coward and abandon their Faith. When Cyprian returned, he took the lapsed Christians back, disagreeing with the pope, who favored punishing them. He quarreled with another pope (who called the African bishop a "false Christ") over the validity of certain baptisms, which led to the Donatist Schism.

Cyprian retreated again during a second persecution, but returned to stand trial and to set an example to his flock. When his death sentence was announced, he said, "Thanks be to God." He was beheaded after giving his executioner twenty-five gold pieces and snapping, "Hurry up and get it over with."

Cyriacus—August 8
PATRON INVOKED AGAINST EYE DISEASE AND DEMONIAC POSSESSION

The Emperor Diocletian persecuted the Christians of Rome in the year 303 by obliging them to build the city an enormous bathhouse. Nevertheless, Cyriacus, one of the indentured construction workers, took pity on the emperor's daughter Artemia, who was possessed by a demon, and in Christ's name cast out the evil spirit inhabiting her. Impressed, Diocletian granted Our Saint a sabbatical, and dispatched him to Persia, where Jobia, the daughter of Diocletian's ally King Sapor, was likewise diabolically afflicted. Cyriacus not only cured the princess, but converted the king and 430 of his courtiers to the Faith. He then returned to Rome, where for his thanks he was bound in chains, dipped in boiling pitch, and decapitated. He was invoked throughout the Middle Ages as a specialist in exorcising devils; as such he is one of the Fourteen Holy Helpers (*whom* SEE), upon whose collective feast day his personal feast day falls.

Cyricus—June 16
PATRON OF CHILDREN

Little Cyricus—or Cyr, as he is known in France—was but three years of age when his mother, Saint Julitta, was haled before Alexander, governor of Alexandria, and charged with Christianity. When she proudly confessed her Faith, she was stripped, flogged, and racked—before the eyes of her tiny son, whom the wicked Alexander dandled on his knee. "I'm a Twistian too!" lisped the tot, as he kicked and scratched his pious mother's tormentor. Enraged, the wicked magistrate flung the holy child down a flight of stairs, killing him; when Julitta rejoiced in her son's martydom, he gave orders that she be slain as well. Some centuries later, the child "Cyr" appeared— stark naked—to the Emperor Charlemagne, just in time to rescue that worthy monarch from the threatening tusks of a wild boar; for which reason many places, including the French "West Point," are named in his honor.

Cyril and Methodius—February 14
PATRONS OF CZECHOSLOVAKIA, EUROPE, AND THE SLAVS

The Cyrillic alphabet, in which the Russian, Ukrainian, and Slavonic languages are still written, was supposedly devised in the ninth century by these missionary brothers. They spent their lives, when not preaching or translating Holy Scripture, quarreling with German ("Latin") prelates over liturgical rights to all the turf east of the Danube. In a recent (1980) ecumenical gesture, John Paul II, himself a Slav, declared the two "Joint Patrons of Europe," along with Saint Benedict (*whom* SEE).

Damasus—December 11

PATRON OF ARCHAEOLOGISTS

Like his father before him, Damasus was a simple priest in Rome, when at the age of sixty he was elected to succeed Liberius as Supreme Pontiff, in the Year of Our Lord 366. His right to the Chair of Peter was contested by a rival, Ursinus, and the armed adherents of pope and antipope warred in the streets, until Damasus's faction negotiated his support by the imperial authorities. Another staunch supporter of Damasus was the learned Saint Jerome (*whom* SEE), who praised him as "a Virgin Doctor of the Virgin Church." Pope Damasus encouraged devotion to the early martyrs, to which end he ordered that the catacombs in which they were entombed be excavated, drained, adorned, and open to the public.

David—March 1

PATRON OF POETS AND OF WALES

David (whose real name was Dewi) was of royal descent, Welsh style—he was begotten (mid-fourth century) when Sant, a ferocious Celtic chieftain, raped the pure and pious Saint Non. Through this connection, as the eminent historian Geoffrey of Monmouth observes, David was related to King Arthur himself. Young David traveled to the Isle of Wight to study under Saint Paulinurus, and upon his arrival cured that ancient Welsh ascetic of his blindness (which had been caused by excessive weeping). Upon his return to Wales, David began, prolifically, to establish monasteries—the ruins of which may yet be seen at every crossroads west of Herefordshire. A dreadful thing, the Pelagian heresy (a liberal, English, "anything-goes" school of thought), was popular in Britain at that time, but David would have none of it; his life and monastic rule were so severe that he was nicknamed "the Waterman," because he and his monks were all strict teetotallers. He ate nothing but bread, salt, and leeks—which vegetable became the national symbol of the Welsh, to be worn proudly (in the hat) every Saint David's Day.

Demetrius—October 8
PATRON OF BULGARIA, MACEDONIA, AND SERBIA

As a matter of historical fact, Demetrius appears to have been a simple missionary-deacon who was martyred at Mitrovica in Serbia around the year 300. In legend, he is a great warrior-Saint, a knight similar to Saint George (*whom* SEE), invoked by his Balkan clients in their endless wars against the Austrians, Avars, Hungarians, Slavs, Turks, and each other.

Denis—October 9
PATRON OF FRANCE; INVOKED AGAINST FRENZY AND HEADACHES

Denis was the first bishop of Paris, one of the original seven missionaries sent from Rome to minister to the pagan Gauls, in the year 90. He could have been a Greek philosopher named Dionysius, converted and baptized by Saint Paul himself. And then again, maybe not. After Our Saint was decapitated in the somewhat unsavory Montmartre district, he picked up his head and carried it six miles to the present site of the great cathedral that bears his name. "The first step," said the Saint's head, "was the difficult one." "*Montjoie Saint Denys!*" ("Follow Saint Denis!") was for centuries the war cry of the armies of France, who rode to battle behind his banner, the golden oriflamme.

Devota—January 17
PATRONESS OF CORSICA AND MONACO

A Christian maiden of Corsica, Devota was cruelly martyred in 303—after her feet were tied together and she was dragged over rough ground, she was stretched on the rack. Yet she would not deny her Lord, and when she mercifully expired, a white dove was seen fluttering over her body. A priest and a friendly boatman placed her blessed remains in a skiff, and it followed the dove across the sea to Monaco, where she is interred.

Didier—May 23
PATRON OF CHILDBIRTH; INVOKED AGAINST FALSE WITNESS

Queen Brunhilde of Burgundy (534–613) was a real character. When her sister Galeswintha was murdered by her husband, Chilperic, Brunhilde urged her own husband, Sigebert, to exact revenge in the form of a vast land-grab. At the end of the war, Sigebert was dead and Brunhilde imprisoned. Down but not out, the plucky queen seduced and married Merovech, Chilperic's son. The bishop of Vienne, Desiderius (Didier to his friends), denounced this naughtiness; whereupon Brunhilde encouraged a certain woman named Justa to accuse Our Saint of being no saint, and he was banished from his diocese for some time. Didier was eventually restored to his bishopric, and martyred (in 607) by thugs acting on behalf of Brunhilde's grandson, King Thierry II. She herself came to no good end when, at the age of 80, she was dragged to death at a horse's tail in 613.

Diego Alcalá—November 13
PATRON OF COOKS

Born near Seville early in the fifteenth century, Diego was, as a young man, an apprentice to a solitary hermit—together they grew vegetables and fashioned kitchen utensils for sale. He then joined the Franciscans as a laybrother, and was sent to a friary in the Canary Islands, where he was employed as cook and doorkeeper. As a result of his charity to the local poor and his miracle-working care of sick friars, Diego was (to his surprise) chosen as Superior of the house for a term. After another thirteen years of humble service in friaries throughout Spain, he died at Alcalá in 1463. The Saint was raised from obscurity to canonization by the tireless efforts of King Philip of Spain, who credited the cure of his son to Diego's heavenly intercession.

Dismas ("The Good Thief")—March 25
PATRON OF CRIMINALS, THIEVES, AND UNDERTAKERS

The Gospels assure us that Christ was crucified between two thieves, and that He promised one of them a trip to Paradise. Pious legend, which ascribes the names Dismas and Gestas to the Son of God's fellow victims of capital punishment, further relates that they had all met before—when the two thieves waylaid the Christ Child and His Holy Family on their visit to Egypt. On  that occasion as well, Gestas behaved like a cad, whereas Dismas was a perfect gentleman.

Dogmael—June 14
PATRON OF CHILDREN LEARNING TO WALK

The toddlers of Brittany are placed under the protection of this fifth-century monk. He was a native of Wales, the son of Ithel ap Ceredig ap Cunedda Wledig.

Dometius the Persian—August 7
PATRON INVOKED AGAINST SCIATICA

If there was one group the Emperor Julian the Apostate hated more than Persians, it was Christians. Dometius was both, and people flocked to his humble cave to be cured of their spiritual ills as well as stiffness of the joints, until his fame reached the emperor's ears. Julian traveled to Dometius's hermitage, witnessed a few miracles, and accused Our Saint of being—in so many words—a show-off. Then he had him stoned to death.

Dominic—August 8
PATRON OF ASTRONOMERS AND THE DOMINICAN REPUBLIC

Before Dominic Guzman was born, his mother, a noblewoman of Castile, dreamt that her child would be a dog with a lighted torch in its mouth, and at the time of his baptism she clearly saw a star shining on his breast. No biography of this Saint omits these curious details, and a star is Dominic's emblem, which accounts for his traditional patronage of astronomers. In 1203, when he was thirty-three, the young Dominic visited Languedoc in the south of France, where he was shocked to see shameless heresy—in this case, the Albigensian, or Cathar, heresy—being practiced everywhere with utter impunity. For the next decade, he and a small band of like-minded clerics tramped the dusty countryside around Toulouse preaching a return to Orthodoxy, with wonderful results. In Dominic's wake marched the great army (financed by the pope and the king of France) of Simon de Montfort. Whenever an individual or a community clung stubbornly to Catharism, he, she, or it was put to fire and the sword. (At the city of Béziers, in 1209, the entire population—men, women, and children—was slaughtered for harboring the Albigenses. "Kill them all," ordered Simon. "God will know His own." A Gothic-Roman Catholic church now marks the site.) Dominic always attributed his success against the Cathars to the power of rosary beads, a device he appears to have invented. In the city of Toulouse, finally captured and returned to the One True Fold, in 1215, Dominic founded his religious order, a paramilitary organization of ultraorthodox heretic-bashers at first called the Friars Preachers, but soon to be known everywhere as the Dominicans. Dominic was famous for his miracles: he raised numerous deserving persons from the dead. To settle doctrinal arguments, he would throw books—his own and his opponent's—into a bonfire, where Error would burn, but from which Truth would emerge unscorched. It is also asserted that Dominic met and was admired by the gentle Saint Francis of Assisi (*whom* SEE), but this strains credulity. Dominic had been dead for ten years when, in 1231, Pope Gregory IX instituted the Inquisition; but we can be certain there was joy in Heaven when Our Saint learned that the Dominicans were put in charge of it.

Dominic of Silos—December 20
PATRON OF CAPTIVES AND SHEPHERDS; INVOKED AGAINST INSECTS AND MAD DOGS

Dominic, who was a devout lad, was a shepherd in the Cantabrian Mountains of Spain. He joined the Benedictine Order and became a monk in the abbey at Silos, where he rose to the rank of abbot because of both his piety and his prescient support of the territorial claims of Castile over those of Navarre. His prayers helped a local noblewoman through a difficult pregnancy, and she named her child Dominic (SEE *above*) in his honor. For centuries, Our Saint's staff has been brought to every Spanish queen during her confinement. Following his death in 1073, visions of Dominic often appeared, freeing Spanish prisoners of war being held captive during the long Moorish occupation of the Spanish peninsula.

Dominic Savio—March 9
PATRON OF CHOIRBOYS AND
JUVENILE DELINQUENTS

Dominic Savio holds the record as the youngest (nonmartyr) Saint ever officially canonized. He died in 1857, at the age of fifteen. His mentor and biographer was Saint John "Don" Bosco (*whom* SEE). Thanks to the influence of that wise and kindly man, the teenage mystic from Turin was prevented from becoming an altogether insufferable prig and flamboyant masochist. While the lad enjoyed confiscating and shredding his fellow students' porno magazines, and inserting a crucifix between school-yard combatants, he was, we are assured, no tattletale. Bosco's report to Pope Pius IX of a miraculous vision of Dominic's—he saw people wandering in a fog—allegedly inspired Pius IX to renew the Vatican's attentions to the spiritual plight of the English.

Domitian—May 7
PATRON INVOKED AGAINST FEVER

Upon Domitian's appointment to the bishopric of Maastricht (*circa* 550), he immediately banished the loathsome dragon that had been poisoning the local water supply, a spring at Huy on the Meuse. His popularity increased when, in a time of famine, he successfully predicted a bumper crop, thereby convincing the rich to distribute the grain they had been hoarding.

Donatus—October 22

In 828, the bishop of the Italian city of Fiesole (near Florence) died, and the townsfolk assembled in the cathedral to elect his successor. When an Irish monk (on his way home from a pilgrimage to Rome) entered, the bells all rang and the candles lit themselves. And the Fiesolans acclaimed Donatus their new bishop. Bishop Donatus (the locals called him Dino) befriended the Frankish king, Lothair, and his son, Louis the Pious. On behalf of the latter, Donatus led an army against marauding Saracens, and, for the sake of passing pilgrims from his homeland, he established a hospice, Saint Brigid's in Piacenza.

Dorothy—February 6
PATRONESS OF BRIDES, FLORISTS, AND GARDENERS; INVOKED AGAINST
FIRE, LIGHTNING, AND THIEVES

A beautiful Christian maiden of Caesarea in Cappadocia, Dorothy was desired by the provost Fabricus, but refused his offer of marriage. He sent his two sisters to plead his case, but instead Dorothy converted them to the Faith. She was jailed (and fed by Angels), thrown into boiling oil (which she turned to balm); stretched on an iron bed over flames (at which she smiled). As she was being led to the place of

her beheading, a bystander (Theophilus) sarcastically asked her to send him fruit and flowers from her "heavenly garden." After her
death, a child (an Angel in disguise) appeared
to him bearing apples and roses—in February,
remember—and told him Dorothy was awaiting him in her garden. After tasting one of the
apples, Theophilus was converted, executed,
cut into pieces, and fed to the birds.

Dorothy of Montau—October 30
PATRONESS OF PRUSSIA

In 1364, when she was seventeen, Dorothy married a wealthy
swordsmith, Albert of Danzig. By the constant example of her piety,
she transformed the surly brute into a Christian gentleman. She also
bore him nine children, one of whom survived. Upon Albert's death,
Dorothy retreated to a simple hermitage, where she experienced numerous mystical visions. She was able, for example, to actually *see*
Christ in the Eucharist. Her counsel was sought by the mighty, and
her miraculous curative powers by the infirm.

Drausius—March 7
PATRON OF CHAMPIONS

The magnificent sarcophagus of Drausius is now an exhibit at the
Louvre. (It is empty of his holy relics, which were scattered and dese-
crated during the excesses of the French Revolution.) For centuries,
while it was in the cathedral at Soissons, the sarcophagus was the site
of nightlong vigils made by knights and warriors about to enter combat—champions not only from France, but from Italy and England as
well. Through the intercession of Drausius, they were made invul-
nerable. He himself had led an austere life of church-building and severe bodily mortifications until his death (or Heavenly Birthday) on
this day in 674.

Drogo—April 16
PATRON OF COFFEEHOUSE OWNERS AND SHEPHERDS; INVOKED AGAINST
HERNIA AND GRAVEL IN THE URINE

A posthumous child—his father died before he was born, and his
mother in childbirth—the Flemish Drogo was consumed all his life

with self-loathing. He became a humble shepherd renowned for his sanctity as well as for his remarkable ability to hear Mass in church while simultaneously tending his flocks in the field, which gave rise to the famous Flemish folk-saying, "Not being Saint Drogo, I can't be in two places at the same time." Severe misfortune befell him in the form of an ulcer that emitted so foul an odor it forced him into seclusion. He built a humble hut by the side of the church, which he refused to leave even when the church caught fire. Eventually his bowels putrefied, leading to his death in the year 1186. For reasons of their own, the coffeehouse owners of Flanders long ago took him as their Patron Saint.

Dunstan—May 19
PATRON OF ARMORERS, BLACKSMITHS, GOLDSMITHS, JEWELERS, AND LOCKSMITHS

In Mayfield convent, East Sussex, England, visitors may gaze upon the blacksmith's tongs with which Saint Dunstan caught the Devil (who appeared to him in the guise of an evil woman) by the nose. As archbishop of Canterbury, Dunstan strongly disapproved of King Edwy, whom he openly accused of having sex. Banished by that licentious Saxon monarch, he took up the craft of a smith, and it was in this period that he encountered and bested the Devil. He was restored to high office by, and officiated at the coronation of, King Edgar in 957. Dunstan acted as a sort of secretary of state to him and to his successor, Edward the Martyr (*whom* SEE).

Dwyn—January 25
PATRONESS OF LOVERS AND SICK ANIMALS

This fifth-century Welsh maiden was the child of parents both royal and devout; nevertheless, Dwyn fell passionately in love with a young man named Maelon Mafodril, and he with her. But, following a spat, she asked the Lord up above, "Why must I be a teenager in love?" and an Angel appeared, offering her a heavenly potion to ease her heartache. She drank it, and its effect was to turn Maelon to ice (or stone—accounts differ). Appalled, Dwyn requested and was granted three wishes. Her first was that Maelon be restored to life. Her second was that all true lovers who invoked her name either achieved their hearts' desires or at least recovered quickly from their disappointment . . . and, finally, she asked that she herself never marry nor even wish to. So Dwyn became a nun, serving as abbess of a convent in the place that still bears her name, Llanddwyn. There can be found a miraculous spring, wherein, from the movements of the fish, the adept can tell the future. Its waters also work wonders with sick animals.

Dymphna—May 15
PATRONESS OF ASYLUMS AND MENTAL-HEALTH WORKERS; INVOKED
AGAINST EPILEPSY, INSANITY, AND SLEEPWALKING

In Belgium, near the town of Geel, can be found one of Europe's largest and most "progressive" hospitals for the care and cure of the emotionally disturbed. It was founded on the site of Saint Dymphna's martyrdom, and is named in her honor. Dymphna was the teenage daughter of Damon, an Irish warlord. When his wife died, Damon was inconsolable. He searched, they say, the Western world in vain for another bride as fair, until his grief-crazed gaze fell upon his wife's living image—their own daughter.

No sooner had he made his depraved desires known to Dymphna than the maiden fled Ireland for far-off Belgium, aided and accompanied in her escape by Father Gerebran (an old and holy priest), as well as by her father's court jester and his wife. Spies sent by Damon followed the trail of Irish coins the runaways paid or gave to the poor, and found the fugitives living in a hut in the woods at Geel. The mad Damon himself then crossed the sea, surprised his daughter, demanded she accede to his monstrous demands, and, when she refused, drew his sword and slew her where she stood. At her grave, miraculous cures of epileptics and other "lunatics" soon began to occur; Dymphna has ever since been invoked by all who suffer emotional and nervous disorders. But the obvious connection between the sexual abuse of children and mental illness, made in the sixth century, would not be discovered again for 1,300 years.

Edmund—November 20
PATRON INVOKED AGAINST PLAGUE

Edmund became king of the Angles (that part of England known as East Anglia, which juts into the North Sea) at the age of fourteen, and took the Old Testament's King David as his role model, memorizing all his psalms. The Viking princes Hingvar and Hubba, mistakenly thinking Edmund had murdered their father, Lodbrod ("hairy breeches"), invaded England. Edmund's army was roundly defeated and he offered himself to the enemy, hoping to save his people. He was scourged, shot with arrows, and finally beheaded. The Vikings, afraid that his head would be worshipped, took it to another part of the forest in which he had died, where a wolf came to protect it. A year later Edmund's men found the body and started looking for the head, crying, "Where art thou?" In time the head answered, "Here! Here! Here!" The men found it (with the wolf still on guard) and were able, miraculously, to join the head to the body. Edmund's still incorrupt corpse was taken to Bury St. Edmunds, where his shrine and cult became an inspiration for the art and literature of the time, embodying as it did the heroic ideals of the period.

Edmund Campion—December 1
PATRON OF PRINTERS

History calls the last Catholic monarch of England "Bloody Mary." She was succeeded by "Good Queen Bess." By order of the latter, Edmund Campion was the first of hundreds to be hanged,

drawn, and quartered for adhering to their religious beliefs. Campion was born in London in
1540, the son of a London printer-bookseller. A
brilliant writer and speaker, at seventeen he became an Oxford fellow, but in the persecutions
that followed the queen's excommunication he
fled to France, where he joined the Jesuits. In
1580 he returned to his homeland as a sort of
secret agent for the Faith. He was the object of
a year-long manhunt, all the while ministering
to Catholics in hiding and publishing "underground" pamphlets, including his famous autobiographical "Brag." Betrayed, captured, tried,

and convicted of treason, he was executed on the first day of December 1581. Along with thirty-nine of his fellow martyrs—priests, lay-
men, and laywomen—he was canonized in 1970.

Edward the Martyr—March 18

The son of the English King Edgar by his first wife, at thirteen Edward assumed the throne upon his father's death in 975. His mentor
and spiritual advisor was the great Saint Dunstan (*whom* SEE). When
he was all of sixteen, he unwisely paid a visit to the home of his half
brother Ethelred. There his "wicked but beautiful" stepmother "al-
lured him with her female blandishments" (as the *Anglo-Saxon Chronicle* nicely phrases it) until her henchmen stabbed the lad. So Ethelred
became king and, when a rash of flamboyant miracles broke out in
the vicinity of Edward's grave, had the decency to order the nation-
wide observance of his Sainted brother's feast. His stepmother joined
a nunnery.

Eleutheris of Tournai—February 20

An extremely handsome man, Eleutheris was made a bishop by
the age of thirty. The daughter of the governor of Tournai—both of
whom were pagan—was madly in love with him, interrupting his
prayers one day to declare her passion. She grabbed his robe, and,
when Eleutheris ran away, leaving her holding the garment, she
dropped dead on the spot. Eleutheris went to the grieving governor
and promised to bring his daughter back to life if he would convert to
Christianity. The governor agreed, but insincerely, and it took three

more tries before the governor, this time *really* seeming to convert, made it possible for Eleutheris to raise the girl from the dead. After his conversion, the governor reverted to his former ways, and a plague broke out. Eleutheris was thrown into prison, and the plague worsened. Truly contrite yet again, the governor released Eleutheris and promised to stay faithful to Christianity. The plague ceased, and 11,000 citizens became Christians. In his later years, the bishop was attacked and killed by a band of heretical Arians. Eleutheris's emblem is, for no apparent reason, a heated oven.

Elias—July 20
PATRON INVOKED AGAINST EARTHQUAKES AND DROUGHT
Several Old Testament figures, including Enoch and Elias (Elijah), are venerated as Saints simply for the reason that they are, the Bible says, in Heaven. Elias, a ninth-century (B.C.) prophet, traveled there in style, in both a chariot of fire and a whirlwind (2 Kings 2:11). His cause has been strongly promoted by the Carmelite Order, who claim him as their founder. He was hiding from an earthquake in a cave on Mount Carmel when he heard "a still, small voice" urging him to denounce King Ahab and Queen Jezebel.

Elizabeth—November 5
PATRONESS OF PREGNANT WOMEN
Elizabeth was an aged, barren woman, related to the Blessed Virgin and married to the righteous Zachary. Luke, in telling her story, borrows from the Old Testament tradition of hero births: an Angel (Gabriel—*whom* SEE) announced to Zachary that the elderly Elizabeth would give birth to her first child. On hearing the news, Zachary was struck dumb. When the Blessed Virgin, also pregnant, came to visit Elizabeth, John the Baptist (though yet unborn) leapt in the womb, recognizing Christ. At the circumcision, after Zachary and Elizabeth defied the Temple by naming the baby John instead of after his father, Zachary's speech returned. Immediately afterward, escaping Herod's persecution of newborns, Elizabeth fled with the baby to the foot of a mountain. She cried, "Mount of God, receive a mother with her child," and the mountain miraculously opened up and gave them shelter. When Herod had Zachary killed, Elizabeth went into the desert and raised John alone. After Elizabeth's death, her firebrand son emerged from the desert to begin his short but memorable career.

Some historians feel that Elizabeth's veneration is an outcome of the Church's tendency to impart holiness to the mothers of major Saints and biblical figures.

Elizabeth of Hungary—November 17
PATRONESS OF BAKERS; INVOKED AGAINST THE PLAGUE

A princess, Elizabeth of Hungary, who was born in 1207, was engaged at the age of four to Ludwig of Thuringia, and went to live with her fiancé and his family as a child. The betrothed children called each other "brother" and "sister," but Elizabeth's mother-in-law-to-be was not so benign, sneering, "She may be a king's child, but her mother was a concubine!" After her marriage and ascension to the throne, the courtiers still persecuted Elizabeth, but her relationship with Ludwig was described as an "idyll of enthralling fondness, of mystic ardor." The young queen threw herself into the performing of charitable acts, wearing dowdy clothes as she tended the sick—behavior that further isolated her from the court. Elizabeth would often return from a day of nursing, change into her royal robes, and preside over a court banquet. She named *both* her daughters after her mother-in-law in a futile attempt to gain that woman's approval. Elizabeth fell under the influence of a sadistic confessor, Conrad of Marburg, who abused her physically and mentally for the rest of her life. Conrad held most of the country in thrall as well, leading a pack of fanatics, shaving heads, and burning "heretics" alive. After King Ludwig died—felled by the heat and bad air on a Crusade—Elizabeth was disconsolate: "Dead! Dead! Dead! The world is dead to me!" she would wail. Her melodrama continued when her brother-in-law threw her and her children (including her son, who was the rightful heir) out of the castle, forcing them to live in a pigsty. Orders were given throughout the country that the former royal family be shunned, and Elizabeth was comforted only by occasional visions of Christ. She was eventually given a settlement, and Father Conrad took this opportunity to assert total control over her life. On Good Friday, 1525, Elizabeth renounced the world, her family, and her children, and submitted herself to Conrad's authority, causing rumors to spread suggesting their relationship was of a sexual nature. She wore rags, scrubbed floors, and enlisted virgins to follow her. When her father, the king of Hungary, saw her, he cried and begged her to come home, but she refused. It was generally agreed that Conrad's brutal

treatment was responsible for Elizabeth's death at the age of twenty-six. Just before she died, she heard a heavenly choir—and at her funeral Conrad lost no time in collecting depositions for her sainthood, while the devout, eager for relics, groped in her coffin, cutting off her hair and nipples. Her son was poisoned by his uncle nine years after

Elizabeth's death. She is the Patroness of bakers because the ubiquitous story of concealed bread being turned into roses is attributed to
her as well as to other Saints.

Elizabeth of Portugal—July 4
PATRONESS OF PORTUGAL AND OF THE THIRD ORDER OF SAINT FRANCIS

Elizabeth of Portugal was the daughter of King Peter III of Aragon; Saint Elizabeth of Hungary (*above*) was her great-aunt. At
twelve, she married the reluctant King Denis, who complained of
her large ears. A benevolent monarch, skilled in the art of fandango
dancing and expert on the castanets, Elizabeth established hospitals
(where she personally washed feet), orphanages, and homes for
wayward women. Family feuds consumed her life, beginning with
that between her father and grandfather, continuing with her son
and husband, and concluding with her son and grandson. When her
son and husband took up arms against each other, Elizabeth rode a
mule down the center of the battlefield to attempt a reconciliation.
Like Saints Zita and her Great-Aunt Elizabeth, she hid bread for the
poor in her apron, bread that turned to roses when she was confronted by her irate husband. A unsavory scandal occurred when an
evil-minded page told King Denis that Elizabeth was having an affair
with another page. The king (who himself obliged Elizabeth to raise
his illegitimate children) ordered her alleged lover thrown into a
lime kiln, but, in a happy mix-up, the evil page was thrown in instead! This convinced King Denis that Elizabeth was innocent. One
miracle cited at her canonization told of a carpenter who, falling
from a roof onto a beam, invoked Our Saint on the way down and
was miraculously restored (with the beam) to his original position.
Another miracle told of a wet nurse who went dry but who, after
drinking wine according to the Saint's prescription was able to nurse
two more children. Elizabeth's feast day, *Rainha Santa*, is cause for
great celebration in parts of Portugal.

Elmo—June 2
PATRON OF SAILORS AND WOMEN IN LABOR; INVOKED AGAINST COLIC,
SEASICKNESS, AND STOMACHACHE

The real name of this enormously popular Saint seems to have
been Erasmus. He is said to have been a Syrian bishop who fled, in a
time of persecution, to a cave on Mount Lebanon, where he was fed

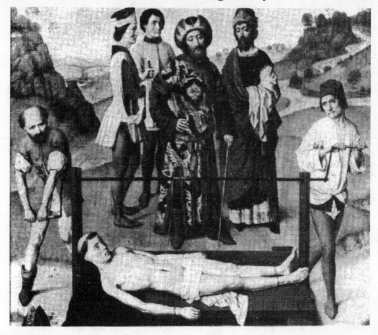

by a raven. Finally captured by the pagan police, he was rolled in pitch and set alight; his experience as a human torch may account for his association with the maritime phenomenon known as "Saint Elmo's fire"—the blue light surrounding ships' masts and prows during electrical storms. Elmo survived this ordeal and escaped in a boat piloted by an Angel, crossing the Mediterranean to Italy, where he died of his wounds. Elmo is represented in sacred art standing beside a ship's windlass, which, during the Middle Ages, inspired among the Faithful the quaint notion that Elmo had been tortured by having his intestines extracted by means of such a device. His aid is therefore invoked by those suffering abdominal pain, including women in childbirth and on behalf of infants with colic.

Eloy—December 1

PATRON OF BLACKSMITHS, COIN COLLECTORS, FARRIERS, GARAGE WORKERS, GOLDSMITHS, JOCKEYS, HORSES, JEWELERS, AND METALWORKERS

This popular seventh-century Patron of "all who work with hammers" is an actual historical figure, an artisan employed by the Frank

ish King Dagobert I as master of the
mint. Eloy's reputation for honesty was
enhanced when he was commissioned
to design and fashion a throne for
Dagobert's son, Clotaire II. Rather than
pocketing the excess materials—gold
and jewels—Eloy (French, Eloi; Latin, Eleqius) constructed for the
heir Clotaire a pair of chairs. His most famous deed as a farrier—that
is, a shoer of horses—involved an animal possessed by a devil. Eloy
blessed the beast, removed its legs, applied the shoes, and grafted the
limbs back on, better than new.

Elzear—September 27
PATRON OF CHRISTIAN GENTLEMEN

Elzear's mother consecrated him to God when he was an infant,
and even as a child he mortified himself by wearing a knotted cord
around his waist. He was married at sixteen to the heiress Delphina,
an equally devout lady who shared his passion for Holy Communion
and had only slight difficulty convincing Elzear to agree to a virgin
union. The holy couple set up housekeeping in Delphina's castle, following a strict moral code that forbade dice, backbiting, and oppression, and included daily Holy Communion services. As lord of the
manor, Elzear won over vassals who had been loath to serve him,
and cured Prince Charles of vanity. In gratitude, Charles appointed
Elzear to public office, but Elzear continued to work among the
poor. Once, when offered a bribe, the Saint sagely observed, "When
one begins to take gifts, an appetite for receiving grows and becomes
insatiable." When Elzear was sent on a mission to Paris, Delphina
voiced concern about his virtue, but Elzear pointed out that if he
hadn't fallen into evil ways in Naples (where he had served as tutor to
the king's son), he wasn't likely to in Paris. But he did, in fact, fall sick
there, made his last confession—he had no mortal sins—and died.
Fifty-one years later, he was canonized by his nephew and godson,
Pope Urban V.

Emerentiana—January 23
PATRONESS INVOKED AGAINST STOMACHACHE

When the relics of a martyr by this name were discovered in
Rome near the shrine of Saint Agnes (*whom* SEE), the faithful piously

conjectured Emerentiana to be Agnes's foster sister. As the legend developed, the maiden was still a catechumen—that is, someone preparing to become a Christian—when Agnes was slain, but she received a "baptism of blood" when she was stoned to death by pagans while praying at her foster sister's tomb. As a miracle worker, she specializes in intestinal disorders.

Emilian—December 6
PATRON OF DRUGGISTS

A fourth-century theologian named Arius taught that, since there is only one God—God the Father—the Savior Jesus Christ could not have been "God" as well. At the Council of Nicaea in 325, "Arianism" was debated and condemned as a heresy, and the truth of the Trinity affirmed. But among Arius's disciples were the Vandals, a marauding Germanic tribe. They were, so to speak, both Aryans and Arians. The Vandals, after sacking Rome, established a kingdom of their own in, of all places, North Africa. There, for a century or so, they gave themselves over to rape, pillage, piracy, and the persecution of the indigenous orthodox Christians. On this day in the year 484 the beautiful and chaste Saint Dionysia was tortured in the arena and burned at the stake for her unswerving faith in the Divinity of Christ. During the same public entertainment and for the same cause her cousin Emilian, a physician and pharmacist, was flayed to death.

Emillion—November 12
PATRON OF SPAIN; INVOKED FOR HELP IN FINDING LOST OBJECTS

Aragon and Castile both claim this minor patron of Spain as a native son. Emillion lived a happy hermit's existence for forty years until a bishop summoned him to serve as parish priest. He was dismissed for being impractical after he gave all the church goods to the poor. The relieved Saint returned to his cell, where he lived to be over 100 and became known as "the cowled one." In art, he is generally represented doing something he never did in real life: fighting the Moors on horseback.

Emygdius—August 9
PATRON INVOKED AGAINST EARTHQUAKES

A citizen of Trier, and therefore a Teuton, or German, Emygdius was converted to Christianity in the year 300 or so, and immediately began rushing about destroying the idols of the locally popular but nevertheless false gods. Then, one step ahead of the enraged pagan clergy, he fled to Rome, where he was made a bishop. His legend is, all authorities agree, historically worthless. But since he is a protector of those in danger from earthquakes, his feast is to this day vigorously celebrated through Italy, and by Italo-Americans living along the earthquake-prone San Andreas Fault in California.

Enda—March 21

Much to the dismay of his sister, the Abbess Faenche, Enda was a (fifth-century) Irish warrior of the most violent class. In answer to Faenche's tearful petitions that he amend his militant ways, Enda vowed to do so only if she would give him, in marriage, the loveliest novice-nun in her care, to which terms she reluctantly agreed. But as fate (or Divine Providence) would have it, the comely virgin in question expired that very night, and when Enda arrived next day to claim his bride, his holy sister unveiled, dramatically, the corpse. This inspired him to depart for Wales, where he studied for Holy Orders under Saint David (*whom* SEE), and thence for Rome, where he was ordained. Upon his return to Erin, Enda, now a model of piety, established a monastery on the barren island of Aranmore, in Galway Bay—a full 1,400 years before it was discovered by the Protestant playwright John Millington *"Playboy"* Synge.

Ephraem—July 9
PATRON OF SYRIA

When the Persians (Iranians) overran Mesopotamia (Iraq) in 363, Ephraem, a Christian deacon and schoolteacher, took to a cave, wherein he wrote the numerous hymns that earned him the title "Harp of the Holy Ghost"; he also wrote many defenses of the doctrine of the Immaculate Conception. He never, we are assured, laughed or smiled.

Eric IX—May 18
PATRON OF SWEDEN

Eric IX became king of Sweden in 1150, and caused his nations's laws to be codified and its first cathedral (in Uppsala) to be erected. He believed that the neighboring Finns should either be baptized or die, and saw to it that a great many of them did one or the other. An army of Danes, aided and abetted by Swedish traitors, put an end to his glorious reign (by beheading him) in 1161.

Ethelbert—May 20
PATRON INVOKED AGAINST THIEVES

This prince of East Anglia sought the hand of the Princess Alfreda, of the neighboring (and hostile) kingdom of Mercia, to which honorable end he visited, in the year 794, the castle of her father, King Offa. Thither he was made welcome by Offa's cunning queen, who showed him to his chambers, wherein a large and inviting chair had been placed upon a trapdoor. Ethelbert sat down, and was never seen or heard from again. Offa, after annexing East Anglia, caused a cathedral to be built at Hereford, which he piously dedicated to Ethelbert.

Eugenia/Eugenius—December 25

The thirteenth-century collection of saints' tales known as *The Golden Legend* tells us Eugenia was the beautiful daughter of the pagan Duke Philip of Alexandria. To preserve her chastity, she disguised herself as a man—"Eugenius"—and fled her father's house to join a desert monastery. Sometime later, the young "monk" was accused of rape by a woman of the neighborhood—at whose motives we can scarcely guess. "Eugenius" was haled before the judge—who happened to be her own father!—and sentenced to death. At which point, says our author, "she rent her coat and showed to him that she was a woman and his daughter." (What proof she showed of the latter we are not told.) Overwhelmed, the duke became a Christian, and, making an utterly happy end to the tale, "the lady that had falsely accused Eugenius . . . was burnt with fire of hell."

Eulalia—December 10
PATRONESS OF BARCELONA, SAILORS, SEA VOYAGERS, AND WOMEN IN LABOR; INVOKED AGAINST DROUGHT AND STORMS AT SEA

This devout virgin, beloved throughout all of Catalonia, was but twelve years old (in the year 304) when she decided to publicly denounce the pagan authorities. She was arrested, naturally, and during her trial was so bold as to trample beneath her feet a cake sacred to the heathen Roman idols. She was sentenced to be cruelly executed—but luckily for her a torch held by her would-be tormentors set her long hair on fire and she smothered in the smoke. Thereupon a white dove flew out of her mouth and ascended to Heaven, and a sudden fall of snow covered her innocent ashes. Her aid has been invoked by all who sail the seas off the Costa Brava.

Eulogius of Córdova—March 11
PATRON OF CARPENTERS AND COPPERSMITHS

A scholar-priest in Muslim-occupied Spain, Eulogius was betrayed by a treacherous bishop and taken prisoner by the Infidels in the year 850. In his cell, he composed the moving "Exhortation to Martyrdom," which inspired his fellow prisoners, Saints Flora and Mary, to die bravely for the Faith. Eulogius himself was then set free. For sheltering a Muslim convert (Saint Leocritia), he was rearrested, and at his trial allegedly offered to convert the *kadi*, the Muslim magistrate, as well. He was beheaded.

Eurosia—June 25
PATRONESS OF CROPS; INVOKED AGAINST DROUGHT

In the Pyrenees of southern France and northern Spain, Eurosia is petitioned against drought and blight by the local farmers at this important time of the agricultural year. She was a pure and virtuous maiden of Bayonne (or perhaps Bohemia), martyred for refusing the bestial advances of a Saracen pirate.

Euseus—February 15
PATRON OF SHOEMAKERS

Because this fourteenth-century hermit in the Piedmont plied the cobbler's trade, he is accounted their Patron.

Eustace—September 20
PATRON OF HUNTERS AND OF MADRID; INVOKED IN CASE OF FAMILY TROUBLES

The story of this Saint, now demoted from the official Church Calendar, was enormously popular throughout the Middle Ages. Eustace was, it seems, a wealthy and powerful Roman general—a captain of the guards under the Emperor Trajan—who, while hunting one day in the woods near Tivoli, Italy, encountered a stag with a luminous crucifix between its antlers, while a heavenly Voice prophesied, "Thou shalt suffer many things for My sake." The huntsman immediately converted to Christianity, as did his wife and their two sons.

The prophecy came true with a vengeance. Eustace was drummed out of the army, and reduced to abject poverty. His wife was kidnapped by pirates. His sons were carried off by wild beasts. Years later, in time of need, the emperor recalled his trusted officer. Back in Rome, Eustace was overjoyed to discover that his sons had miraculously survived and were actually serving under his command. And by a greater miracle, his wife reappeared, alive and not much the worse for wear. But the family's celebration was short-lived. Ordered to worship idols, they refused. They survived exposure to lions in the amphitheater, only to be roasted to death in the belly of a brass bull. Something in the tale touched the heart of medieval man—the Happy Ending? In Germany, Our Saint was considered one of the Fourteen Holy Helpers (*whom* SEE). The Spanish city of Madrid is dedicated to him, as is the magnificent church of Saint-Eustache in Paris, Rome's ninth-century church of Sant' Eustachio, and the Swiss cathedral where his relics are still venerated.

Expiditus—April 19
PATRON OF EMERGENCIES; INVOKED AGAINST PROCRASTINATION

Although Expiditus's cult is venerable and he has answered many a plea for speediness in the execution of errands, this Saint may or may not have existed. According to one theory, he was an Armenian martyr. But a persistent rumor concerns a packing case once shipped from Rome to a convent of Parisian nuns. It contained the skeleton of an authentic but anonymous Saint, and was labeled in Italian SPEDITO, that is (as we would say) SPECIAL DELIVERY. But the good sisters assumed QUICKLY (in Latin, EXPIDITUS) to be the name of the Saint within. This tale has an envious-Protestant or malevolent-agnostic ring to it.

Fabian—January 20
PATRON OF LEAD FOUNDERS AND POTTERS

This twentieth pope was a layman, elected to the Chair of Peter in 236 because a pigeon landed on his head. After a fourteen-year reign, he was martyred.

Faith of Agen—October 6
PATRONESS OF PRISONERS AND SOLDIERS

The charred remains of this virgin martyr, stored in an ornate reliquary at Conques, France, were long an object of pilgrimages, especially by Crusaders on their way to Holy War. Her cult still remains strong in Bogotá, Colombia. Her impregnable virtue was rewarded by her being immolated on a brazen bed during the third-century persecutions conducted by the Roman governor of the Aquitaine, the notorious Dacian. The English call her "Saint Foy"—and her legend is sometimes confused with an earlier Greek martyr of the same name.

Felicity—March 7
PATRONESS OF MOTHERS; INVOKED AGAINST INFERTILITY

It was in Carthage, in the year 202, that the noble and beautiful matron Perpetua and her pregnant slave Felicity were arrested and charged with the crime of believing in the One True God, as their *Acts*, written by Perpetua herself, testify. They were both, naturally, eager to suffer and die for their Faith, but feared the authorities would spare Felicity, due to her delicate condition. Together they prayed, and luckily ("Felicity" means "fortunate") the slave-girl gave birth prematurely. The sweet patience with which she endured the pangs of labor inspired a jailor, Pudens, to convert to the Faith. Then both women were led into the arena, where they happily submitted to being flogged by gladiators, and thrown, not to the lions, but to a wild cow. Saint Augustine of Hippo (*whom* SEE) was not actually present at the execution; nevertheless he assures us that even as they were being tossed on the horns of the savage beast, they carefully kept their skirts down.

Felix of Nola—January 14
PATRON INVOKED AGAINST PERJURY

There are more than sixty Saints called Felix in the Roman Martyrology. This one, a priest of Syrian descent, was, at the time of the Emperor Decius's persecution of the Christians (around 250), assistant to Bishop Maximus of Nola. The old bishop went into hiding; the police arrested Felix, and tortured and imprisoned him. With the help of an Angel, Felix escaped, eluding his pursuers by hiding in a cave across the entrance of which an obliging spider spun a web. He tracked down Maximus, and carried the sick old man back home to be cared for; despite popular demand, Felix declined the bishopric after Maximus's death. All this we know from a poem written by a later bishop of Nola, Paulinus, who assures us that, in Heaven, Felix has a special sympathy for innocent victims of false testimony.

Ferdinand—May 30
PATRON OF ENGINEERS, GOVERNORS, RULERS, AND MAGISTRATES

For a thousand years the Iberian peninsula was a patchwork of petty feuding fiefdoms, the whole in the heathen power of Africa. It was under San Fernando that the nation of Spain emerged. He inherited the kingdom of León from his father, and Castile from his mother. Andalusia he took for himself, city by city, siege by siege, from 1215 to 1272. At the Battle of Xeres (now Jerez), which was the climax of the *reconquesta,* Saint James himself, or Santiago, as he was known to the Spaniards, came down from Heaven on a white horse to lead the charge. The Moors were utterly routed; only ten Spanish lives were lost. In peace as well as war, Ferdinand was the model of a Catholic ruler. He begat, by succeeding wives, nine sons and three daughters. In thanksgiving for his victories, he ordered the Great Mosque at Seville turned into a Real Church. The Jews of his realm, so long as they wore funny hats and paid large fines, were not unduly persecuted. He was as diligent in ransoming Christian slaves from the Infidels as he was in selling infidel slaves to the Christians.

Fermin—July 6
PATRON OF PAMPLONA

To commemorate the unusual manner of Fermin's martyrdom (he was dragged through the streets by bulls), his annual fiesta on this day features the world-famous "running of the bulls," during which the young men of the town (and Hemingway fans from America) are gored and trampled.

Ferreolus—September 18
PATRON OF SICK POULTRY; INVOKED AGAINST RHEUMATISM

Ferreolus was a tribune and secret Christian who was exposed when he refused to arrest Christians or worship idols. He was placed in chains in the prison cesspool, aptly called the "barathrum." On the third day, he slipped from his chains and made a daredevil escape through the sewer, only to be recaptured and beheaded. What any of this has to do with chickens is anybody's guess.

Fiacre—September 1
PATRON OF CABDRIVERS, GARDENERS, AND NEEDLE MAKERS; INVOKED AGAINST HEMORRHOIDS AND VENEREAL DISEASE

Because a hackney stand in Paris was located in front of a hotel named in honor of this Saint, French taxis are called "*fiacres*." Thus, Fiacre is the Patron of cabbies. By a lucky coincidence, "*fic*" (meaning "fig") is a French slang term for hemorrhoids—a common complaint of taxi drivers, against which Fiacre's aid is invoked. Fiacre was an Irish hermit who resettled in Brittany, and a gifted horticulturalist. When the local bishop offered him as much land as he could plow in a day, Fiacre, using only his staff, cleared several acres, on which he erected a church and hermitage, and planted an extensive vegetable garden. A neighboring shrew first

complained to the bishop about this land deal, and then harangued
Fiacre to his face. Her tirade left the Saint so downhearted that he
sat heavily upon a stone, leaving thereon the imprint of his buttocks.
(This stone was later moved to the church of Saint-Fiacre-en-Brie,
where generations of pilgrims sat on it to be cured of the piles.) The
incident confirmed the Saint as a militant misogynist: all women
were banned from his chapel, and when a noblewoman of Paris defied this rule, she grew to elephantine proportions and went mad.
Another peeped inside and her eyes fell out. Nevertheless, Anne of
Austria, queen to Louis XIII, was greatly devoted to Our Saint, and
credited him with the safe delivery of her son the Sun King.

Fidelis of Sigmarignen—April 24

Fidelis, whose real name was Mark Rey, was a Renaissance Franciscan friar with a doctorate in law and philosophy, renowned as "the
poor man's lawyer." Thoroughly disgusted with the law, Fidelis
abandoned it to concentrate on preaching and caring for the sick. He
wore a hair shirt, abstained from wine, and was sent from Italy to
combat the Zwinglian heresy in Switzerland. He was preaching in a
Swiss church when a bullet flew by him, but he kept on with his sermon. Shortly afterward he was killed with knives, and his head and
arm were cut off. A few days before his assassination he signed a letter "Brother Fidelis, who will soon be food for worms."

Fillian—January 19
PATRON INVOKED AGAINST INSANITY

An eighth-century English hermit of Irish descent, who could
(they say) study all night by the light of his glowing left hand, Fillian
had, during his lifetime, a calming effect on the mad. Long after his
death (up until the nineteenth century) the mentally ill of Scotland
were dipped in a pool (called Strathfillan) and left, tied up, overnight
in the ruins of the Saint's chapel nearby. If they were found loose in
the morning, they were considered cured.

Fina—March 12

Fina was christened Seraphina, but everyone in Tuscany knew her
as Fina, the shy and beautiful daughter of a poor widow. At the age of
six, paralyzed by an illness, she asked not to lie on a cot, but on a hard
board, in emulation of Jesus on His cross. Nor did she utter a word of

complaint when rats and mice nibbled on
the many sores she developed, for the dead
Pope Gregory the Great (*whom* SEE), had appeared to her and promised the child a
happy death on his feast day (which used to
be celebrated on this date). And so it came
to pass. And when the neighbors came to

bury Our Saint, they discovered that the board she lay on was cov-
ered, not with scabs and pus, but with sweet-smelling white violets.

Finnbar (Barry)—September 25
PATRON OF CORK

Originally named Loan, Finnbar was the illegitimate son of a
metalworker and a royal lady. He was the shame of the court until a
group of hermits spirited him off. While cutting the boy's hair one
day, a hermit exclaimed, *"Finnbar! Shining hair!"* thus changing his
name. ("Finnbar" actually means "white hair.") Finnbar in his youth
rescued a small town that was being terrorized by a serpent as large
as a hill: he sprinkled the beast with holy oil, causing it to flee, roaring, into the sea, tearing up the land in its wake and forming a river. It
was there that Finnbar built his monastery, which attracted a large
following and created what is now the city of Cork. His reputation as
a miracle worker grew after he healed the blind and mute daughter of
King Fachtna the Angry and returned the king's dead wife to life.
Finnbar could make hazelnuts appear on a tree, instantly ripen, and
fall into his lap. When the pope wanted to travel to Ireland and conse-
crate Finnbar a bishop, the Saint refused him, explaining that Heaven
Itself wished to perform the ceremony. Which Heaven did—and during it, Finnbar was airlifted by Angels above the altar, and oil poured
forth, covering the feet of those nearby. Then Christ appeared, and
took Finnbar by the hand, after which Finnbar's right hand always
emitted rays of light. Sometime later, crossing the English Channel in
Saint David's boat, the *Horse,* he spotted Saint Brendan (*whom* SEE)
heading in the other direction on his way to discover America. When
Finnbar died, the sun didn't set for two weeks.

Fintan—February 17

This early-seventh-century Irishman led a strict order of monks,
who ingested nothing but woody bread and muddy water—and that

only after sunset. In addition to possessing the gift of prophecy, when Fintan prayed he was surrounded by a light so brilliant it once struck a fellow monk blind. The severed heads of vanquished Celtic warriors were buried near Fintan's monastery in the belief that proximity to such holy men would hasten their salvation. The members of neighboring monasteries were intimidated by Fintan's austerities, and in the hopes of persuading him to relax his restrictions, requested a colloquy with him. On his way to meet them, Our Saint, encountering a deaf-mute, blessed and cured him. The first words out of the man's mouth urged Fintan to accommodate "the weaker vessels," which Fintan then agreed to do—exempting himself from any liberal reform.

Flannan—December 18

The son of an Irish chieftain, Flannan made a pilgrimage to Rome (to which he sailed, Saint that he was, on a floating stone) and, once there, was consecrated bishop by the pope himself (John IV, who died in 642). Flannan returned to Ireland, and became a wandering preacher, famous as well in Scotland and in the Western Isles—a group of which desolate rocks still bear his holy name. It had been predicted by Saint Colman of Cloyne (*whom* SEE) that Flannan's father would beget seven kings, all named Brian. (Which, by the way, he did.) Despite *not* being named Brian, Our Saint feared all earthly honors, and prayed to be made physically repulsive. Merciful God heard his pleas, and afflicted him with rashes, boils, and scars about the face. It is also believed that Flannan invented the delicious Irish practice of praying seven times a day while immersed to the neck in icy water, the better to banish carnal temptations.

Florentius—November 7

PATRON INVOKED AGAINST GALLSTONES AND RUPTURE

Florentius was a peripatetic Irishman who settled down as a hermit in Alsace. When he reentered society, Florentius preached and worked miracles, including healing the king's daughter, a deaf-mute. He set up a monastery for his countrymen, in the Irish tradition, at Strasbourg. The

monks of Bonneval sold his relics to the abbot of Peterborough, England.

Florian—May 4
PATRON OF AUSTRIA, BREWERS, CHIMNEY SWEEPS, FIRE FIGHTERS, POLAND, AND SOAP BOILERS; INVOKED AGAINST DROWNING, FIRE, AND FLOODS

An officer in the Roman army of occupation in Austria, Florian confessed his own Christianity rather than take part in the persecution of the Faithful. He was scourged twice and the skin was entirely flayed from his body before he was tossed, with a millstone around his neck, into the river Enns, in the year 304. He is alleged to have extinguished a raging conflagration by pouring a single pitcher of water on it—hence his Patronage of fire fighters; the pitcher he is shown holding in sacred art explains his association with brewers; his death by drowning explains his being invoked against danger from water; he is a Patron of Poland by virtue of the fact that his holy relics were bestowed by Pope Lucius III upon the city of Cracow. Why he is prayed to by soap boilers—in fact, what soap boilers are—remains a mystery.

The Four Crowned Martyrs—November 8
This team of stonemasons in Yugoslavia—traditionally named Claudius, Nicostratus, Simpronian, and Castorius—created a number of ornate carvings for the building-mad Roman Emperor Diocletian. But, being Christians, they refused to make an idolatrous statue of Aesculapius, the pagan god of healing, and were arrested. When the judge conducting their trial suddenly dropped dead, his influential family blamed the four masons, who were forthwith placed in lead boxes and drowned. (A fifth mason, Simplicius, died along with them, but was not granted the Crown of Martyrdom, for he had only pretended to become a Christian in order to improve his carving skills.) Understandably, they were taken as Patrons by the medieval stonemasons' guild. There is a great church, the Quattro Coronati in Rome, and, ironically, a London lodge of the (militant anti-Catholic) Freemasons with the same name.

The Fourteen Holy Helpers—August 8
These fourteen worthies are the most powerful of all the miracle-working Saints. Miraculously (for instance), they number nineteen:

Acacius, Antony of Padua, Barbara, Blaise, Catherine of Alexandria, Christopher, Cyriacus, Denis, Elmo, Eustace, George, Giles, Leonard, Margaret of Antioch, Nicholas of Myra, Pantaleon, Roch, Sebastian, and Vitus—*all of whom* SEE. Their cult reached its (well-nigh idolatrous) height (understandably enough) during the Black Plague (1347–51); it was strongly discouraged by the Council of Trent (1545). This feast itself, like the feasts of many of the individual Saints, has been officially suppressed in the ecumenical interest of making Roman Catholicism less fun.

Fra Angelico—February 18
PATRON OF ARTISTS

Born Guido di Pietro, this Dominican friar and painter of the Italian Renaissance created many frescoes for the monastery of San Marco in Florence, most notably the *Annunciation* (1440). He was venerated as "Blessed" even by his contemporaries, but not officially recognized as a Saint until 1984, when Pope John Paul II, despite the objections of the Congregation for the Causes of Saints, bypassed the usual channels of canonization and unilaterally declared him to be the Patron of Artists. Art historians in general agree with the poet Browning: "Brother Angelico's the man, you'll find."

Frances of Rome—March 9
PATRONESS OF MOTORISTS AND WIDOWS

Had there been—which there were not—society pages in Rome in 1397, they would have banner-headlined the nuptials of the beautiful and aristocratic Francesca dei Roffredeschi, aged thirteen, to the dashing Lorenzo, heir to the vast Ponziano castle and estates in Campagna. In truth, the marriage got off to a rocky start, and the bride, who would have preferred the life of a nun, waxed pale and sickly. Only after Saint Alexis (*whom* SEE) appeared to her in a vision did she resign herself to the married state, recover, and swiftly bear three children. But these were the days of the Great Schism, and when the wicked forces of the antipope attacked Rome, the family castle was pillaged and burned, and Lorenzo himself was badly wounded. The once-wealthy Ponzianos now wore rags and begged for scraps. Two of the children died of plague; then an Angel appeared to Frances. (She described him as blond, blue-eyed, and with very clean feet.) This Being's unearthly radiance, visible only to her, enabled Our

Saint, throughout her life, to see in the dark—hence, one supposes, her Vatican-confirmed Patronage of motorists. With the Angel always at her side, she bravely endured her husband's death and her surviving son's unfortunate marriage. She eventually joined a convent, where in her old age she experienced (and described) many entertainingly graphic visions of Hell.

Frances Xavier Cabrini—November 13
PATRONESS OF EMIGRANTS, HOSPITAL ADMINISTRATORS, AND
IMMIGRANTS

Frances Xavier Cabrini was the first American citizen to be canonized, doubtless as much for her business acumen as for her holiness. Frances (she added the Xavier herself), was born in Italy, the youngest of thirteen children. A bout of smallpox prevented her from entering the convent, so she became a celibate teacher in an orphanage managed by a mad nun. She boldly took charge, and the pope was so impressed by her managerial skills that he approved her newly founded order of missionaries. Her lifelong dream (after reading the *Annals of the Propagation of the Faith*) was to be a missionary to China, but the pope, saying "Go West, not East," sent her to New York. The tiny Frances, who spoke very little English, came to America in 1889 to tend the 50,000 Italian immigrants there. The school and orphanage she expected to manage never materialized, because the archbishop of New York had a falling out with his benefactress, the Countess Cesnola, so His Eminence suggested Frances and her nuns vacate their vermin-infested room in Gotham's slums and return home to Italy. Instead she herself maneuvered funding from the countess, and built her first orphanage on the shores of the Hudson River. By 1917, the astute businesswoman had expanded operations into eight countries and built numerous hospitals, schools, and convents. Critics point to her extreme narrow-mindedness—illegitimate Catholic children as well as Protestants were unwelcome in her schools. Controversy raged around her in Italy—a lawsuit was filed against her in Italian courts and she was the cause of riots in Milan. Frances died of malaria in 1917 and her canonization process was quickly undertaken by her friend and compatriot Pope Pius XI. At her canonization ceremony in 1946, Pope Pius XII stressed that her accomplishments were supernaturally extraordinary—since they were beyond the normal strength of any woman. Her body, originally (and mistakenly) thought to be incorrupt, lies, under glass, in the Washington Heights section of Manhattan.

Francis Borgia—October 10
PATRON OF PORTUGAL; INVOKED AGAINST EARTHQUAKES

Alexander VI was, without doubt, the worst of the "Bad Popes" of the Renaissance. Among his children by his various mistresses were the unscrupulous Cesare Borgia—Machiavelli's model for *The Prince*—and Lucretia Borgia, evil incarnate. Among his great-grand-children was Saint Francis Borgia, the third Father General of the Jesuits. He was a Spanish nobleman, a duke, happily married, the father of eight, the viceroy of Catalonia, fabulously wealthy, and enormously fat. Then one day, for reasons of state, he chanced to glance into the coffin of the late Queen Isabella and see the putrefied face of that once-beautiful monarch. It made him think. When his own wife died, Francis, then forty years old, settled his estate upon his eldest son and, with the permission of Saint Ignatius Loyola (*whom* SEE) himself, joined the Society of Jesus. As a preacher, this duke-turned-Jesuit was especially popular among the Catholics of Portugal, and disliked by the Inquisition. In 1565 he was elected to lead the Society. He built, at his own expense, the Roman College, now the Gregorian University in Rome, and dispatched Jesuit missionaries to as far away as Poland and North America.

Francis de Sales—January 24
PATRON OF EDITORS, JOURNALISTS, AND WRITERS; INVOKED AGAINST DEAFNESS

The militantly Catholic duke of Savoy had a problem—the majority of his subjects along the shores of Lake Geneva had, by 1593, become militant Calvinists. Furthermore, the wily Protestants, taking advantage of an outbreak of literacy among the innocent peasants, were distributing copies of the Bible, newly translated into French—although the Vatican had expressly forbidden the printing of the Good Book in any language but Latin. Clearly, this was a job for Francis de Sales. Our Saint was a local boy, and by most accounts a scholar and a gentleman, notwithstanding his youthful indiscretions with one Mlle. de Vezy. After an unsuccessful (if papally sanctioned) attempt to bribe the Calvinist clergy into submission, Francis began wandering among the heretical Savoyards, passing out copies *not* of

that obscure and dangerous text, the Bible, but of his own personal writings, which included that early classic of self-help literature, *Introduction to the Devout Life*. After failing in a number of attempts to assassinate the Saint, the Savoyard population en masse (so to speak) returned to the fold of the One True Faith, and Francis became the bishop of Geneva.

Francis of Assisi—October 4

PATRON OF ANIMALS, ECOLOGY, ITALY, AND TAPESTRY MAKERS;
INVOKED AGAINST FIRE

Francis of Assisi's great popularity, even among unbelievers, has never waned—he remains a subject for garden statuary and Hollywood movies. Born at Assisi in northern Italy in 1181, the son of a wealthy cloth merchant, Francis was christened John. Because his mother was French, he was given the then rare nickname of Francis ("Francesco," meaning "little Frenchman"). In his youth he was extravagant and carefree, a troubadour and knight-at-arms. But on a pilgrimage to Rome, he impulsively exchanged his rich attire for a beggar's grimy garb. And on his return to Assisi, he took to dismounting from his horse and passionately kissing lepers. When he was twenty-six, while praying in a ruined chapel, he heard an image of the Crucified say to him, "Repair My falling house." Taking Him literally, Francis immediately began restoring the building. In need of funds, he sold bolts of cloth taken from his father's warehouse. His angry parent haled him before the bishop, and disinherited his apparently mad son. Francis happily removed the clothes he was wearing at the time and gave them back. The bishop clad the naked Saint in the rough brown tunic of his gardener; this was the origin of the distinctive Franciscan habit. Francis departed, singing, and was immediately (to his great delight) beaten and thrown into a ditch by a band of ruffians. The knight-troubadour had found his True Love: "My Lady Poverty," he called her. With a few like-minded companions ("friars"), he wandered the countryside, begging and preaching. Within fifteen years, he was the leader of 5,000 Friars Minor and a growing sister order of nuns, the Poor Clares. Francis wrote a very strict Rule for them to live by, emphasizing absolute poverty, humility, and discipline. During his life, and in the following centuries, that Rule has been (acrimoniously) liberalized, conserved, reformed, and modified many times. But Francis himself is not so much a religious organizer as a charismatic example—a hero. He preached a sermon to the birds; he made a peace treaty with a wolf; he instituted the tradition of the Christmas crib. And in 1224, while praying, he was granted the Stigmata—the marks of Christ's five wounds on his own body. In 1226, nearly blind and very ill, he composed and sang his *Canticle of Brother Sun,* and joyfully went to meet "His Sister Death." He had wished to be buried in a paupers' field, but was enshrined in the lavish basilica in Assisi which bears his name.

Francis of Paolo—April 2

PATRON OF NAVAL OFFICERS, SAILORS, AND SEAFARERS

At thirteen Francis of Paolo became a friar; at fifteen a solitary hermit in a cave by the sea; and at nineteen the founder of an order, the Minims ("the lowest ones"), who specialized in feats of fasting—denying themselves not only meat, but eggs and milk. Although he never wore shoes, washed, or changed his clothes throughout his lifetime (nearly the entire sixteenth century), Francis was renowned as a miracle worker, mind reader, and advisor to kings and popes. No one he met ever failed to comment on his peculiar heavenly odor. Chronically short of funds, he was once berated by a blacksmith for nonpayment, and commanded his horse to kick off its new shoes—which it did. Stranded in Sicily without passage money, Francis spread his cloak on the waves, stepped aboard, and floated home to Calabria. For this miracle, his aid is invoked by all who sail. He was impervious to heat and cold—able to hold burning coals in his hands, and walk barefoot in the snow. He was summoned to aid and advise two succeeding French kings, Louis the Spider and Charles the Affable. Canonized within a decade of his death, Francis was long a favorite of artists—appearing (posthumously) in works by Goya, Velázquez, Victor Hugo, and Franz Liszt.

Francis Patrizi—May 12

PATRON OF RECONCILIATIONS

A nobleman of Siena, Francis heard, at an impressionable age, a sermon by a member of the Mendicant Servites, which inspired him to join that order after his blind mother's death. He achieved instant fame and popularity as a confessor; fabulous sinners came to him from miles around to tell all, which made many of his fellow Servites understandably jealous. Luckily, the Blessed Virgin appeared to Our Saint, admonished him to use "his tongue, not his ears," and struck him deaf. Thereafter, Francis became a celebrated extemporaneous preacher, whose sermons had the wonderful effect of reconciling the bitterest of enemies.

Francis Xavier—December 3

PATRON OF FOREIGN MISSIONS, GOA, INDIA, JAPAN, OUTER MONGOLIA, AND TOURISM

Except (perhaps) for Saint Paul, Francis Xavier was the greatest Christian missionary. A Basque Spaniard, he was born in 1506 into a new, round world, in which rich untamed lands lay to the east and west of Europe. As a student in Paris, Francis met Ignatius Loyola (*whom* SEE) and upon being asked by that Saint what it would profit him to gain the world but lose his soul, signed on as one of the seven original Jesuits. By papal command, Francis set out for the newly discovered East Indies. After a ghastly thirteen-month voyage around Africa, he arrived in the Portuguese colony of Goa in May of 1542, and labored for seven years to reform the corrupt colonists and to convert the natives in southern India and throughout the Malay peninsula. There remains some question as to whether Francis mastered the Malabar language, preached through interpreters, or was possessed of the gift of tongues, but he certainly took his vow of poverty seriously, living on rice and water and sleeping in a hut. Among the Indian poor, therefore, he had great success—but none with sophisticated Hindus of higher caste. When he heard from mariners about the land of Japan (which they had glimpsed, but dared not enter), he sailed thither, becoming the first European to set foot upon those islands. For two years he preached with astonishing success to the Japanese, establishing a thriving Christian colony before setting out for the even more forbidding nation of China. But it was God's will that Francis die on an island within sight of that country, worn out from his labors, an old man at the age of forty-six. He is alleged to have personally baptized several hundred thousand people. Often, at day's end, his arms ached from administering the sacrament. His work, of course, was of supreme urgency, for like all Catholics, he knew that the soul of any mortal anywhere on earth who dies unbaptized proceeds directly to eternal Hell.

Fridolin—March 6
PATRON OF OPTOMETRISTS

Nicknamed "the Traveler," this sixth-century Irish monk journeyed as far into darkest Europe as the Rhine. On his way through Gaul, he visited a monastery at Poitiers, which had recently been sacked by the pagan tribe whose very name is a byword for vandalism, the Vandals. While there, he was miraculously granted a sort of X-ray vision, through which he discovered, buried in the rubble, the holy remains of Saint Hilary (*whom* SEE).

Frumentius—October 27

PATRON OF ETHIOPIA

With his younger brother, Aedesius, this Syrian-Christian philosophy student arrived by ship in Ethiopia in the year 330. While the lads were ashore, sitting under a tree studying and praying, the Ethiopians slaughtered everyone aboard, and then fetched the two survivors before the king at Axum. His Majesty was much impressed by the dignity and bearing of the boys, and made them members of his court—Aedesius as his cupbearer, Frumentius as his secretary. Upon the king's death some years later, the brothers were set free. The younger returned to Tyre to tell this preposterous tale, while Frumentius journeyed to Alexandria, was anointed bishop, and made his way back to Ethiopia, where he had considerable success Christianizing the natives. "Abuna" ("Our Father"), the name by which he was known, remains to this day the honorific title of the Primate of the Ethiopian Orthodox Church.

Gabriel Possenti—February 27

PATRON OF COLLEGE STUDENTS

Gabriel's father was a lawyer and the leading Catholic layman of Assisi, begetting thirteen children by his wife before she died. Orphaned at four, the boy (whose name was originally Francis) was raised by Jesuits, and in his youth was nicknamed "Il Damerino" ("The Ladies' Man"). Twice in his teens he was afflicted with serious illnesses, and on both occasions vowed to enter the priesthood if cured, but on recovery he delayed his decision. In 1856 (when he was eighteen) an epidemic of cholera broke out. A Holy Picture of Our Lady of the Sorrows was paraded through the streets, which put a quick end to the plague, but as it passed Francis, the Blessed Mother looked at and spoke to him. He immediately joined the Passion-

ist Order, taking the name "Gabriel of Our Lady of the Sorrows." Until he died of tuberculosis at twenty-two, he was, by all accounts, a model novice—humble and obedient, his body wrapped at his own request in chains set with sharp points, the better to mortify his sinful flesh. Small wonder that the Sacred Congregation of Rites, confirming his Sainthood in 1932, recommended him as Patron of college students.

Gabriel the Archangel—March 24

PATRON OF CHILDBIRTH, DIPLOMATS, MESSENGERS, POSTAL WORKERS, STAMP COLLECTORS, TELEPHONE AND TELEVISION WORKERS

After Michael (*whom* SEE) the second most glorious of all the Heavenly Host, Gabriel has acted throughout history as God's envoy to humankind. It was he who explained to the imprisoned prophet Daniel the meaning of his visions, who advised the father of John the Baptist (*whom* SEE) that his barren wife was with child, and who announced the news of her being In the Holy Family Way to the Blessed Virgin (coining, in the process, the most frequently repeated phrase in history, "Hail, Mary"). By tradition it is said that Gabriel led the singing Herald Angels in proclaiming Christ's birth to the shepherds. Muslims call him Gibrail, and believe he dictated the Koran. Pope Pius XII, in 1951, declared him Patron of everyone employed in the telecommunications industries. Paul VI, in 1982, put mail carriers under his protection—and, by extension, stamp collectors.

Gall—October 16

PATRON OF BIRDS AND OF SWITZERLAND

There are several possible reasons for this Saint's traditional Patronage of our feathered friends. Gall once performed an exorcism on a young girl, and the dispossessed demon flew out her mouth in the form of a black bird. He and Saint Columba (*whom* SEE) lived for a while near Lake Zurich on a diet of waterfowl. Furthermore, "*gallo*" is Italian for "rooster." By destroying their idols and wrecking the vats in which the sacred beer was brewed, this

Irish missionary offended the Swiss people and their pagan deities. He did constant battle with the local water sprites (called "nixes"). Finally, Gall settled in an Alpine cave (which he shared with a bear) near the town of Arbon, where he died in 645.

Galmier—February 27
PATRON OF LOCKSMITHS

A locksmith in Lyons, Galmier (aka Baldomerus) lived in great poverty and gave everything (including his tools) to the poor. His holiness inspired the monastery of Saint-Justus to give him a cell and the birds to eat out of his hand. Eventually, against his will, he was made subdeacon and inspired this piece of verse by a fellow monk:

> In chastity, clean
> In friendship, firm
> In charity, benign
> In reading, intent
> In watching, solicitious
> In almsgiving, prompt.

Gelasius I—November 21

African by birth and believed to be the illegitimate son of a bishop, Gelasius I was the first pope to be called "the Vicar of Christ." A tough administrator in the tradition of Pope Leo, he battled schisms and barbarism. He was less than infallible when he insisted that all babies who died before receiving Holy Communion would go straight to Hell—a dictum that was overruled by the Council of Trent. His self-described Gelasian Renaissance demanded, among other things, that bishops turn over half their revenue to the Vatican and that wine be taken at Mass—a pointed affront to the sober Manichaeans. Gelasius argued for separation of Church and State, plainly telling the emperor to stay out of his affairs, but exercised his own right to make civil decisions, even banning the harmless festival of Lupercalia. His landmark ruling (in 493) against women serving at the altar remains in effect.

Gemma Galgani—April 11
PATRONESS OF HOSPITAL PHARMACISTS

Roman Catholicism at the end of the twentieth century featured a flurry of flamboyantly holy female mystics, such as the Fatima children, Louise Lateau, and Therese Neumann, but Gemma Galgani was the only one to be canonized—and not without considerable opposition within the Church. Her popularity, especially among Italians, is immense, but the Vatican remains somewhat embarrassed by the supernatural phenomena attributed to her. The daughter of a pharmacist, she was born in Tuscany in 1878. She was afflicted by ill health (paralysis and deafness) in her youth, as well as temptations against holy chastity, but she was soon cured of both

after making a novena to Saint Gabriel of Our Lady of the Sorrows (Gabriel Possenti, *whom* SEE). Although she was still considered too physically weak to enter a convent, the nuns were kind enough to give her a pamphlet entitled "An Hour with Jesus Agonizing on the Cross," and no sooner had she read it than the Blessed Virgin Mary, accompanied by an Angel, appeared to her, bestowing upon her the gift of the Stigmata. Thereafter, Gemma's hands, feet, and sides regularly gushed blood. She was also blessed with the wounds of the Crown of Thorns and of Christ's scourging; so severe were they that her bones were exposed and her hair was frequently drenched with blood. The Devil never ceased to torment her with visions of earthly comforts, and even pleasures; once a demon actually *possessed* her, causing her to break a rosary and spit on a crucifix. In 1903, at the age of twenty-five, the tubercular Gemma died—with her arms outstretched, as if on the cross. According to the inscription on her tomb, this "most pure virgin, consumed more by the fire of Divine love than by her wasting disease," is now and for eternity "in the bosom of her celestial Spouse."

Genesius—August 25

PATRON OF ACTORS, COMEDIANS, LAWYERS, AND SECRETARIES;
INVOKED AGAINST FREEZING AND EPILEPSY

For the sake of amusing the wicked Emperor Diocletian, a blasphemous "comic" play was once staged in Rome. In it, Christians

and their practices were to be parod-
ied and ridiculed. But one performer,
Genesius, was—in mid-act—suddenly
converted to the very Faith he was
mocking! Forsaking his foolish role,
he stepped forward and proudly proclaimed himself a Believer. He was
forthwith dragged from the stage,
stretched on the rack, burned with
torches, and beheaded. His heroism is
the subject of a play by the great Spanish dramatist Lope de Vega; Saint

Genesius medals have been worn, devoutly or superstitiously, by any
number of movie stars and other beloved entertainers.

Geneviève—January 3

PATRONESS OF PARIS; INVOKED AGAINST DROUGHT, FEVER, FLOODS,
AND PLAGUE

In 429, on his way through the little town of Nanterre, the Bishop
Saint Germain (for whom the Parisian boulevard is named) "discovered" the seven-year-old Geneviève, and predicted great things for
her if she remained "clean and untouched." At fifteen, she moved to
Paris and received from his very hands the veil of a dedicated virgin.
The young nun proceeded to declaim visionary prophecies of doom
for the sinful city, which made her unpopular at first, especially as
Paris was at the time under siege by the Franks. Then, much to everyone's surprise, the gloomy prophetess personally ran the blockade, returning with several boatloads of wheat to feed the starving
populace (although she herself was able to subsist on two meals a
week of barley and beans). This improved her reputation. In 451, the
advance of Attila the Hun and his savage horde upon Paris threatened even worse disasters until the murderous pagan army inexplicably bypassed the city—at which point it was generally agreed that
only Geneviève's prayers has saved them. Among her emblems in art
are the Devil, who employed a bellows to extinguish her lantern, and
an Angel, who relit it. Since her death, in the year 500, Geneviève has
continued to protect her city. In 1129, when an epidemic of ergot-
poisoning raged in Paris, her holy relics were disinterred and paraded
through the streets, which put an end to the plague, and in 1206 they
caused the overflowing Seine to subside.

Gengulf—May 11

PATRON INVOKED AGAINST UNHAPPY MARRIAGE

Gengulf was a noble knight of Burgundy, and a close comrade-in-arms of the Frankish King Pepin the Short, privileged to sleep in that monarch's tent when on campaigns. He was troubled by rumors that his highborn and beautiful wife was unfaithful to him. He confronted her in the garden of their castle, and she denied his allegations; he asked her to plunge her arm into the cool water of a well, thereby to confirm her innocence, which she did; the water immediately boiled, scalding the adulteress. The pious Gengulf did not slay her in her shame, but rather withdrew to another of his castles, where he undertook a life of charity and penance; to which retreat the notorious woman sent her paramour, who surprised Our Saint in his bed and hacked him to pieces. Gengulf is invoked against cuckoldry in France, Holland, and Belgium.

Gentian—December 11

PATRON OF INNKEEPERS

Two Roman missionaries (Fuscian and Victorious) once traveled to Gaul to visit their friend Saint Quentin (*whom* SEE). On their way to his church at Amiens, they took lodgings for the night at Sain, in the home of an aged pagan named Gentian. It was their host's unpleasant duty to inform them that their friend had been recently, and most cruelly, martyred. The following morning, the Roman governor of the province sent a troop of soldiers to arrest Gentian's guests. The hospitable old man stood in his doorway with his sword drawn—and was beheaded on the spot. Fuscian and Victorious were seized and likewise executed, but the looks on their (decapitated) faces drove the governor stark staring mad.

George—April 23

PATRON OF ENGLAND, PORTUGAL, GERMANY, CAVALRY, HORSES, EQUESTRIANS, FARMERS, BOY SCOUTS, KNIGHTS, ARCHERS, AND ARMORERS; INVOKED AGAINST THE PLAGUE, LEPROSY, AND SYPHILIS

George was a Palestinian soldier martyred during the persecution of Diocletian; his cult flourished not only in the Middle East but in England during the Crusades—it was probably the Crusaders who who brought it with them from Palestine. King Edward III made George Patron of England, and Henry V invoked him at the Battle of

Agincourt. The story of George and the dragon—the triumph of good over evil—varies. In the classic version, George, young and handsome, confronts the dragon-with-poisonous-breath who is holding a princess captive. (She drew a short straw in the town lottery and/or was perishing in a castle from lack of water.) George pierces the dragon with his lance, leads it captive through town in the princess's girdle, and instantly converts 15,000 people. In the East, George is depicted as a quasi-god who endures a series of tortures, including running in red-hot shoes, but always miraculously recovers the next day. In the Western version, George is a prince of Cappadocia who is tortured daily for seven years and whose bravery is so great that he converts 40,900 people, including the Empress Alexandria. An ignoble George does exist, however: in Gibbon's *Decline and Fall,* which portrays him as a brigand dealing in black-market bacon and rising to power as a Primate of Egypt. This George was arrested and thrown into the sea. In art, George is depicted dressed in armor, carrying a banner with a red cross, and slaying the dragon. The British flag, the Union Jack, includes a variation of the red cross of Saint George. "Riding Saint George"—that is, sexual intercourse with the female on top—was long believed to be the certain method of begetting a bishop.

Gerard—September 24
PATRON OF HUNGARY

Gerard was living in Venice when he walked to Hungary wearing only a pair of wooden clogs. There he befriended Saint Stephen (*whom* SEE), the king, who appointed the intellectual monk tutor to his son in 1035. Gerard became bishop, renowned for such acts of charity as taking lepers into his own bed. At the same time he was a noted wine connoisseur who carefully selected the wines used at Mass. After Stephen's death, pagan factions claimed the throne of Hungary. The evil Duke Vatha, an avowed enemy of Our Saint, ordered his soldiers to pelt Gerard's carriage with stones. The Saint stood up, made the Sign of the Cross, and the stones remained suspended in midair. He was then dragged from the carriage and killed.

Gerard Majella—October 16
PATRON OF CHILDBIRTH AND MOTHERS

The Redemptorist Order relentlessly promotes devotion to this Saint, "invoking his powerful assistance against the forces of evil which attack the sanctity of Marriage and the dignity of Motherhood," as it says in the Constitution of the League of Saint Gerard. Born near Naples in 1726, Gerard was in his youth properly devoted to his own (widowed) mother, whom he supported by his work as a tailor's apprentice. (He sometimes supplemented the family larder with miraculous loaves of bread donated to the pious lad by a statue of Our Lady.) Because Gerard was both tubercular and simpleminded, the Redemptorists were at first unwilling to accept him. "A useless brother," he was called. But the order's leader and founder, Saint Alphonsus Mary de' Liguori (*whom* SEE), recognized in Gerard that rare and highly useful thing, a miracle worker—someone who could (for example) cause food and/or money to materialize and/or multiply. There was ample eyewitness testimony at the time of his canonization proceedings that Gerard could heal the sick, be in two places at once, become invisible at will, read minds, fly through the air, and walk on water. All of these abilities are (come to think of it) expected of your average mother—but Gerard's special Patronage of them arises from one particular incident. Once, when visiting friends, he left his handkerchief behind. The daughter of the house picked it up to return it to the Saint, but he said, "Keep it, it may be useful to you." Years later, the young woman was dying in childbirth when she remembered Gerard's hanky. It was brought to her, she gripped it and prayed—and lived, the mother of a healthy infant. Although he was a laybrother, not a priest, Gerard was the spiritual director to several communities of nuns. In 1754, an ex-novice, Neria Caggiano, accused Our Saint (the Patron of *mothers!*) of having taken scandalous liberties with her person in the course of his ministry. She was, naturally, lying.

Gerard of Brogne—October 3
PATRON INVOKED AGAINST SCROFULA AND JAUNDICE

The marquis of Flanders chanced, while attending a Mass said by this military-man-turned-Benedictine, to pass an enormous and painful kidney stone. Understandably grateful, he assigned Gerard the task of traveling from abbey to abbey thoughout his realm to enforce

much-needed monastic reforms, and to restore, miraculously, if need be, the sickly monks therein to holy vigor.

Gereon—October 10
PATRON OF SOLDIERS; INVOKED AGAINST HEADACHE

An exquisite mosaic in Cologne Cathedral portrays the heroic martyrdom-by-beheading of Gereon and 318 other brave Christian soldiers, known locally as "the Golden Saints." They were (like Saints Maurice and Victor, *both of whom* SEE), among the 6,660 newly baptized members of Rome's Theban Legion who, in the year 290, gave up their lives rather than obey an order to worship the "divine" Emperor Maximian.

Gertrude of Nivelles—March 17
PATRONESS OF CATS, GARDENERS, AND TRAVELERS; INVOKED AGAINST MICE

This seventh-century nun is still invoked against rodents in her native Belgium—water from her well and cakes baked in her convent are said to repel vermin—and she is traditionally pictured holding a pastoral staff up which a pair of mice scamper. She was famous for her hospitality to strangers (Belgians call a drink for the road "Saint Gertrude's cup") and some believe that the souls of the departed spend the first night of their afterlife in her tender care. Her power over rodents accounts—one supposes—for her traditional patronage of cats.

Gertrude the Great—November 16
PATRONESS OF THE WEST INDIES

Gertrude, who was born in Saxony *circa* 1356, was placed with cloistered nuns at the age of five, and never left the convent. She had her first mystical experience at twenty-six, when Christ appeared to her. He reproached her for studying too hard, gave her the traditional nuptial ring, and introduced her to His Mother. Her biographer, Mechtilde, and other nuns who witnessed her visions often found Gertrude staring at an image of Christ with "greatest ardor," no doubt because He promised her that "My divine delights shall be as wine to you." During one of these ecstasies, the Devil was spotted nearby, groveling on the floor in chains. Much of Gertrude's writings, which are believed to have been ghosted by Mechtilde, stressed the humanity of Christ; her devotion to the Sacred Heart grew after she placed her head on Christ's Chest and listened to the beating of His Heart. Immediately after Gertrude's death, a host of souls was released from Purgatory to accompany her to Heaven. She was never formally canonized, but became famous through her writings; Pope Innocent XI added her name to the Roman Martyrology in 1677.

Gervase and Protase—June 19
PATRONS OF HAYMAKERS; INVOKED AGAINST RAIN

In 386, on the eve of dedicating a basilica in Milan, the bishop Saint Ambrose (*whom* SEE) was led in a vision to the nearby site where the holy remains of Saints Gervase and Protase lay buried. Many miracles immediately ensued, which added greatly to the occasion. Ambrose concluded, on the basis of forensic evidence and private revelation, that they were twins, martyred by Nero. Gervase had been flogged to death with a lead-tipped whip, his brother Protase merely beheaded. Three centuries later, their relics were sent to Paris; because their feast falls at the traditional time of the first grain harvest, they were invoked by French farmers for fair weather on that day.

Ghislain—October 9
PATRON INVOKED AGAINST TWITCHING

This seventh-century Frankish monk once hung his cloak on a tree while gardening. A she-bear, escaping from hunters, hid herself in it. The danger past, the ungrateful brute seized a basket containing Ghislain's Mass vestments and made off with it. Providentially, Our Saint was led to the beast's den by a friendly eagle, and recovered the sacred garments. In some mysterious way, this tale is said to account for the founding of the city of Mons.

Gildas the Wise—January 29
PATRON INVOKED AGAINST DOG BITES AND RABIES

This wholly admirable monk was born in the year 500, in Britain—a Celtic-Christian nation abandoned by the Roman army of occupation, and not yet invaded and corrupted by Anglo-Saxons. Gildas wrote a history of those times—the only firsthand history we have, *Concerning the Ruin and Conquest of Britain*. In it, he praises King Arthur's heroic stand against the Saxon dogs in the battle of Bredon Hill, and otherwise excoriates, in the strongest possible terms, the cowardice and hypocrisy of his contemporary clerics and rulers toward their new square-headed overlords. Gildas fled his debauched homeland (as did most good Britons) for Armorica—the land that came to be known as Brittany. In art, Gildas's emblem is a snarling dog—a tribute to his vitriolic literary style. By reason of this, his protection is invoked against attacks by man's best friend.

Giles—September 1
PATRON OF BEGGARS, BLACKSMITHS, CRIPPLES, HERMITS, HORSES, AND
NURSING MOTHERS; INVOKED AGAINST LAMENESS, LEPROSY, AND
STERILITY

A deer fed milk daily to this gentle hermit, who lived in the depths of the forest. When a famous king—Charlemagne, Chilbert, Wamba, or Flavius, depending on the version you read—was hunting Giles's deer, he shot the white-haired Saint instead. Filled with remorse, the king built Giles a monastery that became a popular pilgrimage site. Charlemagne once went to Giles for confession, but couldn't articulate a particularly intimate offense—so an Angel revealed the sin to Giles, enabling him to absolve the emperor. In Rome, the pope gave Giles a gift of two enormous doors made of cypress wood, which the Saint cavalierly threw into the Arno, instructing them to float to Provence. They washed ashore shortly before he arrived there himself. Giles's powers of healing were so strong that a fatally ill man was cured simply by wearing the Saint's coat. Numerous churches and hospitals are dedicated to him, and he is known as the chief patron of poor folk (except in Poland, where, for some reason, he is the Saint of the princely elite). He is shown in sacred art pierced with an arrow, his doe at his side. A poem about him reads:

> Gracious Giles, of poor folk chief patron,
> Medicine to sick in their distress,
> To all needy, shield and protection,
> Refuge to wretches, their damage to redress,
> Folk that were dead restoring to quickness . . .

In Normandy, women who have difficulty becoming pregnant sleep with a picture or, better still, a statue of the Saint. It works.

Goar—July 6

PATRON OF POTTERS; INVOKED AGAINST WHIRLPOOLS

A parish priest from Aquitaine with a reputation for holiness, Goar retreated into a solitary life, preaching, working miracles, and building up a devoted following. Some detractors, however, declared him to be a "humbug who ate a big breakfast before noon," and they reported him to the local bishop, Rusticus. The bishop then proceeded to declare Goar a sorcerer. At this point a three-day-old child was brought into the proceedings and testified that Bishop Rusticus was its father! The bishop was unfrocked, but Goar fell ill for seven years and died, his home becoming a place for pilgrimages. He is invoked against whirlpools because Gewirr, on the Rhine, is a whirlpool near his town; it might also explain his name. Like Saint Brigid and others, he had the ability to hang his cloak on a sunbeam.

Godberta—April 11

PATRONESS INVOKED AGAINST DROUGHT AND EPIDEMICS

The parents of this beautiful maiden brought her to the sixth-century Frankish court to find a husband, but there the bishop, Saint Eloy (*whom* SEE), intervened. He slipped his own episcopal ring onto her finger, and declared her a bride of Christ. King Clothaire officially recognized the marriage, and bestowed upon Godberta a convent, where she and twelve companions lived a life of mortification and prayer. Our Saint once halted an outbreak of plague by fasting for three days, and on another occasion quenched a raging fire by making the Sign of the Cross at it.

Godeleva—July 6

PATRONESS OF FLANDERS; INVOKED AGAINST SORE THROATS AND IN TIME OF DROUGHT

Godeleva was born near Boulogne around 1045. After her marriage to the Flemish nobleman Bertulf, her new mother-in-law called her a "black crow" because of her dark hair and eyebrows. In the middle of the wedding feast the groom deserted Godeleva, leaving her to live with her mother-in-law, who gave her nothing to eat except bread that had already been chewed by the dogs. Godeleva escaped and asked the local bishop to help, which he did—by forcing her husband to take her back. This time Bertulf, anxious to marry again, convinced Godeleva that the cure for their marital distress was a love potion. When she was on the trail of such an elixir, two of Bertulf's henchmen killed Our Saint by putting a thong around her neck and sticking her head in a pond. The site of her murder became famous as a place to go in search of a cure for sore throats. Bertulf, after fighting in the Crusades, repented and entered a monastery.

Gomer—October 11

PATRON OF UNHAPPY HUSBANDS AND WOODCUTTERS; INVOKED AGAINST HERNIA

Gomer, or Gummarus, was born in 717, in a castle in Brabant. A knight of King Pepin's court, he was miserably married to a shrew named Grimnaira. When Gomer was away on business, his wife was unpleasant to his retainers and employees. Once, for instance, she denied liquid refreshment to the reapers, obliging her husband to create a miraculous well to slake their thirst. Gomer eventually set out on a pilgrimage to Rome, and on his way, it is said, he cut down a tree "to serve as a pillow." The owner of the tree waxed wroth with Gomer, but Our Saint replanted the tree, reattaching its branches with his sash, and it was good as new! During Gomer's yearly festival at Lierre, Belgium, he works wonders for hernia sufferers.

Gontran—March 28

A Burgundian king (561–92) with a typically unsavory career that included a scandalous divorce and the high-handed execution of a court physician on the flimsiest pretext, Gontran turned (at an advanced age) to a life of penance and edifying generosity to the local clergy's building fund.

Gregory the Enlightener—September 30

PATRON OF ARMENIA

When his father killed the Armenian ruler Chosroes sometime in the middle of the third century, the newborn Gregory was sentenced to death along with the rest of his family. A nursemaid gave the infant to a traveling merchant for safekeeping; the merchant was a Christian, and Gregory was brought up in that faith. After he married and had two sons, he and his wife separated to join respective religious orders. On a visit to court, Gregory encountered Tithridates, the son of King Chosroes. When Tithridates discovered who Gregory's father was, Gregory was horribly tortured: he was hung up by one foot while noxious odors were placed under his nostrils, then flung into a vermin-infested sewage pit, where he remained for thirteen years. Gregory's faith eventually won the king over and the two became fast friends, even going on pilgrimages together. In a symbolic version of the story, Gregory transforms the king from a boar to a man by virtue of his prayers. Gregory's own son became a bishop (centuries of Armenian bishops were descendants of Gregory) and together they converted most of the nation. Then, his task completed, Gregory went to a hollowed-out juniper tree and died. His body was discovered by shepherds and his head was taken to Naples, along with the chains he had worn when imprisoned.

Gregory the Great—September 3

PATRON OF MUSIC, SINGERS, TEACHERS, POPES, AND SCHOOLCHILDREN; INVOKED AGAINST PLAGUE

Gregory, who is generally credited with ushering in the glorious Middle Ages, was born to a wealthy patrician family and quickly climbed the ranks to become prefect of Rome. Soon after his mother became a nun, he turned to a life of piety and contemplation, becoming a monk and using his considerable fortune to build monasteries. He emerged, after several years in the cloister, to become a cardinal and, eventually, in 590, pope—a role he resisted and termed "the height of embarrassment." He inherited a Rome in ruins, but reformed the clergy and strengthened the papacy, asserting its right to intervene in secular affairs—within ten years he had deposed both an emperor and a king. He supported missionary work, sending Saint Augustine of Canterbury (*whom* SEE) to successfully convert England and the Anglo-Saxons after seeing a group of fair-haired children in a slave market and making the memorable joke, "Not Angles, but Angels." Gregory was less successful in converting the Jews, even though he reduced by a third the rent of any Jew who became Christian. He suffered lifelong indigestion and gout as a result of drinking, in his youth, resin-flavored wine. Perhaps best known as the ultimate music lover, Gregory is credited with promoting plainsong, later called Gregorian chant, which subjected ancient church melodies to the rules of harmony. His heightened aesthetic provided a sharp contrast to the rigidity of his moral teachings: he held that sex is always evil ("pleasure can never be without sin"), even when it produced children; he forbade it during menstruation, pregnancy, and lactation. After a man slept with his wife, he was forbidden to enter church until he had purged himself by penance and washing. To further illustrate his point, he liked to tell the story of a married woman who attended church soon after intercourse and promptly went insane. Gregory took Saint Paul literally when that Saint said, "In Adam, all have sinned," and held that babies are born as the damned fruit of their parents' lust. He was known in his lifetime for his huge bald head, which today many cities, including Prague, Lisbon, Sens, and Constance, claim to possess.

Gregory the Wonderworker—November 17
PATRON INVOKED IN DESPERATE SITUATIONS AND IN TIMES OF
EARTHQUAKE AND FLOOD

Gregory, who was born *circa* 213, preached in the neighborhood of Caesarea (modern-day Turkey), working spectacular miracles that included changing the course of a river, transforming himself into a tree, and once even moving a mountain. (When Gertrude the Great—*whom* SEE—was added to the liturgical calendar, there was talk of moving Gregory's feast day, but the pope felt that a Saint who had moved mountains shouldn't himself be moved.) Known as a second Moses, Gregory used his power to determine civil matters as well: when two brothers were in dispute over the rights to a lake, the Saint resolved the matter by drying up the lake. Gregory was enormously successful in converting Caesarea, although he naively thought that recent converts would enjoy having pagan festivities replaced by the feast days of solemn martyrs.

Guardian Angels—October 2
PATRONS OF THE POLICE

Every Catholic school child has been taught that he or she is accompanied through life by a personal Angel, an invisible immortal Spirit divinely assigned at birth to his or her case. In the interests of instilling habits of modesty, even when one is "alone," one's Angel is invariably of the opposite sex. (The gender of Clarence, the Angel looking out for Jimmy Stewart's welfare in the movie *It's a Wonderful Life* is a film-flub much commented upon by Catholics.) Neither is this a quaint metaphor or extradoctrinal superstition. Pope Clement X, in 1670, declared October 2, the feast of the Guardian Angels, to be a Red Letter Day in the calendar—one to be observed by the Universal Church. And in 1926, the Sacred Congregation of Rites officially designated the Guardian Angels as Patrons of the (Spanish) police.

Gudula—January 8
PATRONESS OF BRUSSELS; INVOKED AGAINST TOOTHACHE

The daughter of Count Witger, this somewhat obscure eighth-century maiden seems to have spent her life performing devotions and charitable works. Once, on her way to church at night, Gudula's latern went out—and was miraculously relit as a result of her prayers. A great church in Brussels is dedicated to her, and in it are all of her teeth, before which the dentally distressed are wont to pray for relief.

Guignolé—March 3
PATRON INVOKED AGAINST IMPOTENCE AND INFERTILITY

In England, where many of his relics rest and several churches are dedicated to him, this Saint is known as Winnol, Winwaloe, or Gwenno. In France he is Guénolé or Guignolé. He was a typical Celtic monk of the sixth century, much given to the wearing of hair shirts and other self-mortifications; he is said to have carried a bell, which he rang to attract fish. In a church in the city of Brest is an ancient and most peculiar wooden statue of this Saint—its most prominent characteristic being a rigidly protruding male member. What's more, for over a thousand years, the faithful of both sexes, eager for charms against inadequacies, have been whittling bits off it—yet Guignolé's prowess remains to this day miraculously undiminished. It is an ongoing miracle. So great was the reputation of this hyper-virile Saint throughout the Middle Ages that he became (rod at the ready) the star of a sex-and-violence puppet show; he is the French equivalent of the English Punch. Thus, since the nineteenth century, the theater in Paris specializing in the lewdly grotesque has called itself le Grand Guignol.

Guy—September 12
PATRON OF HORSES

On the outskirts of Brussels there is a field of wheat that Saint Wyden, as the Flemish call him, once caused to grow overnight. This holy simpleton, known and revered as "the Poor Man of Anderlecht," Saint Guidon (in English, Guy) was a wandering rustic peasant who found employment as a church sacristan in Laeken, near Brussels. He shared the pittance he earned with those less fortunate than himself. One day Guy was offered a business opportunity—a chance to invest in a commercial venture—and, thinking only of the works of charity he could perform when his ship came in, Guy gave his all. The (literal) ship sank in the harbor, and dejected, not to mention destitute, Guy set out on foot on a seven-year pilgrimage that took him as far as Rome and Jerusalem, until, in 1012, he staggered back to Anderlecht to die. Conclusive evidence of his sanctity was soon provided by a horse, which profaned Guy's newly dug grave in some vulgar equine manner and was instantly struck dead. This miracle is allegedly the reason Our Saint is still venerated by the drivers of Brussels's many picturesque horse-drawn cabs.

Gwen—June 1

PATRONESS OF INFANTS AND NURSING MOTHERS; INVOKED AGAINST CRADLE CAP

Statues of this remarkable Breton woman clearly show the miraculous asset for which she is honored by nursing mothers—a third breast, which was granted her on the occasion of her giving birth to triplets. The heads of infants are customarily bathed in the waters of a rock spring near her shrine, protecting them against the form of eczema called cradle cap, or *mal de Sainte Gwen*. In England, she is also known by the names Whyte and Candida.

Hallvard—May 15

PATRON OF OSLO AND OF INNOCENCE

The object of a Norwegian cult, this young prince was, one day in 1043, about to launch his boat upon the river when a slave woman rushed up and implored his aid. She had been falsely accused of theft, she said, and needed to escape. As she boarded Hallvard's boat, an angry mob arrived on the quay, demanding custody of the woman. Once more she vowed her innocence, and the prince bravely cast off, only to die in a hail of arrows from the shore.

Harvey—June 17

PATRON INVOKED AGAINST BLINDNESS, DEMONS, FOXES, AND WOLVES

Harvey's father was a famous Welsh minstrel who, on his way home from the court of the Frankish emperor, met and fell in love with a beautiful Breton maiden. Harvey, their son, was born blind, but he, too, became a harpist, poet, and singer of great skill, whose music had charms even for animals. A wolf who attacked and slew Our Saint's white seeing-eye dog repented and became his guide and companion; a fox who stole a chicken from him returned the fowl unharmed; even frogs could be silenced by his songs. He is a popular Saint in Brittany, long invoked for the protection of flocks and herds, and against eye troubles.

Hedda—April 10

In 869, the Vikings went too far. They invaded England, killed the noble Edmund, king of the East Angles, then sailed up the Thames, looting as they went, slaughtering monks and civilians along the banks. At an abbey near Peterborough they brutally massacred the abbot, Our Saint Hedda, together with all eighty-four members of his community. But when the Danish berserkers arrived at a convent of nuns at Coldingham, they were intent on worse than pillage. Yes, rape! Brilliantly, Saint Ebba, the abbess, and all her sisters cut off their mouths and noses with razors, which quelled the ardor of the Norsemen, who then merely torched the place. This is obviously the sort of thing that made Alfred the Great an absolute necessity.

Hedwig—October 16
PATRONESS OF BAVARIA AND SILESIA

At the age of twelve, Hedwig was married to Henry I the Bearded, duke of Silesia, and bore him six children—a miracle in itself, given Hedwig's aversion to her husband and to sex. It is said that she never spoke to him in private, and convinced him of the sinfulness of intercourse in Lent, on all Sundays and holy days, and during her pregnancies. Finally, after twenty-five years of wedded grief, she moved into a nearby convent. There she distinguished herself by habitually kissing the seats of chairs, pews, and stools. She also enjoyed washing the feet of the nuns, then drinking the dirty water. She herself, as she wandered the dukedom doing good deeds, never wore shoes, and her feet were a mess. Her estranged husband sent her a pair of shoes, commanding her never to appear in public without them. Thereafter, clever Hedwig carried them everywhere . . . under her arm. (Thus she is pictured in sacred art).

Helena—August 18
PATRONESS OF ARCHAEOLOGISTS

Helena was either the daughter of that celebrated British monarch Old King Cole or a barmaid in a Turkish saloon. About the year 270, she married Constantius, an officer of the Roman forces then occupying her homeland, whichever it was. She returned with him to Rome, and gave birth to a son, Constantine. Then, given the chance of marrying the emperor's daughter and succeeding him as Caesar, her husband divorced her and sent her into exile. Remember, these people were pagans. Young Constantine sided with his mother, naturally, and upon his father's death in 306, when he became the emperor, recalled her from exile, declared her to be "Augusta," that is, empress, and had coins struck in her honor. When a certain General Maxentius disputed Constantine's imperial claims, a winner-take-all contest

of arms between their armies was scheduled for
October 28, in the year 312, at the Milvian
Bridge over the Tiber. The night before that battle, Constantine had a famous vision: he beheld a
cross in the sky, surrounded by the words *"in hoc
signo vinces,"* "by this sign you shall conquer."
The next day, the bridge collapsed under Maxentius's advancing army, and Constantine, while
not actually converting to the Christian religion
himself, nevertheless legalized it. His middle-aged mother, Helena,
however, took to the Faith with a passion. After being baptized by
Pope Saint Sylvester (*whom* SEE), she caused numerous costly
churches to be built in Rome; then, as her son continued on his conquering ways to the East (moving the empire's capital to Byzantium,
which city he modestly renamed Constantinople), Helena accompanied him, until, in her eighty-fifth year, she arrived in the Holy Land,
where she had a vision of her own: the location of the long-lost True
Cross on which Christ had died was revealed to her. Under her direction, it was duly excavated, along with other priceless relics such as
the Holy Nails and Our Savior's own seamless cloak, the Robe—
hence this noble lady's traditional patronage of archaeologists. A surprising number of pieces of the True Cross are, to this day,
commercially available, and the Robe was made into *The Robe*, the
first movie in CinemaScope.

Helier—July 16
PATRON OF JERSEY, CHANNEL ISLANDS

   The capital city of Jersey, largest of the Channel Islands, is named
for this Belgian hermit who took up his abode in a cave there sometime in the sixth century. Helier was martyred by a band of passing
pirates whose spiritual condition he attempted to improve.

Henry of Uppsala—January 19
PATRON OF FINLAND

   An Englishman serving as a bishop in Uppsala, Sweden, Henry accompanied the Swedish king Saint Eric (*whom* SEE) on his highly successful expedition to neighboring Finland in 1152. Henry zealously
attempted to instruct in the True Faith the few Finns who had somehow survived Eric's visit, but was soon himself martyred by one of
his prospective converts.

Henry the Emperor—July 13
PATRON OF FINLAND

The son of Henry the Quarrelsome of Bavaria, Our Saint was as a young man favored with a vision of Saint Wolfgang (*whom* SEE), who pointed to the words "AFTER 6." The prince assumed this to be a foretelling of his death, but its true meaning became evident six years later, in 1014, when he was crowned Holy Roman Emperor. (Actually, in a pre-Napoleonic gesture, Henry took the crown from the pope's hands and coronated himself.) He became a staunch advocate of clerical celibacy—once it occurred to him that the lands of childless priests reverted to the crown—and to set an example he lived in ostentatious chastity with his queen, Saint Cunegund (*whom* SEE). On his deathbed, he returned his bride to her troublesome family with the words "Receive back again the virgin you gave me." By means of many battles (he prayed before each one) Henry succeeded in reuniting the German empire. Some edifying tales of his personal life concern his childhood friend Meinwork, whom he appointed his royal chaplain. Father Meinwork once appropriated Henry's royal cup and robes, and by saying Mass with them, consecrated them. Henry retaliated by altering the text of the book Meinwork read at Mass, so that the chaplain prayed not for mercy but for mules. Meinwork was briefly excommunicated, but it was all in good German fun. Henry was formally declared Patron of Finland in 1961, for the Vatican's own mysterious reasons.

Herbert—March 16
PATRON INVOKED IN TIME OF DROUGHT

Herbert, a German cleric, served as chancellor to Emperor Otto III, but quarreled with that monarch's successor, Henry II (Henry the Emperor, *whom* SEE), who was the husband-in-name-only of Saint Cunegund (*whom* SEE). A terrible drought that occurred in Cologne in 1000 was generally assumed to be a sign of the impending end of the world, but Herbert's prayers brought rain.

Hermes—August 28
PATRON INVOKED AGAINST INSANITY

There was, no doubt, a Roman martyr with this name, but we know nothing certain about his life and death. Many of his surprisingly abundant relics wound up in Renaix, Belgium, to which site lunatics have long made pilgrimages. Possibly his curative powers arise from a confusion of this Saint with the Greek god Hermes, whose name he shares.

Hilary of Poitiers—January 13
PATRON OF BACKWARD CHILDREN AND LAWYERS; INVOKED AGAINST
INSANITY AND SNAKEBITE

Born into a wealthy pagan family in Gaul *circa* 315, Hilary was thirty-five years old, a married man with a daughter, when he became a Christian and—over his strong objections—was made a bishop, in the year 350. His politically incorrect but theologically sound opposition to the then-dominant Arian heresy resulted in his banishment to Phrygia, and thence back to Gaul, where he died. His bed was given a place of honor in the cathedral at Poitiers, and throughout the Middle Ages it was widely believed that any madman who could be enticed to spend the night in "Hilary's cradle" would rise up cured. He once banished all the snakes from an island he was visiting, for which reason he is invoked against danger from snakebite. The "Hilary term" at British universities is so called for commencing on or about his feast day; Our Saint himself had taken an interest in the education of slow learners.

Hippolytus—August 13
PATRON OF HORSES AND PRISON GUARDS

According to legend, when the famous martyr Saint Lawrence (*whom* SEE) was imprisoned, Hippolytus was assigned to guard his cell, and was both converted and baptized by the Saint. After Lawrence's ghastly execution, Hippolytus managed to gather and preserve many of his charred relics—for which crime he himself was sentenced to death: he was tied by his feet to a team of horses, and dragged through thistles and thorns until he joined his mentor in Paradise. In Greek mythology, by a curious coincidence, a son of the hero Theseus, likewise named Hippolytus, died in the same manner.

The Holy Innocents—December 28
PATRONS OF BABIES AND CHOIRBOYS

The Bible (Matthew 2: 16–18) tells us that, upon hearing from the Magi that a new king had been born in Bethlehem, Herod took the precaution of ordering the slaughter of all male children under two years of age in that city. These "Holy Innocents" have long been honored as the first martyrs, and their commemorative feast ("Childermas") was celebrated in England until the seventeenth century by whipping the children of the household while they lay abed. In Europe, December 28 was "the Feast of Fools," a day on which a highly satirical sort of anarchy was permitted in the churches; a blasphemous parody of the Mass was sometimes celebrated, in which the congregation brayed the responses like donkeys; the youngest member of any religious community was placed in absolute authority; and a good time was had by all. (An elaborate description of the day's excesses is provided by Victor Hugo in his novel *The Hunchback of Notre Dame*.)

Homobonus—November 13
PATRON OF GARMENT WORKERS AND TAILORS

Homobonus, a happily married cloth worker, was the prototypical "good man"—prudent, diligent, charitable, and devoted to Saint Giles. Homobonus even worked the occasional miracle, but is most noted for his dramatic passing: during the Gloria of the Mass, he stretched out his arms in the shape of the cross and fell flat on his face. It wasn't until Mass was over that people realized he had dropped dead. Pope Innocent hastened his canonization in an effort to shore up the nonmartyr, nonclergy quota of Saints, describing Homobonus as one who did "ordinary things extraordinarily well."

Honoratus—May 16
PATRON OF BAKERS AND MILLERS

Rue Saint-Honoré in Paris is named for this Saint, who was bishop of Arles *circa* 600. His patronage of bakers is traditional, but hard to explain; perhaps it arises from the pious legend that he once received the Eucharist, "the Bread of Angels," from the hand of God Himself.

Hormisdas—August 8

PATRON OF STABLEBOYS

King Varannes of Persia was a pagan tyrant of the tolerant, liberal ilk, with a "live-and-let-live" attitude toward his Christian subjects. However, their bishop, Abdas, was a hard-liner, with a policy of destroying wholesale pagan shrines, temples, and statues. Overreacting, perhaps, Varannes ordered Abdas and his flock rounded up and fed live to rats. However, one of that flock, the

youth Hormisdas, was, although a Christian, of noble stock. By royal decree, his punishment consisted of being assigned the post of sanitary engineer in the royal camel stables. One day, His Majesty chanced to espy young Hormisdas, now reduced to a ragged, begrimed, and malodorous urchin. Moved to pity, the king approached Our Saint, offering him a bath and a clean linen tunic if he would but deny His Savior. The boy refused, in the strongest terms, and Varannes had him immediately executed.

Hubert—November 3

PATRON OF HUNTERS, MATHEMATICIANS, MACHINISTS, AND
METALWORKERS; INVOKED AGAINST DOG BITES AND RABIES

Hubert was an affable and shallow hanger-on at the court of King Pepin, content to do little but indulge his passion for hunting until an event (remarkably similar to the experience of Saint Eustace, *whom* SEE) changed his life. One Good Friday, after Hubert passed up church for a hunting trip, he encountered a stag in the forest with a crucifix between its antlers. The tiny figure on the crucifix warned him, "Turn to the Lord, or thou wilt fall into the abyss of Hell!" Soon after this, his wife died in childbirth and the chastened Hubert placed himself and his newborn son in the service of the bishop, Saint Lambert (*whom* SEE). After Lambert's assassination, an Angel appeared to the pope, citing Hubert as Lambert's successor. Allied with Charles Martel, Hubert converted the region, working miracles and casually exorcising the possessed by making the Sign of the Cross over them. Hubert also had a vision in which Saint Peter gave him a stole the Blessed Virgin Herself had embroidered in Heaven. Hubert's son succeeded him after his father's death, and rabies victims came to the older man's tomb seeking a successful, if complicated, cure: a thread was taken from the stole the Virgin had given to Hubert and placed in an incision in the forehead of the patient, who, among other things, was forbidden to comb his hair for forty days, and ordered to eat only pork and bacon from a boar.

Hugh of Lincoln—November 17
PATRON OF SICK CHILDREN

Born in France, this monk attracted the attention of Henry II of England, who asked him to lead one of his monasteries and later promoted Hugh to be the bishop of Lincoln, the nation's largest diocese. From Lincoln, Hugh defied, in succession, three Plantagenet kings in defense of justice. He helped build the cathedral with his own hands, nursed lepers, and single-handedly defended the Jews against angry mobs. The controversial bishop excommunicated Henry II's foresters for mistreating peasants and refused to levy money for King Richard's war against France. This was the first time a money grant had been refused a king, and Hugh, seeking a reconciliation with Richard, went to him, saying, "Give me a kiss." The king refused but the Saint overcame him with a kiss, and went on to defy King John as well, thus earning his nickname—"Hammerking." Hugh kept a wild swan as a pet: the bird followed him everywhere, attacked anyone who approached, and would "bury its head and long neck in Hugh's wide sleeves." In one of his extant sermons, Hugh attests that the virtuous laity have a place in Heaven along with the clergy. From his deathbed, he gave instructions for the completion of his new cathedral and made his own funeral arrangements. Three kings and three archbishops were his pallbearers, and in attendance were fourteen bishops, a hundred abbots, and assorted dukes, princes, and commonfolk. His cult became widespread after his death, and the sick—in particular, children—were brought to his shrine for a cure. The shrine was dismantled during the Reformation and his body was removed and lost.

Hunna—April 15
PATRONESS OF LAUNDRESSES

Although married to the noble Count Huno of Strasbourg, Hunna took in the washing for her needy neighbors, which earned her the title "the Holy Washerwoman." Hunna died in 679, but was not formally canonized until 1520.

Hyacinth—August 17
PATRON OF LITHUANIA

A native of Poland, this thirteenth-century Dominican preached both the Gospel's message of peace and the bloody Crusade against the Prussians through his homeland and as far as Kiev. His connection with the flower of the same name is a curious one—his name was Jacob, which the Poles pronounce "Jacko"; this in turn was rendered into Latin as *"Jacinthus,"* which means "hyacinth."

Ignatius Loyola—July 31

PATRON OF THE MILITARY AND OF RELIGIOUS RETREATS; INVOKED
AGAINST BEING OVERLY CONSCIENTIOUS

The founder of the Society of Jesus (the Jesuits) was raised by his noble Basque parents to be a soldier and a courtier—a knight. He was the youngest of eleven children, a five-foot-two, swaggering redhead, "a man given to the vanities of the world," as he later wrote of himself. Rumors persist that he had fathered an illegitimate daughter before his shin was shattered by a cannonball at the Battle of Pam-

plona in 1521. Ignatius was confined to a lengthy bed stay. He asked for something to read—his tastes ran to romance novels—but his pious sister-in-law gave him a book on Saints' lives. He forthwith dedicated himself to God, dressed as a beggar, and retired from the world to a mountain cave, where he began to practice his original metaphysical-fitness program, the "Spiritual Exercises." He prayed for seven-hour sessions, during which time his hair and fingernails grew to unseemly lengths. Then, at thirty-three years of age, Ignatius went back to school, studying Latin with a class of eleven-year-olds. By forty-three, he was a Master of Arts in Paris, where he was twice imprisoned (and released) by the Inquisition for his unorthodox evangelical methods; but his disciples remained loyal to his cause, and, after becoming priests, they (Bobadiela, Favre, Lainez, Rodrigues, Salmeron and Xavier) became, in 1540, the first members of the Society of Jesus, the original Jebbies. Our Saint is traditionally invoked by those troubled with scruples, that is, suffering from an overly delicate conscience. Although throughout their glorious history the Jesuits have been accused of many faults, having scruples has never been among them.

Imelda—May 13
PATRONESS OF FIRST COMMUNICANTS

In 1322 a daughter was born to the Count and Countess Lambertini of Bologna. As an infant, little Imelda amused herself by erecting and decorating tiny altars around the castle. At nine she was sent to be educated by nuns, to whom she continually expressed her passionate desire to make her First Communion, lisping prettily, "How can anyone receive Jesus into his heart and not die?" Yet Imelda was deemed too young for the Eucharistic Sacrament. After the Mass on the Ascension Day of her eleventh year, however, the Host Itself flew out of the tabernacle and hovered over the devoutly praying maiden, which the officiating priest took as a sign. He plucked the Divine Wafer from the air, and placed it on the dear child's tongue, whereupon she expired in rapture.

Irene—April 3
PATRONESS OF PEACE

Three sisters, Agape, Chionia, and Irene—whose names respectively mean Charity, Snow, and Peace—were arrested in Macedonia, in the year 304, for possessing Holy Scriptures in defiance of an Imperial edict. One night the drunken governor Dulcitius, who lusted after all three, groped his way into their dark cell and was tricked by the chaste but mischievous trio into kissing kitchen utensils. For this prank, Agape and Chionia were burned to death. But a crueler punishment awaited Irene, who was committed to a brothel (like Saint Agnes—*whom* SEE—and many beautiful and modest Christian virgins before her) and (like them all) she emerged *intacta*. She was then mercifully chained naked to a pillar, and shot through the throat with an arrow. Her cult remains strong in the Eastern Rite—a painting (icon) of this Patroness of peace in New York City is believed to weep real tears in time of war.

Isidore—May 15
PATRON OF FARMERS, FARM WORKERS, AND RANCHERS

"Isidore the Husbandman" is a Spanish favorite. Born near Madrid in the twelfth century, he spent his whole life as a hired hand, working the lands of a rich man, Juan de Vergas. Our Saint was (as was his holy wife, Maria) famous for the hours spent daily in prayer, churchgoing, and good works—so much so that his employer began to wonder when any farm work was getting done. He paid a surprise visit to his fields and discovered, sure enough, Isidore rapt in prayer beneath a tree . . . while Angels behind a team of snow-white oxen plowed the south forty. In winter, they say, Isidore would empty sacks of grain to feed the starving birds, and those sacks would be be miraculously refilled with grain that yielded twice as much flour.

Ivo of Kermartin—May 19
PATRON OF BRITTANY, JUDGES, LAWYERS, NOTARIES, AND ORPHANS

"Saint Yves was a lawyer, and a Breton as well/ But not a liar, strange to tell," goes the French nursery rhyme about this wholly admirable thirteenth-century character. After studying law in Paris and Orleans, Ivo returned to practice in the courts of his native Brittany, as a (free) advocate for the poor and oppressed, and later as a just, merciful, and incorruptible magistrate. He was always especially concerned with the welfare of orphans. His (unique) emblem in art is a cat. He is not to be confused with Saint Ives (made famous in the rhyme "As I was going to Saint Ives, I met a man with seven wives"). The town of Saint Ives was named for an Irish maiden who sailed to Cornwall on a leaf.

James Grissinger—October 11
PATRON OF GLASS PAINTERS

In 1432, at the age of twenty-five, this native of Ulm, Germany, enlisted as a mercenary in the army of Naples. Appalled at "the license of military life" (in the words of Alban Butler), he resigned and found employment as a lawyer's secretary at Capua, where he stayed for five years. After another brief stint in the army, this time in Bologna, he joined, at the age of thirty-four, the Dominican Order as a laybrother. For fifty years, Brother James painted edifying pictures on glass for the fiscal benefit of all, while experiencing ecstasies and performing a miracle here and there.

James Salomonelli—June 5
PATRON INVOKED AGAINST CANCER

Shortly after his birth in Venice in 1231, James's mother abandoned him to join a convent. This might account, in part, for Our Saint's lifelong powerful devotion to Our Lady. He became a Dominican priest in Folgi, a town near Bologna, and was soon famous for his miraculous cures—of blindness, gout, tuberculosis, and especially cancer. Ironically, he himself died of that very disease on March 31, 1814. Within twenty-eight months of his death, 338 authenticated miracles were ascribed to his intercession.

James the Greater—July 25
PATRON OF GUATEMALA, SPAIN, NICARAGUA, VETERINARIANS,
HORSEMEN, LABORERS, FURRIERS, AND SOLDIERS; INVOKED AGAINST
ARTHRITIS AND RHEUMATISM

James was one of the original twelve Apostles, brother of Saint John the Evangelist, and is believed by some historians to be Christ's cousin, since his mother, Salome, may have been Mary's sister. In a famous scene from Bible history, James and his brother were re-

cruited by Christ when they were fishing with their father Zebedee. James
and John were part of Jesus' inner circle
(He named them "Boanerges," or
"Sons of Thunder"), and at one point
Salome pressed Christ to have her sons
sit on His right and left side in Paradise.
James once brought back to life a boy
who had been unjustly hanged and had
been dead for five weeks. When the
boy's father heard of the miracle, he

sputtered that his son was no more alive than the roasted fowl on the
table. The fowl rose up from the plate, became refeathered, and flew
away, and the man was reunited with his son. James was the first
Apostle martyred by King Herod Agrippa I. After his death, his body,
alone in a sailboat, was transported by a concourse of Angels to
Spain, where it lay on a stone that closed over it. His relics were discovered in the year 800 and taken to Compostella, where miracles
took place in the name of Sant'Iago—to this day the rallying cry of
the Spanish army is "Santiago!" His cult was fostered by the kings of
Spain until, centuries after his death, James emerged as the defender
of Christianity against the Moors. This transition is described by Gibbon: "From a peaceful fisherman of the lake of Gennesareth, he was
transformed into a valorous knight, who charged at the head of the
Spanish cavalry in their battles against the Moors." The pilgrimage
and arduous journey to James's shrine at Compostella became so
popular that his emblems became the pilgrim's hat and scallop shell.
The shells were so highly valued that they were often handed down
as legacies. It's extremely unlikely, however, that, dead or alive, Saint
James ever visited Spain.

James the Lesser—May 3
PATRON OF THE DYING, HATTERS, AND URUGUAY

The younger (hence "the Lesser") of the two Apostles named
James became, after the Ascension of Our Lord into Heaven, the
bishop of Jerusalem. According to a pious legend, he resolved to fast
until the Second Coming, and might have starved, had Jesus not appeared to him and personally cooked him a nice meal. As a result of
his constant kneeling in prayer, James's knees, it is said, resembled

those of a camel. In the year 62, James was captured by the Pharisees and flung from the pinnacle of the Temple in Jerusalem—in Divine Retribution for which deed that edifice was destroyed. James survived the fall long enough to forgive his murderers, after which he was beaten to death with a club.

Januarius (Gennaro)—September 19
PATRON OF BLOOD BANKS; INVOKED AGAINST THE EVIL EYE

Around 305, Bishop Januarius was beheaded after wild lions refused to touch him and he had emerged from a burning furnace unharmed. In the fifth century, Naples inherited his relics, including two vials of his blood that had been collected by followers. In 1389, a thousand years after Januarius's death, a priest holding the flasks of his coagulated blood noticed the contents beginning to bubble and liquefy. Since then the blood liquefies and boils whenever it is in close proximity to the bust containing part of Januarius's skull. This phenomenon, this "standing miracle," repeats itself on various feast days eighteen times a year, except during times of strife, famine, oppression, and the election of a Communist mayor in Naples. The miracle occurred off-schedule during a visit from Cardinal Cooke of New York (coincidentally the home of the world-famous San Gennaro fair). Although spectroscopic beams of light through the vials have revealed the presence of hemoglobin, skeptics maintain that there is wax in the blood or that the heat generated by the emotional spectators results in the liquefaction. The liquefaction is inconsistent—sometimes bubbling furiously, sometimes sluggish, and the color varies from dull rust to vivid crimson. If the blood does nothing during the ceremony, the spectators, particularly a group of excited women known as "the aunts of Saint Gennaro," have been known to shout "Boil! Boil! Boil, damn you!"

Jerome—September 30
PATRON OF LIBRARIANS AND STUDENTS

The most learned of the Latin fathers, Saint Jerome, who was originally named Hieronymus, was born in Yugoslavia. He traveled with the smart patrician set in Rome, and was a man known for his sarcastic wit and aggressiveness. Once, however, after reading Cicero, Jerome dreamed it was Judgment Day and that he was standing before God, declaring himself a Christian. But the Deity huffed,

"Thou liest . . . thou art a Ciceronian!" Transformed by the dream, Jerome moved his library to the desert and lived there as a hermit, writing books and learning Hebrew, but often tormented by impure thoughts of his former life. He emerged from the desert, emaciated and burned black, after four years, returned to Rome, and joined the priesthood. He worked as the pope's secretary and became an advisor on cel-

ibacy to a group of wealthy Roman women. Jerome befriended Saint Paula (*whom* SEE), treating her daughters as his own. His relationship with Paula lent itself to scandalous gossip and contributed to his already immense unpopularity. In later years, he and Paula—and Paula's fortune—founded a monastic settlement in Bethlehem, and it was there that Jerome did most of his writing, including his most famous work, the Latin version of the Bible that came to be known as the Vulgate. His genuine devotion to Paula aside—he was inconsolable at her death—Jerome emerged as the foremost critic of marriage and sex, and is credited with laying the Church's foundation of sexual asceticism. Saying "It must be bad to touch a woman," he also argued, somewhat oddly, that any man who loved his wife too much was guilty of adultery. Not even Saint Peter was spared, although Jerome did say Peter "washed away the dirt of his marriage with his martyrdom." Jerome broke ranks with former colleagues, who held that Mary had other children after Jesus, maintaining, moreover, that Her hymen had remained intact even after the Virgin Birth. A gentler side of this fierce Saint is revealed in the story of the lion with the thorn in its paw, who came limping to Jerome for aid. Our Saint removed the thorn, domesticated the lion, and put it in charge of his donkey.

Jerome Emiliani—February 8
PATRON OF ORPHANS

After a carefree, not to say dissolute, youth, Jerome joined the Venetian army in the war of the Italian city-states and was taken prisoner. Held captive in a dungeon by a ball and chain, he repented his former ways and prayed fervently to the Blessed Virgin Mary. At

length She appeared bearing a key, un-
bound the captive, and led him from
the prison in disguise. He proceeded directly to Her Shrine in Treviso, hung
his fetters upon the wall of the chapel,

and entered the priesthood in 1518. He was devoted to the care of
plague victims and reformed prostitutes, but especially to poor orphans and abandoned children, and is credited with having devised
the question-and-answer "catechism" style of religious education for
their enlightenment.

The Jesuit Martyrs—October 19
PATRONS OF CANADA

The first brave missionary priests (known to the natives as "Blackrobes") came from old France to New France in 1608 for the purpose
of harvesting untold thousands of heathen souls. They began their
work among members of the peaceful Huron tribe, and in 1637 the
first adult Indian—a Huron—was instructed, converted, and baptized. At that rate, who knows how many souls they might have
saved? But by 1650 the entire as yet unredeemed Huron nation had
been sent to Hell and seven saintly Blackrobes to Heaven by the
neighboring Iroquois. *Pères* Brébeuf, Chabanel, Daniel, Garnier, La-
lande, Lalemant, and Jogues, S.J., heroically endured their martyrdoms as they were variously flayed, mutilated, scalded,
dismembered, decapitated, incinerated, and/or eaten. Their Patronage of Canada was confirmed by the Sacred Congregation of Rites in
1940.

Joan de Lestonnac—February 2

Joan's mother, a sister of French Renaissance author Michel de
Montaigne *(Essays)*, embraced the Calvinist movement then cur-
rently in vogue and pressured her daughter, who was born in 1556, to
do the same. Joan remained steadfast in her Catholicism, although
she did marry. At forty-seven, after her husband's death, Joan left her
almost-grown children and entered a Cistercian monastery. That
order proved too rigorous for the frail Joan, and she received Divine
instructions, while at prayer, that she was to start her own less austere order. She proceeded to her estate, collected some novices, and
founded the Congregation of Notre Dame of Bordeaux with herself

as Mother Superior. The nuns nursed plague victims and lectured against Calvinism, living lives of poverty and mortification. Joan's world collapsed, however, when a fellow nun with the unlikely name of Blanche accused her of unspeakable acts and began to attack her physically. The cardinal believed Blanche, appointing her Mother Superior and deposing Joan. Shortly before dying, Joan was vindicated; after her death her body remained fresh, emitting a sweet odor. A heavenly light surrounded her funeral bier. Years later, during the French Revolution, extremists dug Joan's body up, profaned it, and reburied it . . . with a horse.

Joan of Arc—May 30
PATRONESS OF FRANCE AND THE MILITARY

Like the gods about whom Homer sang, the Saints in Heaven have been known to take a partisan interest in mortal politics—as when, in 1426 (the eighty-ninth year of the Hundred Years' War), Saints Catherine, Margaret, and Michael (*all of whom* SEE) decided to assist the Valois party of Charles of Orléans against his rivals the Burgundians and their English allies. It was their wish that the dauphin Charles of France (to all appearances a treacherous and cowardly toad) become the king of France; They chose as their instrument of policy a teenage farm girl named Jeanne d'Arc, to whom They appeared (infrequently) and spoke (constantly). Thanks to many hundreds of books and plays and films, everyone knows what happened next: Jeanne, clad in white armor, rode at the head of the dauphin's army, while he himself remained prudently at the rear. She raised the siege of Orléans, and was wounded by an arrow in the breast. The dauphin was crowned. Jeanne attacked Paris, and was wounded by an arrow in the thigh. Charles dallied at court. She was captured at Compiègne by the Burgundians, and sold to the English. Her king expressed no interest in her plight, attempting neither ransom nor rescue. Because she would not deny her Saints, inquisitors found her guilty of heresy, and turned her over to the civil authorities. Because she had opposed their occupation of her country, the English concluded she was a witch. She was burned at the stake on May 30, 1431. She was almost nineteen years old. Over the centuries, such cantankerous agnostics as Mark Twain and George Bernard

Shaw have fallen madly in love with her. Joan was officially canonized by the Catholic Church in 1920. We invite anyone who has a word to say against her to step outside and say it.

Job—May 10
PATRON INVOKED AGAINST DEPRESSION AND ULCERS

Among the Old Testament figures venerated as Saints was Job, the long-suffering hero of a Persian fairy tale that made its way mysteriously into the Hebrew Bible. Prosperous and pious, Job was the object of a bet between God and Satan, and subjected to a succession of catastrophes, not the least of which was the "comfort" of his friends. In the end, God explained Job's sufferings to him by bragging about how He, not Job, had created crocodiles and hippos. Isn't it remarkable that medieval people understood the "psychosomatic" connection between depression and ulcers?

John-Baptist de la Salle—April 7
PATRON OF SCHOOLTEACHERS

Born in 1651 into a wealthy family of Rheims, John-Baptist entered the religious life at eleven, and at sixteen was granted the prestigious and lucrative office of canon of the cathedral there. His heart became touched by the plight of the many poor and ignorant children of the city, and he resolved to devote his life, as well as his considerable fortune, to their education. The pedagogical innovations of this seventeenth-century French priest were many, including the training of teachers, lessons taught in the vernacular, and dividing classes into grades. He also founded technical schools and humane reformatories. The teaching order he founded, the Brothers of the Christian Schools, suffered early from interior conflicts and exterior opposition. He weathered lawsuits and even riots, but in the end prevailed. Thanks to this man, there are today more than 20,000 "Christian Brothers" terrorizing and otherwise educating Catholic boys in parochial schools around the world.

John-Baptist-Marie Vianney—August 4
PATRON OF PARISH PRIESTS

In the year 1859, Charles Darwin published *On the Origin of Species,* Karl Marx issued his *Critique of Political Economy,* and 100,000 French pilgrims traveled to the village of Ars-en-Dombes to confess their

sins to a pious simpleton. "The Curé of
Ars," as he was known through Christendom, was a farm boy whose family had remained staunchly Catholic throughout the
dreadful anticlerical excesses of the French
Revolution. Young Jean-Baptiste-Marie, although stupid to a remarkable degree, was
studying (with great difficulty) for the
priesthood when, at the age of twenty-
four, he was conscripted (by mistake) into
Napoleon's army. After an amnesty for
draft dodgers was declared, Our Saint
emerged from the barn where he had been
hiding, and resumed his studies. Ordained
at last, he was posted to Ars, a backwater
parish of 250 souls. There, subsisting on a
diet of nothing but potatoes, he established a miracle-working shrine to the (utterly mythological) Saint Philomena, and
by means of a series of emotional sermons
sought to eradicate such offenses against
common decency as dancing. But it was
primarily as a hearer of confessions that he

gained worldwide renown. He was gifted, it seems, at "reading
hearts"—which meant he knew one's sins without being told. This
presumably saved penitents both time and embarrassment. On an average day, the curé spent twelve to eighteen hours in the confessional. Sinners made appointments months in advance; a special train
service was laid on from Paris to Ars. But the Devil wasn't about to
stand idly by while all of France was shriven of its sins—the Evil One
frequently attacked the little parish priest, administering fearful beat-
ings to his body, and once going so far as to set the curé's bed on fire.
The curé did not, understandably enough, enjoy his life as an object
of intense international and Infernal attentions. He yearned to
become a cloistered monk, and on three separate occasions ran away
from his church to do so. Each time his Ecclesiastical Superiors
obliged him (most sadly and altogether unwillingly) to return. Seventy years after his death, the curé of Ars was papally declared to be
the Patron Saint of parish priests.

John Berchmans—November 26
PATRON OF ALTAR BOYS AND TEENAGE BOYS

John Berchmans was virtuous from early childhood, preferring the company of adults to that of other kids. By the time he was nine, John was serving Mass twice a day. "If I don't become a Saint when I am young, I never will," he would explain, poignantly. Although his father wanted John to join him in his shoe-repair business, the boy signed on with the Jesuits. (Curiously enough, his widowed father soon joined the priesthood, too.) As a novice in Rome, the young Belgian succumbed to the fever-inducing summer heat, and after a short illness fulfilled his childhood wish by dying at the age of twenty-two. Miracles were attributed to him as early as his funeral, and thousands of holy cards bearing his image were distributed in Rome as well as in his native land. His relics rest in an urn alongside those of his role model and fellow Jesuit "Boy Saint," Aloysius Gonzaga (*whom* SEE).

John Bosco—January 31
PATRON OF APPRENTICES AND EDITORS

Giovanni "Don" Bosco was, by any definition of the word, a Saint. His mission was to the urban poor of his native city of Turin, especially to children, particularly boys. To the new, neglected underclass of exploitable and expendable street urchins (Dickens was a contemporary of Don) he provided food and shelter, education, and recreation—although his work was ferociously opposed by corrupt clergymen and fanatic anticlericals alike. For the boys' amusement, he performed magic tricks; for their welfare, he performed miracles. Although the order he founded, the Salesians, spread across Europe and around the world, Don Bosco never left Italy. Once, in a dream, he flew over a great city, and the next day described it in detail. He had seen, an American visitor was amazed to discover, Boston.

John Chrysostom—September 13
PATRON OF ORATORS

The son of a Latin father and Greek mother, John set aside his classical education to pursue the life of a monk-hermit. The dampness of the monastery proved too much for the young holy man and he turned to preaching, earning his name "Chrysostom," meaning "golden mouth." He theorized that asexual reproduction must have occurred in Eden, and that Adam and Eve had remained in that perfect state, virginity. In one of his speeches, John said, "Virginity is as superior to marriage as Heaven is to earth or Angels to men." When he became patriarch of Constantinople, then a nest of intrigue, John attacked the loose morals of the city and clergy, as well as the behavior and appearance of the women at court. Jews weren't spared in his oratory either, for he flatly stated, "I hate the Jews. God hates the Jews and always did." His attempts at reform earned him the enmity of the empress, whom John pointedly referred to as "Jezebel." He particularly objected to her statue outside his cathedral and her participation at the races on Good Friday. The emperor had him exiled, but superstitiously recalled him after an earthquake occurred. He was then banished a second time, on foot, to the extreme end of the empire, and died on the way. Right after he died, a strong hail fell on Constantinople, and four days later, his nemesis, the empress, the Jezebel, died as well. He is one of the four Greek Doctors of the Church, and in his most famous writings holds forth on the dangers of women and "their ready inclination to sin. For the eye of the woman touches and disturbs our soul, and not only the eye of the unbridled woman, but that of the decent one as well." In later writings, using Paul as a source, he urged that women be veiled at all times. (Actually, Paul had been thinking of hairstyles.) At best, John felt that all women were "weak and flighty" and their only hope was "salvation through children." A fifteenth-century Church doctrine on witchcraft quotes John: "For what is woman but an enemy of friendship, an inescapable punishment, a necessary evil . . . painted with beautiful colors?"

John Climacus—March 30

Fourteen hundred years before there was a twelve-step program to sobriety, there was a thirty-step program to sanctity, as detailed in the book *Scali Paradisi (Ladder to Paradise)*, written by this holy Syrian hermit at Mount Sinai. The reason for his interesting nickname is that *"klimax"* is the Greek word for "ladder."

John de Brito—February 4
PATRON OF PORTUGAL

Born of noble parents, John de Brito was the favorite page of the Portuguese prince Don Pedro. As a child he fell seriously ill and his mother prayed to the Apostle of India, Saint Francis Xavier (*whom* SEE), promising to dedicate her son to him. When the child recovered, she began dressing the eight-year-old in priest's vestments, making him something of a curiosity at court. At sixteen he entered the priesthood in earnest, joining the Jesuit Order. In 1673, Don Pedro, now King Pedro, found himself at odds with both the pope and Dutch traders over land rights in southern India. He sent his childhood friend John to Goa, ostensibly to baptize the natives, and just possibly to solidify his territorial claims there. Surviving some early bouts of torture by the local heathens, John again made friends in court. He even succeeded in converting the rajah, and persuaded His newly Christian Highness to divest himself of at least his youngest wife. This irked the deposed lady, who complained to the local Hindu clergy. They conspired against Our Saint, and slew him. His head, after being displayed on a pole, was returned to King Pedro of Portugal. Pedro naturally ordered a Mass of Thanksgiving to be celebrated, to which ceremony John's proud mother wore a festive gown.

John-Francis Regis—June 16
PATRON OF ILLEGITIMATE CHILDREN, LACE MAKERS, AND SOCIAL WORKERS

A seventeenth-century French Jesuit, *Père* Jean-François desired to be sent to Canada and tortured to death by the savages there. He was assigned, however, to a mission to the savages of southeast France. There his works of pragmatic charity were many: he founded orphanages, improved the lot of prisoners, and established a lace-making industry so that prostitutes might have a more honorable way of earning a living (which made him unpopular among pimps). He was a famously popular preacher, although (or because) his sermons were full of "trivial and indelicate language . . . satire and savage invective." His Jesuit superiors sought to restrain his activities, but he responded by performing numerous miracles, curing the blind and infirm and multiplying food supplies. The martyrdom he had longed for in the snows of Canada he found in the snows of the Pyrenees; on a mission to La Louvesc in the winter of 1640 he died of exhaustion, pleurisy, and exposure.

John Gualbert—July 12
PATRON OF FORESTERS AND PARK KEEPERS

When he met his brother's killer in an alley in Florence, John drew his sword, but found himself unable to take his revenge. He proceeded to the nearest monastery, where Jesus (on a crucifix) nodded to him three times. John therefore cut off his hair and joined a religious order. He soon sensed some irregularity among his superiors, however (simony? nepotism?), and departed to found an order of his own. He and his monks became the self-appointed monitors of the lax and corrupt clergy, destroying degenerate institutions by fire and thunderstorm. John's greatest triumph came when he learned that the new bishop of Florence had bought his office. John and his monks stirred up a mob against this offense, the police became involved, and the pope himself visited Florence to defend the beleaguered bishop. John lit a great bonfire in the town square, and challenged the bishop to walk through it, which he declined to do. John then ordered one of his own monks to submit to trial by fire, praying he be spared only if the bishop "had obtained his episcopal throne by means of money." The monk emerged unsinged from the inferno, the crowd went wild, and the bishop was forced to resign. When not walking through fire, John's monks busied themselves transforming the desolate lands around their monastery into a parkland of evergreen trees, so that Our Saint has always been regarded as the Patron of foresters.

John of Beverley—May 7

This Englishman, bishop of York from 705 to 717, both baptized and ordained to the priesthood the historian Saint Bede (*whom* SEE); and the author was not stinting in the praise of his mentor's holiness. Among John's more spectacular miracles was his cure of a peasant lad afflicted both with a severe speech impediment and baldness caused by ringworm. After a session with the bishop, the boy became quite garrulous, and grew (says Bede) "a beautiful head of hair."

John of Bridlington—October 21
PATRON INVOKED AGAINST COMPLICATIONS IN CHILDBIRTH

A native of the town of Thwing in Yorkshire (he is sometimes known as "John Thwing"), this Augustinian prior led a life "absolutely devoid of a single incident of interest," in the words of British hagiographer Sabine Baring-Gould. Nevertheless, many pilgrims' prayers have been answered at his tomb, including, one supposes, from his traditionally sanctioned Patronage, that of pregnant women.

John of Capistrano—October 23
PATRON OF MILITARY CHAPLAINS

A man of the world, a lawyer, and the governor of the city of Perugia, John got religion at the age of thirty. How he managed to get rid of his wealthy wife is not known, but since his first pious act was to ride through town on a donkey, backward, wearing a paper hat with his sins written on it, perhaps the lady did not object much. He joined the Franciscans, and studied holy rabble-rousing under Saint Bernardino of Siena (*whom* SEE) before setting out on his own career—a gaunt, shoeless, withered, doomsday-is-at-hand-preaching evangelist. Our Saint could get very testy if his arrival was not celebrated with a parade. According to his official biographer, "His heart blazed with hate against three species of men, to wit, Jews, heretics, and schismatics." Impressed by John's no-nonsense reputation, the pope appointed him to the Inquisition. In Vienna, many a heretical Hussite was brought back to Orthodoxy or sent straight to Hell, courtesy of Our Saint. Strict, he was. Zealous. And how delightful was the division of confiscated Jewish property! Then, in 1453, the Turks captured Constantinople. John realized that this new Muslim peril was worse than all the Hebrews and Hussites in Austria, and with the Holy Father's blessing hastened to Hungary, there to take the field beside the noble Christian general Hunyadi. In 1456, they both led an army that slew 120,000 infidels, raised the siege of Belgrade, and saved Christendom forever—or at least until 1521, when the city fell to Suleiman the Magnificent. But by then Saint John of Capistrano, a fightin' chaplain if there ever was one, was long dead, of plague he contracted wandering happily among the corpses on the battlefield.

John of God—March 8
PATRON OF BOOKSELLERS, HOSPITALS, NURSES, AND PRINTERS;
INVOKED AGAINST ALCOHOLISM AND HEART DISEASE

By the time he was forty (in the year 1535) this Portuguese soldier of fortune had "done it all"—fought against the French in Spain and the Turks in Hungary, sold slaves in Morocco, even herded sheep in Spain. In Granada, where he ran a little shop that sold holy pictures and religious books, he one day chanced to hear a stirring sermon by the traveling preacher John of Ávila, and went suddenly, spectacularly mad, right there in church. Visiting him at the asylum, John of Ávila recognized the symptoms of lunacy as a form of penance, and urged the guilt-crazed bookseller to undertake a career of charitable works. Upon his release, John of God opened a hostel for the sick and destitute, for whose benefit he labored for the next fifteen years with astonishing zeal and compassion, despite a debilitating heart condition. Because a hospital for drunks in Dublin, Ireland, is named for him, he is considered the patron of alcoholics.

John of Kanti—December 23
PATRON OF LITHUANIA AND POLAND

He was known as John Cantius, after his Polish birthplace, the town of Kanti. After his ordination to the priesthood and graduation from the University of Cracow, he became a professor there, but his popularity as a lecturer and preacher inspired envy among his colleagues, and they contrived to have the austere intellectual posted to a simple country parish, where he was as miserable as the members of his congregation. He returned to the university as professor of sacred Scripture, which post he held until his death in 1473. John was renowned not only for his academic achievements but for his boundless charity to the poor and the severity of his personal life (he slept on the floor, never ate meat, etc.). In 1737, Pope Clement XII declared him to be the Patron of Lithuania and Poland.

John of Nepomuk—May 16
PATRON OF BRIDGES, BRIDGE BUILDERS, BOHEMIA, CONFESSORS, AND CZECHOSLOVAKIA; INVOKED AGAINST SLANDER

It was long believed that this bishop of Prague died a martyr to the seal of the confessional, because, in 1393, he refused, even under torture, to reveal to King Wen-

ceslaus IV the details of Queen Sophia's confession, and was thrown from a bridge to his death, a hero to his vows and to the Sacrament of Penance. Certainly, Wenceslaus was a bad man: cruel, jealous, and hysterical, not to mention lascivious. (His notorious paramour was Sussanah the Bathwoman.) And by his command, Bishop John of Nepomuk was indeed flung into the Vltava River—a plaque on the bridge in Prague marks the site to this day. Modern scholarship, however, suggests that Our Saint was bumped off for less romantic reasons, the victim of a sordid political squabble between his religious superiors and the court. Be that as it may, during John's canonization process, in 1719, his tomb was opened, and his *tongue* was found to be perfectly preserved.

John of the Cross—December 14
PATRON OF POETS

San Juan de la Cruz is the author of the famous poem "Noche obscura del alma" ("Dark Night of the Soul"). It is *not* about depression, but a description of the Soul's mystical marriage to Christ. Born in 1542, this Carmelite priest was a friend of the great mystic and reformer Saint Teresa of Ávila (*whom* SEE), and was himself actually imprisoned for undertaking to return the Carmelites to their primitive rule of poverty. It was in a jail cell in Toledo that he composed his great poem.

John Roche—August 30
PATRON OF BOATMEN

Although the Spanish Armada (July 1588) failed in its noble mission to rescue the England of Elizabeth I and return it to the True Faith, the persecution of English Catholics continued. That very August a half-mad priest, William Watson, was arrested and thrown into London's Bridewell Prison. Margaret Ward, the devout Catholic servant girl to a fine Catholic family, took it upon herself to visit Father Watson: she brought him, hidden in a basket of food, a clean shirt and a length of rope. The young Irishman John Roche (aka Neal), a friend of Margaret's, was in on the plot. He was a waterman, one of the many who plied their aquatic taxicabs along the River Thames, and he waited in his boat (at two in the morning) to aid the escaping prisoner. But, halfway down the wall, Watson slipped and fell, not only creating a hellish racket, but breaking an arm and a leg as well. Fast-thinking Roche exchanged clothes with the priest, who managed to get away. Roche and Margaret were not so lucky—the rope she had taken to Watson was easily traced. They were, naturally, both tortured, but offered a royal pardon if they would renounce their religion. They declined, and were duly hanged by Good Queen Bess.

John the Baptist—June 24

PATRON OF AUTO ROUTES, CANDLEMAKERS, FARRIERS, HEALTH SPAS, JORDAN, LEATHER WORKERS, ROAD WORKERS, AND WOOL WORKERS

Most Saints are commemorated on the anniversaries of their deaths—their *natales,* or "Heavenly Birthdays." But on June 24—Midsummer Day—we celebrate the *earthly* birth of John the Baptist. After this date the days grow shorter, and the end of the Christian year approaches, until in early winter we celebrate the birth of Christ, and a new Beginning. John is a figure of great importance in the New Testament. All four Evangelists are at pains to praise this contemporary of Jesus (according to Luke, he was Our Lord's cousin). Perhaps this Holy Man of the Desert—preacher, prophet, baptizer—was briefly Christ's rival for the title of Messiah; at any rate, the authors of the Gospels describe John as humbly deferring to their Hero. John, like many an Old Testament prophet before him, had harsh words for the morals of reigning Jewish royalty. King Herod had him arrested, imprisoned, and, so the story goes, decapitated—his severed head being awarded to a striptease dancer named Salome. As Patron of Midsummer, John absorbed all the pagan magic associated with that day (and the eve of that day). The bonfires lit to honor the old gods became "the fires of Saint John." The miraculous curative herb *Hypericum* traditionally gathered at that time became Saint-John's-wort—"High John the Conkeroo" to voodoo practitioners. Because he vowed to "make straight the way," he is the Patron of highways and road workers; because he called Christ "the Lamb of God," and is invariably pictured with a lamb, he looks after all those engaged in the wool-working trades. He was always clad in a camel's hide, endearing him to leather workers, and having immersed sinners in the waters of Jordan, he is the Patron both of all health spas and of that Middle Eastern nation.

John the Divine—December 27

PATRON OF TURKEY AND OF WRITERS; INVOKED AGAINST POISON

Scholars dispute whether Jesus' "beloved disciple" John, John the Evangelist (author of the Fourth Gospel), and John the Divine (author of the bizarre Book of Revelation) are one and the same person. Tradition says they were indeed, and that his missionary work

took Our John first to Ephesus, where he
wrote his Gospel. Thence he traveled to
Rome, where he survived immersion in a
cauldron of boiling oil. Back in Ephesus, he
was given a cup of poison to drink, but he
blessed the beverage, and the poison departed it, in the form of a serpent. This led, somehow, to his exile on the island of Patmos, where
he experienced the psychedelic visions he described in Revelation.
(Perhaps he hadn't exorcised *all* the poison from that drink. . . .) The
youngest of the Apostles, he lived to a very old age on Patmos, bor-
ing some of his own disciples by endlessly entreating them to "love
one another." He finally dug his own grave, in the shape of a cross,
and lay down in it. There was a flash of light . . . and, body and soul,
John was gone.

John the Dwarf—October 17

One of the Desert Fathers, hermits who in the fourth and fifth centuries fled the world to live in absolute poverty, humility, and prayer
in the rocky wilderness of Skete, Egypt, John the Dwarf seems to
have been somewhat impetuous, for a monk. One day, while working, he suddenly resolved to become an Angel, tore off his garments,
and ran out into the desert. He returned in a week, hungry and
thirsty. He was gently mocked for his pride by his brothers ("Are you
not an Angel?"), until he apologized. He died on Mount Quolzum,
having been driven away from his cell at Skete by marauding Berbers.

Josaphat—November 12
PATRON OF UKRAINE

In the year 1054, the Pope of Rome and the Primate of Byzantium
excommunicated each other, formalizing the scandalous Great
Schism that divided Catholics of the East and West until 1965. Josaphat (born John Kuncewicz) attempted, in the seventeenth century,
to reconcile the Eastern Orthodox and Roman churches. The Byzan-
tines accused him of "turning Latin." The Vatican was equally suspi-
cious, for Josaphat upheld certain Russian/Greek Orthodox
traditions. When, in 1623, the king of Poland, where Josaphat was an
archbishop, withdrew his support for Our beleaguered ecumenical
Saint, a monk named Elias attempted Josaphat's assassination, and
was arrested. Street rabble, in defense of the monk, stormed the arch-

bishop's home, crying, "Kill the papist!" Josaphat, whose first concern was for his servants, was struck in the head with a halberd, then
shot. When canonized by the Vatican in 1867, Josaphat became the
first Eastern Saint to be recognized by Rome.

Joseph—March 19

PATRON OF AUSTRIA, BELGIUM, CANADA, CARPENTERS, FATHERS, HAPPY
DEATH, HOUSE HUNTING, MEXICO, PERU, VIETNAM, AND LABORERS;
INVOKED AGAINST COMMUNISM AND DOUBT

In many parts of the world, including the
USA, small statues of Saint Joseph are buried in
the lawns of houses for sale when the real estate market is slow. An historical—or at any
rate, biblical—figure, Joseph was the husband
of (and provider of shelter for) Jesus' Mother,
Mary, and "a just man." An elaborate account
of his genealogy is given by the Evangelist
Luke, which establishes his descent from King
David, from whose lineage it was known that the Messiah would
come; but since Joseph was not Christ's biological father, the point
seems moot. When his chaste fiancée announced Her pregnancy,
Our Saint was understandably upset, until a visiting Angel explained
matters, and the nuptials took place as scheduled. The fact that Joseph remained celibate for life and his wife, Mary, a Perpetual Virgin
is a cornerstone of the Catholic Faith—and nothing contradicts this
Essential Doctrine except Mark, Chapter 6, wherein Jesus' four brothers are listed by name. In the Middle Ages, Joseph was pictured as a
feeble old man—eighty-nine years of age at the time of his marriage,
according to the learned Saint Epiphanius (315–403). Among his emblems in art is a crutch, which symbolizes his alleged impotence. He
was considered a slightly comic figure, sometimes known as "the Divine Cuckold," but Joseph became a more positive male role model
in response to the crisis of the Reformation.

Mary of Agreda, a fifteenth-century nun, was favored with a vision
that inspired her to write the true biography of Saint Joseph. In her
Mystical City of God, we learn that he was thirty-three at the time of
Christ's birth, and occasionally ate meat—unlike his wife, who was a
strict vegetarian. Because he was of a somewhat feeble constitution,
Mary prevailed upon him to take an early retirement from his career
as a carpenter. During his final illness, he was constantly attended by

Her, and "if she withdrew for a moment, it was only to serve her Divine Son, who united with his mother in assisting Our Saint, except when He was unavoidably engaged in other works." Thus, it is assumed he enjoyed a happy death. His present image as a red-blooded, blue-collar type of guy was underscored by Pope Pius XI when proclaiming him "Patron of those who combat atheistic communism" in 1933, and by Pope Pius XII's institution of the Feast of Joseph the Worker, which is celebrated on the first of May—a sort of Christian counterdemonstration to the godless-commie May Day.

Joseph Cafasso—June 23
PATRON OF PRISONERS

According to his biographer and protégé John "Don" Bosco (*whom* SEE), Father Cafasso, although physically tiny and somewhat misshapen, worked tirelessly and cheerfully among the poor and neglected victims of society in Turin—including the political activists and other criminals in its dreadful prisons. Before his own death in 1860, Our Saint accompanied no fewer than sixty men to the gallows. Because he had heard the confessions of, and granted absolution to, every one of them, he liked to refer to them as his "hanged Saints."

Joseph Calasanctius—September 25
PATRON OF CHRISTIAN SCHOOLS

A Spanish lawyer and priest, Joseph founded a free school for the poor children of Rome in 1597, which attracted first hundreds, and, by 1621, thousands of pupils. The teachers he gathered were recognized as a religious order, the Clerks Regular of the Religious Schools, with Joseph appointed their Superior General. Professional jealousy, political backstabbing, scandalous tale-telling and all the usual features of faculty-lounge life saddened the later years of this idealistic educator, who died in 1648, and was assigned his present Patronage by Pius XII after exactly three centuries.

Joseph of Arimathaea—March 17
PATRON OF CEMETERY KEEPERS, PALLBEARERS, TIN MINERS, AND UNDERTAKERS

In all four Gospels it is related that Christ was buried in the tomb of this wealthy disciple. According to a pious legend of the tin miners of Cornwall, Joseph was Christ's uncle, and a tin miner himself in Palestine. He liked to drop in on diggings, accompanied by his Divine

Nephew. A more likely story is that Joseph made his way, after the Resurrection and Ascension, in the company of Saint Mary Magdalene (*whom* SEE), to France. Then, alone, he traveled on to Britain, and there established a church at Glastonbury, Somerset. Most important, he brought with him the chalice from the Last Supper—which is how the Holy Grail got to England, and why King Arthur, whose own castle was also at Glastonbury, was so concerned with finding it. For over sixteen hundred and fifty years it was said that Joseph's own staff, which he had planted at Glastonbury, had become the large hawthorn tree that flowered there, miraculously, every Christmas Eve. This was the sort of papist nonsense the Puritans laughed to scorn—but just to be on the safe side, they cut the tree down.

Joseph of Cupertino—September 18
PATRON OF ASTRONAUTS, THE AIR FORCE, AND PILOTS

The famous "flying monk" was born in a garden shed because his father, who died soon after his birth, had sold the house to pay off debts. His widowed mother resented her slow, pigeon-toed son, and other children called him "Boccaperta" ("the Gaper") because his mouth always hung open. Bad-tempered and a failed shoemaker, Joseph was dismissed by the Capuchins and joined the Franciscans as a servant. A lucky break enabled him to become a novice—the exam he was given was based on the only text he was able to read. He became more devout and was so happy to be a priest that he mailed his underwear back to his mother, because his habit was all he needed (he didn't remove it for two years). Soon after he became a priest, his famous levitations began; according to his biographers, Joseph levitated over 100 times. He was able to fly high above the altar and once helped workmen by lifting a huge cross thirty-six feet in the air and then stayed perched on top of the cross for several hours. Fellow friars soon took to flying around on his back. During his flights he would issue shrill cries and afterward would dissolve into fits of laughter. The Spanish ambassador arrived for an interview with the "flying friar," but as soon as Joseph entered the church he spied a statue of Mary (to whom he had a special devotion), and flew over the heads of the Spanish entourage, settled for a while at the foot of the statue, then flew back over the crowd, shrieking, and headed toward his room. Christmas carols were especially moving to him, and as soon as they started, Joseph would fly straight upward in a kneeling position and stay that way until the caroling stopped. Church authorities, disturbed by this phenomenon and accusing him of "drawing crowds after him like a new Messiah," placed him in seclusion, actually making him a prisoner. But pilgrims kept finding him, so Joseph was moved from place to place, his notoriety preceding him. The controversy around the Saint, who could also predict the future, caused him to slip into deep melancholia. His last flight was, appropriately enough, on the Feast of the Assumption a month before his death, in 1663.

Josse—December 13
PATRON OF HARVESTS AND SHIPS; INVOKED AGAINST FEVER, FIRE, AND STORMS

This Saint of Brittany—whose name is pronounced "Joyce"—was a third-century prince and a married man. Upon making a pilgrimage to Rome, Josse decided to renounce his former life, and returned home to live as a simple seaside hermit, praying for the mariners. After his death (at the aptly named town of Saint-Josse-sur-Mer) his body remained incorrupt and the faithful were kept busy trimming his beard and nails. In 902, refugees from Saint-Josse in "Little Britain" arrived in Great Britain, bringing along those trimmings as well as other relics of the Saint, which were eventually enshrined in Winchester Cathedral. His popularity among the English is evidenced by the fact that Chaucer's bawdy Wife of Bath swears "by Saint Joce." A complete alternate set of relics eventually turned up in Flanders (where he is known as "Joost").

Jude—October 28
PATRON INVOKED IN DESPERATE STRAITS

This Apostle's traditional miraculous intervention in impossible, desperate, or "hopeless" cases is widely known, even among non-Catholics and pagans. Jude is frequently "thanked" in the "personal" sections of the sort of newspapers Our Saint himself would doubtless

have spurned. In the New Testament he is introduced as "Judas, the brother of James" (Luke 6:16), and "Judas, the brother of Jesus" (Mark 6:3). Biblical scholars, for reasons of their own, also identify him with the Apostle Thaddaeus, aka Lebbaeus. Jude is generally believed to have accompanied Saint Simon to Persia, where they were martyred—beaten to death with clubs. Because his name—Judas—is identical to that of the infamous disciple who betrayed Christ, this Saint was long neglected by the Faithful as an object of veneration. Consequently, he was available to take interest in even the most impossible, hopeless, or desperate cases.

Judith—May 5
PATRONESS OF PRUSSIA

When her beloved husband lost his life on a Crusade, Judith (also known as Jutta) provided for her many children, and then went off to become a religious recluse in the vicinity of Kulmsee, Prussia, where she died in 1260. Her story is in most details strikingly similar to that of Saint Elizabeth of Hungary (*whom* SEE).

Julia—May 22
PATRONESS OF CORSICA

This Carthaginian maiden was captured and sold into slavery in 439. Her master, a Syrian merchant seaman, was well disposed toward her on account of her beauty and her manner, which was humble and obedient, as befitted a Christian girl. She accompanied him on a voyage to Corsica, where he disembarked to transact some business with the island's pagan ruler Felix, and to take part in an idolatrous orgy honoring the local gods. The Syrian, after a few drinks, began to extol the virtues of his Christian slave to his Corsican hosts. Felix offered him four of his best slave girls in exchange for this paragon, but the Syrian declined. The heathen governor had Julia brought from the ship, and made her an offer: if she would sacrifice to his idols, he would grant her her freedom. She refused, of course, and after a session of cruel torture (her hair was pulled out), she was crucified. Although she is Corsica's patroness, her relics have long been venerated in a splendid church dedicated to her memory in Brescia, Italy.

Juliana—February 16

Another Saint in the great tradition of first-century Beautiful Roman Christian Virgin Martyrs, Juliana refused to marry the pagan provost Eleusius, citing her vow of perpetual chastity. Her father, the pagan Africanus, beat her savagely and turned her over to the civil authorities—none other than the rebuffed and irked provost. Eleusius commenced his investigation by ordering that his beloved be stretched between pillars and doused with molten metal. The undaunted maiden was then thrown into prison, where she took part in a series of debates and wrestling bouts with a devil, self-identified as "the Son of Beelzebub." Although she pinned him to the ground and bound his hands and feet, he escaped, and appeared (disguised as an

Angel) as a surprise witness against her at her trial before the provost. She was condemned and beheaded. In sacred art, Juliana is represented with a rope or chain, binding the devil, who has taken the shape of a dog or small dragon.

Julian the Hospitaler—February 12
PATRON OF BOATMEN, CIRCUS PERFORMERS, INNKEEPERS, AND TRAVELERS

Warned by a stag he was hunting that he would one day murder his own parents, Julian moved to a distant country, where he married a rich widow. Many years later, he surprised a couple in his marriage bed, assumed the worst, and slew them—only to discover they were his visiting parents. (His wholly innocent wife had welcomed them and gone to Mass.) Overcome with remorse, Our Saint decided he was unfit to live with people (except his wife) and together they left their castle and all their belongings. On the banks of a raging river they built a hospice for poor pilgrims whom Julian would ferry across for free. One dark and stormy night they provided transport and shelter to a leper, who turned out to be an Angel who assured Julian he had been divinely forgiven. Because of his legendary hospitality to strangers, he is prayed to by traveling entertainers, such as circus performers.

Justin—June 1
PATRON OF PHILOSOPHERS

Justin was the first in that very long line of Christian philosphers who have argued that there is no irreconcilable conflict between Faith and Reason. Although he was born in Samaria in the year 100, Justin, whose parents were Greek, spoke no Hebrew. In his youth he traveled to Alexandria to study Platonic philosophy, and there, through a chance meeting with an old man on the beach, he first heard of Christianity. After his baptism (at age thirty) he visited many lands, debating with heretics, pagans, atheists, and Jews. In Rome, in the year 165, Justin resoundingly defeated in public debate a Cynic named Crescens, who proved himself to be a very poor loser, for he reported Our Saint to the civil authorities. Justin, together with five other Christians, was executed on the order of the Emperor Marcus Aurelius—ironically enough, a bit of a philosopher himself.

Justina—October 7

PATRONESS OF PADUA AND VENICE

The beautiful daughter of a fourth-century pagan king, Justina was baptized by a (miraculously long-lived) disciple of Saint Peter himself, and went to live with the bishop of Padua. While crossing a bridge over the river Po, she was arrested by soldiers, and knelt to pray for courage—her knees left dents in the stone bridge that remain there to this day, providing a tourist attraction. Her emblem is a unicorn, symbolizing her treasured virginity.

Justina and Rufina—July 19

PATRONESSES OF POTTERS AND OF SEVILLE

During a ferocious electrical storm in the year 1504, the magnificent Moorish tower El Giralda in Seville was *not* struck by lightning. The natives of Seville attribute this miracle to the divine intercession of Our Saints, who were the virtuous daughters of a second-century Christian potter. Rather than supply their father's wares for use in an idolatrous and lewd ceremony honoring the pagan goddess Venus, they smashed his entire inventory; after a mockery of a trial, the sisters were thrown to the lions.

Justus and Pastor—August 6

When word reached these two schoolboys, aged thirteen and nine, that their fellow Christians were being executed, they threw down their textbooks and rushed to the site to profess their faith, whereupon they joined the ranks of the Glorious Martyrs of Spain, at Alcalá, in 304.

Kessog—March 10
PATRON OF SCOTLAND

Before Saint Andrew (*whom* SEE) became Scotland's Patron, it was Kessog (aka Mackessog) whose name the Highland clans invoked when going into battle. Kessog was an Irish prince who, as a boy, lost two friends in a swimming mishap. To appease their angry families, he restored the drowned lads to life. Once ordained, he set out for the wilds of pagan Scotland, where he established himself on Monk's Island in Loch Lomond. Thence he wandered the bonny banks and braes, preaching the Gospel and working miracles. The town of Luss takes its (Gaelic) name from the herbs in which his body was embalmed; the bell he carried is the main tourist attraction in the city of Lennox.

Kevin—June 3
PATRON OF IRELAND

In the wild hilly countryside of Wicklow, Ireland, one may visit a barren cave known as "Kevin's Bed." Near it, your native guide will point with pride to a spot high on a cliff from which Our Saint once threw a woman who had come to tempt him. Since no biography  of this holy hermit was written until 600 years after his death, the facts of his life are scarce. Legends abound, however. Doubtless, he lived to the age of 120. Possibly, he was fed by an otter, employed to catch salmon for him. That he stood unmoving until the egg that a blackbird had laid in his outstretched hand hatched strains credulity.

Kilian—July 8
PATRON OF AUSTRIA AND OF WHITEWASHERS

Kilian (whose name in Gaelic means "church") was an Irish missionary to Bavaria in the seventh century who managed to convert

the local ruler, Gozbert. Unfortunately, after
the baptismal formalities, Kilian informed Gozbert that his—Gozbert's—marriage to his former sister-in-law, Geilana, was invalid in the
eyes of the Church. The chief agreed in theory,
but nonetheless had Kilian assassinated. A
strong cult grew up around the Saint—his
image appeared on local coins and seals, and he
became the subject of the yearly Kilianfest in

Würzburg. This includes a play reenacting the Saint's life, in which
the blame for his murder is placed squarely on the woman Geilana.

Lambert—September 17
PATRON OF DENTISTS, MARITAL FIDELITY, AND TRUSS MAKERS

No sooner had Lambert succeeded the recently assassinated Theodore as bishop of Maastricht, Flanders, in 668, than he himself was sent into exile. He retired to join a monastic order remarkable for its austerity—Our Saint once spent an entire night out in the snow, clad only in a hair shirt, as penance for having broken the Rule of Silence by breaking wind. He was soon restored to his episcopal see by Pepin of Herstal, and then murdered at Pepin's own command. Lambert had openly criticized Pepin for brazenly flouting Catholic Marital Law by wedding his own (widowed) sister-in-law. Lambert wept in his chambers while a henchman climbed on the roof and hurled a spear through his heart. Although his death was politically motivated, Lambert is considered a martyr, and an impressive church still stands on the site of his demise. Pope Sergius (686–87) got word of the crime from a visiting Angel, who instructed him to replace Bishop Lambert with a man called Herbert; and who should His Holiness meet the very next day but a pilgrim of that very name.

Laurence Gustiani—September 5
PATRON OF VENICE

When he was still a child Laurence told his mother of his ambition to be a Saint. Toward that goal, Laurence underwent such fearful mortifications that his desperate mother arranged a marriage in the hope of distracting him. Instead, the Saint fled in horror to the nearby monastery of Saint George, never to return to the wealth of his mother's house, except as a beggar. He went throughout Venice in tattered rags, crying, "Alms, for the love of God!" When an old friend tried to woo him back to the world, even to the point of hiring musicians, the friend became so struck by Laurence's holiness that he himself entered the religious life. After Laurence became a priest, he experienced rapture during prayer and shed copious tears at Mass. He cried tears of protestation when he was appointed bishop of Venice (in 1433), and continued to eat from earthenware dishes and sleep on straw. He founded religious houses, parishes, and churches. He banned stage entertainments. When he knew he was dying, Laurence embarked on a prolonged deathbed farewell, crying, "Behold, the bridegroom cometh!" while the entire population of Venice visited him, asking for his blessing and last-minute advice.

Lawrence—August 10

PATRON OF CEYLON, COOKS, LIBRARIANS, AND THE POOR; INVOKED AGAINST FIRE AND LUMBAGO

Each and every Friday since the year 257, Lawrence has been privileged to lead a suffering soul out of Purgatory and into Heaven, as a reward for his own heroic martydom. A Spaniard by birth, he was archdeacon and treasurer of the Church in Rome, as well as the keeper of the library of sacred books, during the holy papacy of Sixtus II and the unholy reign of the Emperor Valerian. When Sixtus was arrested, he instructed his trusted deacon to gather together all the Church's wealth and distribute it to the poor. Overhearing this talk of wealth, the greedy Roman authorities commanded Lawrence to gather up the Church's treasures and surrender them to the prefect. Lawrence asked for three days to do so—and on the third day presented, assembled before the prefect's palace, thousands of lepers, orphans, the blind, and the lame, as well as widows and virgins. "Here," he announced, "is all the Church's treasure." Far from enlightening the prefect, this gesture appears to have enraged him. Lawrence was subjected to a sequence of tortures nearly unique in the gory annals of martyrdom: he was scourged, branded, clubbed, stretched on the rack, and torn with hooks before being placed on a gridiron and roasted. After a while, Lawrence spoke. "Turn me over, I'm done on this side." His emblem in art is a gridiron, for which reason cooks have taken him as their Patron; but it has recently been suggested that a scribe's error in transcription accounts for his legend: meaning to write "*passus est*" (he suffered) the author of Lawrence's *Life* may have written "*assus est*" (he was cooked). Be that as it may, the gridiron on which he died is on display in his titular church, San Lorenzo, in Rome; and a jar of his melted fat was donated to the Escorial in Spain by Pope Gregory XIII. Four hundred years after his burial, when his tomb was opened to receive the newly discovered bones of Saint Stephen (*whom* SEE), Lawrence moved over to make room for his guest—hence his nickname, "the Courteous Spaniard."

Lawrence O'Toole—November 14
PATRON OF DUBLIN

Lawrence, as the last Saint of Ireland, born *circa* 1128, symbolizes his country's subjugation to England and isolation from Rome. He was the son of a chieftain, taken hostage at the age of ten by his life-long nemesis, King Dermot—a man so depraved he once abducted a nun. Dermot mistreated Lawrence and killed his father, so when Lawrence became bishop of Dublin, he banished the old reprobate to England. The Saint brought order and piety to Dublin, inviting thirty homeless people to dinner each night. Years earlier, the pope (himself an Englishman) had given Henry II of England a bull allowing the king to proceed into Ireland, assume power over its people, and collect a "Peter's Pence" for Rome. Treacherous Dermot convinced the English king to enforce the papal bull, and enlisted the aid of the earl of Pembroke, "Strongbow," to invade Ireland. Strongbow married Dermot's daughter (ironically, Lawrence's niece) to solidify the alliance, and the march on Dublin began. The Irish rallied under their High King, Rory O'Connor, but were defeated by Strongbow's forces, and Henry II came to Irish shores to claim the land granted him by the pope. Lawrence succeeded in negotiating a treaty between Henry and Rory O'Connor, and papal protection for his country from a new pope. With the failure of the treaty and the fall of Rory, Ireland's freedom disappeared and the "Irish problem" began. Lawrence continued to work for peace, traveling constantly to England. On his last mission, he was snubbed by King Henry, who forbade him to return to Ireland. He died in France. His last words were in Irish, which, translated, say, "Alas! you stupid, foolish people, what will you do now? Who will look after you in your misfortunes?"

Lazarus—December 17
PATRON OF HOUSEWIVES, LEPERS, AND SEXTONS

Lazarus was, according to the Gospel of John, the brother of Mary and Martha of Bethany, whom Jesus raised from the dead. And because Lazarus was the name of a leper in one of Jesus' parables, it was assumed that the "historical" Lazarus, too, was leprous. In the lore of the Christians of France, Lazarus, after Christ's Ascension, sailed to Marseilles, and was the first bishop of that city; the Faithful of the island of Cyprus maintain that he sailed thither, and was *their* original bishop.

Lazlo—June 27
PATRON OF HUNGARY

A Christian king of Hungary, the greatest since Saint Stephen (*whom* SEE), Ladislaus, or Lancelot, or Lazlo, reigned from 1077 until 1095. He annexed by force of arms Dalmatia and Croatia to his realm and to the Catholic Faith, and made holy war on the neighboring Poles, Russians, and Tartars. Had this mighty warrior not died on his way to the First Crusade, there might have been a different and far happier outcome to that debacle. Or perhaps not.

Lebuin—November 12
PATRON OF THE DYING

An English missionary, Lebuin had labored long and fruitlessly in the dangerous area of the Saxon Netherlands. Dressed in full regalia and brandishing a cross, he determined to gate-crash the annual Saxon assembly at Marklo on the Wesser. "Listen to the God who speaks through my mouth!" he howled at the assembled warlords, and disparaged their gods—Odin, Thor, and the rest—as "dead, powerless things." Many Saxons determined to kill him on the spot, but an ancient chief named Buto granted Lebuin a sort of idiot's diplomatic immunity. Thereafter, Our Saint preached and traveled freely until his death in 773. His particular Patronage of the dying is explained, perhaps, by the stay of execution once granted him.

Leger—October 2
PATRON INVOKED AGAINST BLINDNESS

This bishop (616–79) involved himself perhaps overmuch with Frankish politics, and was found guilty, on purely circumstantial evidence, of murdering Childeric, heir to the throne. Leger's eyes were removed, as were his lips and tongue. Some years later, he was executed "still protesting his innocence"—which cannot have been easy to do, thus handicapped.

Leocadia—December 9
PATRONESS OF TOLEDO; INVOKED AGAINST PLAGUE

By means of their devotion to her relics in their cathedral, the citizens of the Spanish city of Toledo have been spared many a pestilential epidemic. It is said this holy maiden was inspired by tales of the exemplary death of Saint Eulalia of Barcelona (*whom* SEE) to bravely undergo her own martyrdom, in the year 304. Perversely, the official Church Calendar suggests that Eulalia died the day *after* Leocadia.

Leonard—November 6
PATRON OF CHILDBIRTH, HORSES, AND PRISONERS OF WAR; INVOKED
AGAINST ROBBERY

Leonard was a sixth-century French hermit, the godson of King Clovis. He passed up an opportunity to be made a bishop in order to live in a hut in the forest, eating only fruit and vegetables. When Clovis and his pregnant wife visited the Saint while they were out hunting, the queen unexpectedly went into labor, and Leonard successfully delivered the baby. The grateful king told Leonard he could have for his abbey as much land as he could ride around on a donkey in one night. The king further granted freedom to every prisoner Leonard visited—many of these prisoners went to live with the Saint once his abbey was built. When we invoke Leonard against robbery, it is to be assumed that this is because we hold him responsible in some way for those prisoners who returned to a life of crime after being freed. Leonard's patronage of prisoners of war began when Crusaders visited his shrine to give thanks for their release from Infidel prisons.

Leopold—November 15
PATRON OF AUSTRIA

Leopold succeeded his father as margrave of Austria in 1095, and at twenty-three married the widow Agnes, daughter of Henry IV. The couple had eighteen children and were also active in building monasteries. Leopold resolutely refused the crown when his brother died. He wasn't canonized until 350 years after his death, a Saint more by virtue of his endowments than his piety.

Leo the Great—November 10

One of only three popes called "Great," Leo was a famous Doctor of the Church who consolidated basic Christian doctrine and ex-

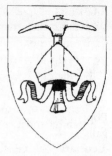

panded the influence and prestige of the papacy, emphasizing its Divine origin. A commanding figure who could calm wind and sea, he fought bizzare heresies within the Church as well as the increasing independence of the patriarch of Constantinople. His most dramatic moment came when he went to confront Attila, "the scourge of God," in 452. Dressed in white robes (and flanked on either side by Saints Peter and Paul), Leo identified himself as "Leo, Pope" and was able to dissuade the Hun from ravaging Rome (with the help of a promise of annual tribute). He was less successful with Genseric and the Vandals, who sacked Rome for fourteen days, even stealing the candlesticks originally stolen from the Temple at Jerusalem. Leo was a bit of a hard-liner on conjugal affairs, banning intercourse for married subdeacons and eventually determining that all marital intercourse was evil (sparing Mary's parents, who conceived without sin).

Leufredus—June 21
PATRON INVOKED AGAINST FLIES

This eighth-century French monk, also called "Leufroy," had a considerable reputation for cursing. When a woman once called attention to his baldness, she and all her progeny became bald. When a thief slandered him, Abbot Leufredus saw to it that he and his descendants were stricken toothless. When he saw farmers blasphemously plowing on a Sunday, he afflicted their fields with perpetual sterility. And when he was interrupted in his prayers by bothersome flies, he banished those insects forever from his house.

Levan—December 24
PATRON OF MALFORMED CHILDREN

Also known as Levian, Selevan, and Selyv, Levan is venerated in southern Brittany and at St. Levan, Cornwall, where the ruins of his chapel and his bench may be seen. Why the Bretons invoke his care for children with birth defects is a mystery, but speaks well of the Saint. In Cornish legend, Levan once caught two fish on a single hook, and cast them back into the sea. But twice more the fish returned to his hook, so he took them home—to discover that his sister and her children had come to dinner.

Liborius—July 23
PATRON INVOKED AGAINST GALLSTONES

Liborius was a fourth-century bishop of Le Mans for fifty years. Pope Clement XI created him a Patron, a Saint to be invoked against gallstones—from which the pope himself suffered.

Louis Bertrand—October 9
PATRON OF COLOMBIA

This Spanish Dominican friar was among the first Catholic missionaries to the New World, traveling to Colombia, Panama, and many Caribbean islands from 1562 to 1568. Although Louis did not speak the language of the natives, he was granted the "gift of tongues" so that they understood his many passionate sermons, and he is alleged to have personally baptized 100,000 of them. To his credit, he was outraged at the soldiers' and colonists' cruel treatment of the Indians, and loudly protested (in vain) to the authorities upon his return to Spain.

Louise de Marillac—March 15
PATRONESS OF ORPHANS, WIDOWS, AND SOCIAL WORKERS

In Paris, in 1625, Mme. Louise le Gras (*née* Marillac), age thirty-four, became a wealthy widow. She might have founded a glittering salon, or, being of a religious nature, joined an austere and cloistered nunnery. Fortunately, her trusted friend and spiritual advisor was Saint Vincent de Paul (*whom* SEE). Customarily, devout and wealthy widows were, for "Monsieur Vincent," a financial resource for his many charitable works. But in Mme. le Gras, delicate as she appeared, he saw real possibilities. Under his direction, she began to do actual *work* among the poor, the sick, the destitute. Eventually she founded and directed the Daughters of Charity, an altogether new sort of order, "whose convent is the sickroom, and whose cloister is the streets." The sisters took no vows. Louise and the women (not all of them, by any means, aristocrats) who gathered to her cause founded and staffed shelters for abandoned women, orphanages, even schools, throughout France. Their operation of the great Hôtel

Dieu hospital in Paris was an acknowledged inspiration, centuries later, to Florence Nightingale. When, 300 years after Louise's death, the Vatican pronounced her a Saint, the act was entirely superfluous.

Louis of France—August 25
PATRON OF BUTTON MAKERS, MARBLE WORKERS, MASONS, SCULPTORS, AND WIG MAKERS

King Louis IX of France (ruled 1226–70) was the very model of a Catholic monarch—he was just, honorable, benevolent, would not abide foul language, and in every way deserved to have a city in Missouri named after him. He waged relentless and successful campaigns against heretics, rebellious nobles, and English invaders (he might be said to have won the Hundred Years' War). He was a loving husband to his queen, Margaret of Provence, with whom he had eleven children. He caused the magnificent church of Sainte-Chapelle to be built as a shrine for his most precious possession, the original Crown of Thorns. As a Crusader, however, Louis was a flop. He was taken prisoner on his first calamitous expedition against the infidels, and died of dysentery on his catastrophic second trip. Historians have assumed he embarked on these lengthy, pointless, overseas wars to get away from his mother, the remarkably obnoxious Blanche of Castile.

Lubin—March 14
PATRON INVOKED AGAINST RHEUMATISM

A peasant boy of Burgundy born early in the sixth century, Lubin sought day labor in a nearby monastery, where he studied by night. Lest he disturb the sleeping inmates, he shaded the light of his candle with his hand. He was a young monk himself in Lyons when the pagan tribe of Franks overran the countryside. In the course of their looting, they captured Lubin, tied his feet together, and lowered him headfirst into the river, demanding the location of the monastery's treasure. The Franks got nothing, and Lubin got rheumatism. He ended his days as bishop of Chartres.

Lucy—December 13
PATRONESS OF GONDOLIERS, GLAZIERS, AND LAMPLIGHTERS; INVOKED AGAINST DYSENTERY, EYE DISEASE, HEMORRHAGE, AND THROAT DISEASE

Lucy's name, appropriately, means "light"—for her feast day fell, in the old calendar, on the winter solstice, the shortest, darkest day of the year. She was a wealthy, beautiful, and affianced maiden of Syracuse, Sicily, whose mother was troubled with an internal complaint. Lucy accompanied her to the shrine of the Virgin Martyr Saint Agnes (*whom* SEE), where a miraculous cure was effected. Lucy vowed then and there to die a virgin, and to give all her worldly goods to the poor. Her acts of charity distressed her fortune-hunting fiancé, who denounced her as a Christian to the authorities. She was condemned to a be despoiled in a brothel, but not even a team of oxen could move her from the place where she stood; she survived an attempted burning at the stake; and, praising God all the while, she was dispatched by a sword in the throat. At some juncture in these proceedings, she plucked out her eyes and made a present of them to her suitor, who had always admired them. She is, of course, the "Santa Lucia" about whom the gondoliers of Venice interminably sing.

Ludger—March 26
PATRON OF SAXONS

A native of seventh-century Friesland (now the Netherlands), Ludger was educated and ordained priest in England before returning home to Christianize his fellow Frisians. He gladly shared the loot from the pagan temples he sacked with the Emperor Charlemagne. Driven out by an invasion of heathen Saxons, Ludger toured France and Italy before returning to Friesland as a missionary bishop to those very Saxons. Apparently a changed man, Ludger now began distributing to the poor the money that had been destined for use in decorating the churches. Charlemagne was outraged, and demanded an audience with the bishop, but Ludger kept him waiting while he finished his devotions, much to the emperor's edification. Münster in northern Germany is named for the monastery he founded there.

Ludmila—September 16
PATRONESS OF CZECHOSLOVAKIA

Ludmila and her husband, Borzivoi, the duke of Bohemia, converted to Christianity after Saint Methodius told the ambitious duke that, if he converted, "his enemies would be made his footstool." Ludmila and Borzivoi became such forceful advocates for the new religion that there was soon an insurrection. Her eldest son, Wratislaus, married a pagan, "the disheveled one"—Drahomira, mother of Saint Wenceslaus (*whom* SEE). Before he died, Wratislaus entrusted Wenceslaus to Ludmila and her confessor, Paul (another disciple of Methodius). In time Ludmila exerted her influence over her grandson to seize the government from his pagan mother. Too late, Drahomira tried to separate her son and mother-in-law, and then ordered Ludmila strangled with her own veil. The wicked queen, in a hypocritical attempt to expiate her crime, dedicated the murder site to Saint Michael and made it a church.

Luke—October 18
PATRON OF BUTCHERS, DOCTORS, GLASS-INDUSTRY WORKERS, GOLDSMITHS, LACE MAKERS, NOTARIES, PAINTERS, AND SCULPTORS

The author of the Third Gospel and the Acts of the Apostles was a Greek-speaking native of Antioch, Syria. He was Saint Paul's disciple, faithful companion, and personal "beloved" physician (Colossians 4:14). Luke's Gospel, which is the most quotable and "poetic," was obviously written for an audience of gentiles rather than Jews—it emphasizes the universality of Christ's message, rather than His fulfilling of Hebrew prophecies. Luke's heavenly interest in graphic artists arises from the legend that he himself painted. His portrait of the Madonna and Child has been lost. Likewise, tradition alleges he never married, and was crucified in his eighty-fourth year alongside Andrew (*whom* SEE) at Patras. Luke's emblem is, inexplicably, a winged ox—which earned him the veneration of butchers.

Lupus—July 29
PATRON INVOKED AGAINST STOMACHACHE

The Frenchman Lupus was born in the third century, and married a sister of Saint Hilary (*whom* see), but after six years they separated, donating their estate to the poor. Lupus became the monk who accompanied Germanus to England to help fight the Pelagian heresy. As bishop of Troyes, he confronted Attila in 451, asking him to spare that province and submitting himself as hostage. Unfortunately his countrymen misinterpreted his motives, believing him to be a collaborator, and Lupus was ostracized and forced to become a hermit.

Lydia—August 3
PATRONESS OF CLOTH DYERS

She is known as Lydia "Purpuraria," that is, "the seller of purple," for that was her employment in the city of Thatira, Turkey, once famous for its dye works. She chanced to be in Philippi at the time of Paul's visit there, and had the honor to become the great Apostle's first convert; subsequently, he was frequently her houseguest.

Lydwina—April 14
PATRONESS OF SKATERS

During her life (1380–1433) Lydwina lived up to her name, which means "friend of suffering." Like Saint Brigid (*whom* SEE), she successfully prayed to become less beautiful, and a fateful skating accident as a teen changed her life. She fell and broke a rib, which pierced the flesh, resulting in an abscess that became an open sore that never healed. A fissure extended from the top of her forehead to her nose, and her lower lip fell off her chin. All this did not deter her from adding to her misery by wearing a horsehair girdle. Understandably, she took to her bed for the next thirty-three years, applying plasters to her wounds and the worms they bred. She generally used eel fat in her plaster, but once demanded the curate give her the fat from one of his capons. When he refused, she shouted, "Well, I hope the mice will eat your chickens!" which they did that very night. Although a band of mercenaries once broke into her room to look at her sores, her most frequent visitor was her Guardian Angel. He took her on trips to Paradise, and enabled her to become invisible so she could assist at High Mass. Once, when a Communion wafer descended from Heaven and headed in her direction, the local priest refused to serve it to her, incurring the wrath of the townspeople, who chased him into the local cemetery. In later years, she received what her biographer termed "the gift of television." One day Lydwina choked on her own phlegm, died, and was buried in her parish church. Her emblem is a pair of ice skates.

Macarius of Alexandria (the Younger)—January 2
PATRON OF PASTRY COOKS

Macarius, a confectioner by trade, retreated to the desert in 335 to spend sixty years in penitential basket making. He was so ascetic that he wore sandbags on his shoulders in the desert, and his diet consisted of raw beans (except during the forty days of Lent, when it was reduced to a couple of cabbage leaves). He once denied himself a bunch of grapes, passing them on to other monks; eventually they landed back with him, and he still refused to eat them. He disdained nursing the sick in hospitals, since he believed it to be grandstanding under the guise of charity. He hated money so much that when a fellow monk died, leaving 100 crowns to the order, Macarius decided not to give the money to either the Church or the poor, but buried it with the monk instead. Racked with guilt over killing a fly, he retreated naked into the desert for six months, allowing himself to be bitten by insects continually. In art he is sometimes shown with a hyena, because he once cured a young hyena of blindness. In gratitude, the hyena's mother brought Macarius a sheepskin.

Macra—January 6
PATRONESS INVOKED AGAINST BREAST DISEASE

A maiden convert to the Faith in Rheims, France (Gaul to the third-century Romans), she was subjected (when she would abandon neither her Faith nor her chastity) to fiendish torments, not the least of which was the shearing off of her virginal though substantial mammaries. Apparently Macra was something of a scholar, for in sacred art she is depicted carrying her breasts on an open book—not to be confused with Saint Agatha (*whom* SEE), who displays hers on a plate.

Madern—May 17
PATRON INVOKED AGAINST LAMENESS

On a desolate moor in Cornwall stand the ruins of this hermit's chapel. Inside is a stone bench—"Madern's Bed"—and nearby is a well. The afflicted who bathe in the waters of the well and sleep the night on the bed rise up cured. Sabine Baring-Gould (*Lives of the Saints,* Volume 5) provides a moving account of the miraculous recovery of a severely injured football player, *circa* 1640.

Magnus of Füssen—September 6

PATRON OF CROPS; INVOKED AGAINST CATERPILLARS, HAIL, AND VERMIN

Magnus was a disciple of Columban (*whom* SEE) and was working out of Kempten, Germany, where he freed the neighborhood of serpents before proceeding to Füssen, where he expelled a dragon and founded an abbey. On a walk, he encountered a bear who showed him a vein of iron ore. Magnus rewarded the bear with a piece of cake. The pair went back to the abbey, and the bear led Magnus, now carrying his tools and accompanied by his fellow monks, to the mountains. They found other veins of iron ore, thus founding the most profitable industry of that region. His cult, however, remains popular among the local farmers.

Magnus of Orkney—April 16

PATRON OF NORWAY AND OF FISHMONGERS

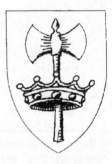

When this twelfth-century Viking prince was captured by King Magnus Barefoot of Norway, he refused to join in pirate raids, preferring to stay on board ship reading psalms. Later he escaped to Scotland and, after the king died, returned to the Orkneys to share the government with his duplicitous cousin Haakon. Although Magnus and Haakon would occasionally join forces to fight common pirate enemies, his cousin remained jealous of Magnus's popularity and schemed to destroy him. After inviting him to the islet of Egilsay for a peace conference, Haakon ambushed the Saint as he reached the shore. Haakon ordered Magnus executed on the spot, and when the executioner hesitated, the generous Saint encouraged him: "Do not be afraid, the guilt is not thine, and remember my clothes will be thy perquisite." Another martyr whose death was more political than religious, Magnus appeared to Robert Bruce on the eve of the Battle of Bannockburn, in 1314.

Mamas—August 17
PATRON OF NURSES AND SHEPHERDS; INVOKED AGAINST COLIC

Mamas was a Christian shepherd boy of third-century Caesarea, gifted with a wonderful power over animals both wild and tame. Arrested, he would not deny his Faith, and was thrown to the lions in the amphitheater; rather than attacking the lad, those ferocious carnivores gathered around him "like a flock of sheep." Soldiers were forthwith commanded to slay Mamas with swords, but one especially large and ferocious jungle cat stood guard over Our Saint. Mamas, eager to achieve the crown of martyrdom, ordered the noble beast to behave himself, and while the pagan soldiers did their duty, the lion stood by, weeping.

Marcellinus—April 26

Marcellinus's reputation as pope (296–304) is considerably diminished by certain acts of weakness, the first being his surrender of Church archives to the Roman authorities (which accounts for the lack of documentation of this period). Later, Marcellinus was observed offering incense to Hercules, Jupiter, and Saturn in a public ceremony in the temple of Vesta. Three hundred outraged bishops immediately formed the Synod of Sinuessa, but were unable to depose Marcellinus as pope, and soon found themselves under a death sentence. Marcellinus first denied his guilt over the incense incident, but later repented and was executed along with the other bishops. Saint Augustine, while denying that any of this ever took place, maintained that Marcellinus's papacy established the precedent that the pope must be the only one to judge his own guilt.

Marcel of Paris—November 1
PATRON INVOKED AGAINST VAMPIRES

Educated and ordained in Paris, Marcel showed a flair for dramatics even in his youth—holding hot iron bars in his hand and turning water into wine. He was a welcome relief in 400 as bishop of Paris after his strict predecessor, Prudentius, and the city loved him. When a rich and dissolute woman was buried in a Christian cemetery, a black serpent wormed its way out of her grave, exposing the corpse and nibbling on her grisly remains, which caused quite a scandal. Marcel, in full bishop's regalia and with most of the city following him, confronted the ghoulish serpent. Ignoring its threatening hisses, the Saint clobbered the fiend with his staff, wrapped it in his robe, and dragged it out of the cemetery.

Marculf—May 1
PATRON INVOKED AGAINST SCROFULA

As everyone knows, the touch of a king cures the skin disease scrofula, for which reason it is called "the King's Evil." In France, all monarchs were endowed with this marvelous power through the intercession of Marculf (or Marcoul), a sixth-century Norman monk whose relics were visited and venerated as part of official French coronation ceremonies until 1825.

Margaret—July 20
PATRONESS OF CHILDBIRTH, NURSES, AND PEASANTS

A princess of Antioch, Margaret's father threw her out when he discovered that her nanny (one Theotimus) had made her a Christian; together the maiden and her maid became simple shepherdesses. A stunning beauty despite having consecrated herself to virginity, Margaret was pursued by an amorous prefect, who, upon her rejection of his advances, threw her into jail. There, in her cell, she was visited by Satan, who assumed the form of a dragon and swallowed her. But in the very belly of the beast, a cross she carried grew to such enormous proportions that the dragon was split in two, and Margaret emerged unharmed; for this reason, she is the traditional Patroness of childbirth. On another occasion, the Devil appeared to Our Saint as a man, but Margaret saw through his disguise, knocked him down, and set her foot on his neck, saying, "Lie still, thou fiend, under the foot of a woman." She was eventually beheaded, and went directly to Heaven, where she enjoyed enormous popularity throughout the Middle Ages. Hers was one of the voices heard by Joan of Arc. Among her emblems is a pearl—which is *"magarita"* in Latin.

Margaret-Mary—October 16
PATRONESS INVOKED AGAINST POLIO

In 1654, when she was seven, Margaret-Mary was inspired to take a vow of chastity, without (as she later acknowledged in her autobiography) the vaguest idea what the words "vow" or "chastity" meant. From her eighth to her fifteenth year, she was bedridden with an illness, possibly poliomyelitis, possibly cured by a miracle. As an adolescent, she was tempted to marry until Christ appeared to her and "made [her] see He was the most handsome, the richest, the most powerful, the most perfect and accomplished of lovers." Thus reminded by the jealous Savior of her childhood engagement to Him, she entered the Visitation convent at Paray-le-Monial in central France in 1671. She went to work in the infirmary, where Sister Margaret-Mary, clumsy and slow, and the infirmarian Sister Mary-Catherine, brisk and efficient, became a spiritually edifying trial to each other. It was on the feast of Saint John the Divine (*whom* SEE), December 27, 1673, that Christ again appeared to Our Saint, and invited her to dinner—in fact, to take the traditional place of Saint John at Our Lord's side, leaning on His breast at the Last Supper. For some time thereafter, Jesus continued to appear to Margaret-Mary, invariably opening His shirt to expose a flaming, throbbing, crimson organ—His Sacred Heart—to which she, of all people, had been Especially Chosen to spread devotion. Her Mother Superior took an understandably dim view of these revelations. Her fellow nuns were somewhat resentful when Margaret-Mary informed them that Jesus had personally asked *her* to expiate *their* sins. When Margaret-Mary persisted, a committee of theologians was convened, and concluded she was, at best, delusional. Yet, by the time of her death (in 1690), her convent was perfoming the Devotions to the Sacred Heart she had prescribed—including the now-ubiquitous Catholic practices of the "Holy Hour" and "Nine First Fridays." The Vatican instituted the Feast of the Sacred Heart of Jesus in 1856. Margaret-Mary was canonized in 1920.

Margaret of Cortona—February 22
PATRONESS OF FALLEN WOMEN

While Margaret, who was born in 1247, was living with her farmer father and wicked stepmother, she was seduced by a knight; she went to live with him openly in his castle—without benefit of clergy—at the age of twelve! She was the knight's mistress for nine years, shamelessly parading through the streets of Cortona flaunting her finery and even bearing the knight a son. One day Margaret's dog led her to the spot where the decomposed body of her erstwhile lover (he had been murdered) was hidden. She realized that his death was due to both her beauty and her sinful life, and took her son and retreated to a friary. Here she began her life as a penitent in earnest, threatening to cut off her nose and lips, practicing bizarre mortifications—and some child abuse, as well. She entered the Third Order of the Franciscans, taking as her confessor Fra Giunta, who earlier had been able to persuade her to keep her nose and lips and to tone down her fasting and mortifications. One day, when she was kneeling before a crucifix, the figure of Jesus leaned forward, addressed her as *"la poverella,"* and released her from her penance. The two began a series of dialogues on a wide range of topics. Twice the figure of Jesus gave her messages of an admonitory nature to deliver to the bishop of Arezzo, which she did; but the bishop ignored Margaret's warnings; this resulted in his untimely death just days after her second visit. In time, her past raised its unhappy head—local wags began to cast aspersions on her relationships with the friars, especially with her confessor, Fra Giunta. This scandal caused him to be transferred to Siena, but Margaret prevailed, and in her later years had great success in converting hardened sinners. Aptly called "the Magdalene of the Franciscans," Margaret is part of the long Italian tradition of village saints that includes the great Francis of Assisi (*whom* see). She is invoked to this day by the people of Cortona, who maintain that her only sin was that she loved too much.

Margaret of Scotland—November 16
PATRONESS OF SCOTLAND

Margaret, an eleventh-century ancestress of England's current royal family, was forced to escape to Scotland from England after the Norman Conquest. Malcolm, king of Scotland, became enamored of her beauty and style, and they married soon after her arrival. The royal couple transformed the social and cultural life of Scotland—Margaret, in particular, tried to rid the Church of its Celtic influences. She called a synod to bring Lent, marriage customs, and Holy Communion practices in line with the teachings of the Church of Rome. She succeeded in getting Malcolm to attend Mass, although she failed to teach him how to read. (He would, however, kiss her favorite books.) After Malcolm had conquered an enemy castle, the loser killed the king by putting a spear through his eye. Margaret's family tried to keep the news from her—she was on her own deathbed—but she cried, "I know how it is!" She then rationalized the tragedy as a form of penance—a purification—for her own youthful sins. During the Reformation, her body was moved to Spain to avoid desecration by Protestants.

Maria Goretti—July 6
PATRONESS OF TEENAGE GIRLS

After her father's death, Maria's mother, Assunta, was forced to go back to work, leaving Maria in charge of the family. In 1902, when she was twelve, Maria looked older than her age, and attracted the attention of the next-door neighbor, Alexander Sernelli, who read dirty magazines. On the feast of the Precious Blood, knowing she was alone, Alexander attacked her, growling, "Submit or die!" Maria, repelling his advances, replied, "Death, but not sin!" which so angered Alexander that he fatally stabbed her. She forgave him from her deathbed and Alexander went to prison, where he remained unremorseful until Maria came to him in a vision, dressed in white and gathering lilies. Maria's canonization in 1950 was held outdoors to accommodate the vast throngs. It was the first time both a Saint's mother and a Saint's murderer attended a canonization, for Alexander, now a Capuchin laybrother, was present. The pope, heralding Maria as "the Saint Agatha of the twentieth century," used the occasion to decry the lack of female modesty in the press and cinema. A left-wing journalist, Giordano Bruno, theorized in 1985 that Maria's martyrdom had been an invention of the Mussolini government and that Pope Pius XII's endorsement of her was an effort to counteract the influence of the occupying (predominantly Protestant) American troops.

Mark—April 25

PATRON OF CATTLE BREEDERS, VENICE, NOTARIES, AND GLAZIERS;
INVOKED AGAINST FLY BITES

Mark's mother, Mary, ran a house that served as the meeting place for the twelve Apostles. Mark was converted to Christianity by Peter himself, who called him his son. He went on the first Christian mission with his cousin Barnabas and Saint Paul, but became discouraged and turned back, earning Paul's extreme displeasure. Mark's Gospel, one of the four in the New Testament, is essentially Peter's dictated recollections of the life of Jesus. Writing in awkward Greek with Semitic overtones, Mark was a surprisingly impartial narrator, and made no bones about recounting Peter's defections—surprising especially because Mark himself fled naked on the night Jesus was arrested. Once when Our Saint was aroused by a beautiful woman who kissed his hand, he cut the offending hand off—only to have it restored by the Blessed Virgin. In the eighth year of Vespian's reign, when Mark was bishop of Alexandria, he was dragged through the streets with a rope around his neck, thrown into prison, and strangled. His relics remained in Alexandria until 829, when they were purchased (or stolen) by merchants. When his tomb was opened, a sweet fragrance filled the entire city. Venice laid claim to the Saint because Mark once took refuge in its lagoons during a storm, and an Angel appeared to him, saying, "On this site a great city will arise in your honor." During the construction of St. Mark's Basilica, a workman fell from a steeple, yelled Mark's name, and was saved by a tree branch that miraculously appeared to support him.

Martha—July 29

PATRONESS OF COOKS, DIETICIANS, HOUSEWIVES, AND WAITRESSES

The sister of Mary and Lazarus and "hostess of Christ," Martha was described as having "the courage of a man and the heart of a woman." It was for her that Christ raised Lazarus from the dead and to her that he said, "I am the Resurrection and the Life." He gently chided her for her household bustling, defending the contemplative

life as exemplified by her sister, Mary. After the Resurrection, the sturdy Martha, along with Mary and Lazarus, was deported from Palestine in an open boat that miraculously landed at the port of Marseilles. She began preaching and working miracles throughout Provence, including vanquishing a dragon that was half beast and half fish, longer than a horse, and horned on either side with a tail like a serpent. Martha made the Sign of the Cross over the dragon (later thought to be a crocodile from Egypt), tied it up with her girdle, and rallied the crowd to tear it to pieces. (Curiously, a similar story is told about a pagan goddess from Provence who had subdued a dragon in an earlier
time. She was named Martis.) Martha died not long after she saw her sister ascend into Heaven, and in Divine reciprocation, Christ served at her funeral Mass and burial. In art she is stout, plainly dressed, and holding a ladle or broom. Occasionally she may be depicted in her more heroic form, conquering the dragon.

Martina—January 30
PATRONESS OF NURSING MOTHERS AND OF ROME

Pope Urban VIII is remembered on this day for forcing his one-time friend Galileo to deny that the earth orbits the sun. But he was also a supporter of the cult of the entirely mythical Virgin Martyr Martina, in whose honor he built a church and under whose protection he placed the city of Rome. According to her legend, Martina was flogged with iron hooks, showered with boiling grease, thrown to the lions, and burned at the stake, all of which she survived, praising the Lord. When she was beheaded, not blood but a fountain of milk gushed from her severed neck; hence her association with breast-feeding.

Martin de Porres—November 3

PATRON OF HAIRDRESSERS, PUBLIC-HEALTH WORKERS, PERSONS OF
MIXED RACE, AND PERUVIAN TELEVISION

Born in Lima, Peru, in 1579, Martin was the child of a Spanish knight and a black Panamanian freedwoman. To the distress of his father's family, he resembled his mother. He was apprenticed to a hairdresser, and at fifteen became a Dominican laybrother, working as a barber-surgeon. The rich and poor of Lima flocked to Martin to be cured by his combination of medicine and miracles. (He could heal with a handshake.) It was widely known that he glowed when he prayed, that he could be in two places at once, and that he could fly. He could also resolve marital problems, dispense agricultural advice, and find time to raise a dowry for his niece. A friend to all creatures, Martin raised money for a hospital, an orphange, and a clinic for dogs and cats. He could communicate telepathically with animals, and despaired that the rats scurrying around the friary ("poor little things") weren't getting enough to eat. Despite his great fame, he remained humble, referring to himself as "Brother Broom" or "Mulatto Dog," and once suggested that the Dominican Order sell him to raise money. After his death in 1639, his grave became a site of pilgrimage and miracles. The flamboyant ascetic Rose of Lima (whom SEE) had been his friend and was declared a Saint shortly after her death, but Martin didn't get the official nod until 1963.

Martin of Tours—November 11

PATRON OF BEGGARS, DRUNKARDS, INNKEEPERS, EQUESTRIANS,
HARVESTS, HORSES, THE MILITARY, NEW WINE, AND TAILORS

Martin was the first universally popular Saint, and the first Saint who was not also a martyr; more churches are dedicated to him than to anyone else. He was born in Hungary, *circa* 315, and became a cavalry officer in the Roman army of Constantine. When he was stationed at Amiens, France, he gave half his cloak to a freezing beggar (having slashed it in two with his sword). When Christ appeared to him wearing the very same half-garment, Martin went to the local bishop, Saint Hilary (*whom* SEE), and asked to be baptized. His reputation as "the Soldier Saint" is somewhat ironic—for his first act as a Christian was to conscientiously object. After leaving the army, he spent some time as a hermit, and then set out for the Balkans to combat the Arian heresy there—and was publicly flogged for his preaching. Upon his return to Gaul, he established the first monastery in that country. Martin cured lepers with a kiss, and brought the dead to life. He exposed a bogus local "Saint" with a vision of the dead man in Hell. Although the French bishops complained that Martin never combed his hair, the people of Tours demanded he be made their bishop. Fearful of the honor, Martin fled and hid, until his whereabouts were betrayed by a honking goose. (A goose is among his emblems, and roast goose is traditionally served on his feast day, "Martinmas.") As bishop, Martin continued his monkish ways, wearing animal skins, riding a donkey, and still not combing his hair. He initiated a method of exorcism whereby the afflicted expelled demons through vomiting and defecation. The Devil himself tormented Our Saint, often appearing to him in the shape of a lusty Roman goddess—but reeking of sulfur. Ever the pacifist, Martin defied authorities by preaching against the death penalty, predicting (correctly) that the execution of heretics increased their influence. By chance, Martin died (in the year 400) on the day of the pagan feast of Vinalia, when the new wine is tasted—thus he is considered Patron of drunkards. (In England, "martin-drunk" means *very* drunk indeed.) His funeral was spectacular. Heavenly music filled the air, as two thousand monks followed his coffin. Trees bloomed (in November) as it passed, so that even today, a spell of fine weather in November is known throughout Europe as a "Saint Martin's summer."

Maruthas—December 4
PATRON OF IRAN

   A fifth-century bishop of the "Christians of the East," Maruthas lived in the city of Maiferkat on the Iran-Iraq border, in the days when Iran was called Persia and Iraq was still Mesopotamia. A diplomat, physician, theologian, and composer of hymns, he was able to persuade the Persian king to cease persecuting his Christian subjects, and is to this day revered by members of the Syrian Orthodox Church as their "Father."

Mary Magdalene—July 22
PATRONESS OF CONTEMPLATIVES, FALLEN WOMEN, GLOVERS, HAIRDRESSERS, AND PERFUMERS

History's most famous reformed harlot is, in Catholic tradition, identified as the "sinner with seven devils," who washed Christ's feet with her tears and dried them with her hair before anointing them with perfume. Pope Gregory the Great (*whom* SEE) promoted the notion that she was the languorous sister of Martha and Lazarus, and the sometime fiancée of Saint John the Divine. His Holiness Pope Gregory attributed her fall from grace to her glamour, observing that "the evil beauty of face is wont to uproot modesty of the soul." Nonetheless, she is venerated as the most ardent and loyal of Christ's followers, one of the women disciples with Him when He died and who buried Him. Christian feminists point to her significant role as the first witness to the Resurrection, who announced the Risen Christ to the Apostles. Whether or not she constituted Jesus' "Last Temptation," Our Lord took her side against various maligners—temple elders, her sister, Martha, and Judas, saying, "Her sins, which are many, are forgiven, for she loved much" (Luke 7:47). In French folk tradition, Mary, Martha, and Lazarus sailed to Marseilles after the Ascension. Mary retired to a cave in the wilderness, fed and otherwise attended by Angels. The mountains surrounding her grotto are named La Sainte Baume in honor of her famous ointment.

Mary, the Immaculate Conception—December 8
PATRONESS OF THE UNITED STATES

Catholics get understandably upset when their friends—atheists, pagans, or heretics—confuse the Mystery of the Immaculate Conception (the conception *of* the Blessed Virgin) with the Mystery of the Incarnation (the conception *by* the Blessed Virgin). For centuries, a debate raged within Christendom as to whether the Mother of God was (or was not) born—like all humans since Adam and Eve—in a state of "Original Sin." Popular opinion, and Franciscan theologians, maintained that she was innocent—that she had been "Immaculately Conceived." Most learned Doctors of the Church, including Saints Thomas Aquinas and Bernard of Clairvaux (*both of whom* SEE), argued that Mary's parents, being mortal, *must* have experienced some carnal pleasure in the act of her begetting, thus infecting her (so to speak) with Sin. In 1847, Pope Pius IX declared Mary, under the title of the Immaculate Conception, to be the official Patroness of the United States—but it was not (curiously) until December 8, 1854, that His Holiness infallibly pronounced the Immaculate Conception to be a matter of Catholic dogma—and not (even more curiously) until 1870 that he infallibly pronounced his own infallibility.

Mathurin—November 1
PATRON OF FOOLS

This (very early) Saint's Patronage of clowns and idiots is, in French, proverbial—and apparently inexplicable. A precociously religious lad of the city of Sens, in what was then Roman Gaul, Mathurin was baptized at the early age of twelve, and then managed the conversion of his own pagan parents. Ordained priest (allegedly by the great Saint Polycarp himself), Mathurin acquired a local reputation as an exorcist, and was invited to Rome by the Emperor Maximian (*circa* 300) to expel a devil possessing his daughter. Mathurin's mission was a success, but resulted in the Saint's own death. Buried with great ceremony in Rome, he one day reportedly rose from the grave and returned to his native city to be buried there. Curiously, *"mathurin"* has long been a French slang term for "sailor. "

Matrona—March 15
PATRONESS INVOKED AGAINST DYSENTERY

A Portuguese princess, Matrona was advised in a vision to travel to Capua, Italy, to be cured of the complaint against which she is invoked. She expired of it there, where her memory is still much revered.

Matthew—September 21

PATRON OF ACCOUNTANTS, BOOKKEEPERS, BANKERS, TAX COLLECTORS, CUSTOMS OFFICIALS, SECURITY GUARDS, AND STOCKBROKERS

Matthew was an exile among his own people, a Jewish tax collector, despised by Jews and gentiles alike as an extortionist. Christ challenged public opinion when He gave Matthew the call to "Follow Me," as recounted in Matthew's own Gospel. When Matthew describes Christ dining with "people of ill repute," he is talking about himself. He undertook his Gospel under special instructions from the Holy Ghost, writing it for Jewish Christians and using his wide knowledge of Jewish customs. Matthew's Gospel tells the story of the Star of Bethlehem, the Flight to Egypt, the Sermon on the Mount, and the Passion. It was made into a movie in 1967 by Pasolini. After the Pentecost, Matthew, like all his fellow Apostles, preached the Faith and suffered martyrdom. Before his death he spent some time at court, where some eunuchs pitted him against a dragon. Joining the legions of Saints who vanquished dragons, Matthew made the Sign of the Cross and the monster feel asleep at his feet.

Matthias—May 14

PATRON OF ALCOHOLICS; INVOKED AGAINST ALCOHOLISM

Following the suicide of Judas, Matthias was chosen (by lot) to take the traitor's place among the Twelve Apostles. He was martyred with a halberd or ax (his emblem) on the shores of the Caspian Sea. His most famous mission was to Ethiopia, where he was captured and blinded by cannibals, being rescued in the nick of time by Saint Andrew (*whom* see), who arrived in a boat piloted by Jesus Himself. His Patronage of drunkards is traditional, but of unknown origin.

Maurice—September 21

PATRON OF HATTERS, SARDINIA, AUSTRIA, DYERS, KNIFE GRINDERS, WEAVERS, THE PAPAL SWISS GUARDS, AND INFANTRY; INVOKED AGAINST GOUT AND CRAMPS

Maurice was a (possibly black) officer at the head of the exclusive Theban Legion, stationed in Agaunum (Switzerland) in the third century. The legion included in its ranks such famous Christian soldiers as Besse, Gereon, and Victor (*all of whom* SEE). Before the Emperor Maximian marched against the Gauls, he ordered the legion to sacrifice to the gods. Maurice, as spokesman, refused, and led the army in retreat to what is now Saint-Maurice-en-Valais. The emperor ordered a decimation—killing every tenth man—until the entire legion of 6,660 soldiers was chopped to bits. Later accounts maintain it was only a cohort (600 men) that was massacred, and even deny that the the more famous Saints were part of Maurice's legion and legend. Although Maurice has suffered from revisionist history, his ring and blood are preserved at Saint-Maurice, as is the slab of stone on which he knelt to receive the final blow.

Maurus—January 15
PATRON INVOKED AGAINST COLDS

Born sometime in the sixth century, this twelve-year-old lad was one of the first to be placed in the care of Saint Benedict (*whom* SEE) at his monastery at Subiaco. Maurus grew to be Benedict's personal assistant and later succeeded him as abbot; as an old man he is supposed to have crossed the Alps to found an abbey of his own, Saint-Maur, on the Rhône. But he worked his most famous miracle when he was still a boy. On a cold winter's day, a fellow student, Placid (*whom* SEE), was sent out to fetch wood, tumbled into the lake, and began drifting from shore. Thinking fast, Benedict sent Maurus— who could not swim—to the rescue. Honoring Holy Obedience above all, Maurus ran quickly and fearlessly across the surface of the water, grabbed young Placid by the hair, and hauled him back to land. In the reformed Benedictine calendar, the feast of Maurus has been moved to October 5, although this traditional date in January, falling at the height of the flu season, seems more appropriate.

Maximilian Kolbe—August 14
PATRON OF DRUG ADDICTS;
INVOKED AGAINST DRUG ADDICTION

This Polish Franciscan priest died in 1941 of a lethal injection administered to him in a cell in Auschwitz. Father Kolbe had actually *volunteered* to die— that is, to take the place of a fellow prisoner condemned to death. In his book *Making Saints*, Kenneth Woodward observes that, upon his papal canonization (November 9, 1982), Maximilian Kolbe became a new *kind* of Saint, "a martyr of charity."

Maximus—November 27
PATRON OF BABIES AND THE DYING

Abbot of Lérins, in France, Maximus had a wide reputation for sanctity and miracle working. He is among the very numerous holy hermits who abhorred the very idea of becoming a bishop. Once offered the job, Maximus fled to Italy and hid in a forest during the rainy season. On another such occasion, he took off in a rowboat. Obliged in the end to accept the miter, he continued to live as a monk, and kept right on wearing his hair shirt. In his own infancy he had been remarkably pious—refusing his mother's breast on fast days and Fridays. As an adult, he was especially adept at deathbed healings and conversions.

Médard—June 8
PATRON OF HARVESTS; INVOKED AGAINST RAIN AND TOOTHACHE

If it rains on Médard's feast day, say the French, it will rain for forty days thereafter. Which is why they call Our Saint "the Great Pisser." As bishop of Tournai in Picardy, Médard founded, fourteen centuries ago, the annual Rose Festival, which is still held there on this day, and during which the region's most beautiful and virtuous maiden is crowned. Rain or shine.

Méen (Mewan)—June 21
PATRON INVOKED AGAINST ECZEMA

Near the hermitage in Brittany of this Welsh-born, sixth-century disciple of Saint Samson (*whom* SEE) is a fountain; its waters bring relief to sufferers from eczema, the skin disease known locally as *mal de Saint Méen.*

Meingold—February 8
PATRON OF BANKERS, BAKERS, MILLERS, AND MINERS

Meingold, a ninth-century Belgian noble, incurred the enmity of a certain Duke Albrecht after marrying his sister and claiming her dowry, which consisted of lands coveted by the duke. In the course of their feud, Meingold's castle was razed, and Albrecht died. Convinced of "the vanity of vanities," Meingold gave up his wife, lands, and money to become a beggar and ascetic; nevertheless, he was sought out by old enemies and murdered. His story makes as little sense as his traditional Patronage of the flour industry—his concern with mining and finance might perhaps be accounted for by the sound of his name.

Menas—November 11
PATRON OF CARAVANS AND MERCHANTS

An Egyptian soldier in the Roman army, Menas revealed himself to be a Christian and was horribly tortured, then burned alive, early in the third century. Menas's followers believed he was not in Heaven, but in the shrine they had built for him—an elaborate monastery/church/baths complex near Alexandria. A pilgrim visiting the shrine was horribly murdered by a robber—chopped to bits and placed in a sack—but Menas appeared with some fellow Saints, reassembled the pilgrim, and restored him to life. The shrine was destroyed by Arabs in the seventh century, and it wasn't excavated until the twentieth. Restored, it enjoyed renewed popularity, especially during World War II. The Patriarch of Egypt credited Menas with the Allied victory in the Battle of El Alamein, which rescued his country from the Nazis.

Mercury—November 25
PATRON OF THE MILITARY

Mercury was a Roman army officer who successfully combated a barbarian invasion. His refusal to participate in a post-battle sacrifice to the gods revealed him as a Christian, so he was tortured and killed. What distinguishes Mercury from others with a similar story is that 113 years after his death, at the behest of the desperate Saint Basil, Mercury returned to earth to rout the Emperor Julian the Apostate, descending from Heaven and killing him with a thrust of his sword. He visited earth a second time, to show himself to the soldiers of the First Crusade, along with Saints George and Demetrius (*both of whom* SEE).

Meriadoc—June 7
PATRON INVOKED AGAINST DEAFNESS

At the shrine of this seventh-century hermit-bishop in Stival, Brittany, is a scarf once worn by the Saint himself. Applied to the head of a pilgrim, it is marvelously effective against hardness of hearing. A play written about this Saint in 1504 is the sole surviving example of medieval Cornish literature.

Michael—September 29

PATRON OF BRUSSELS, GERMANY, PAPUA NEW GUINEA, THE BASQUES, POLICEMEN, BANKERS, GROCERS, RADIOLOGISTS, PARATROOPERS, THE DYING, AND CEMETERIES; INVOKED AGAINST PERIL AT SEA

The Archangel Michael figures prominently in Judaism and Islam, as well as in Christianity. He appeared to Moses in the burning bush, discoursed with Abraham, inspired Joan of Arc—and the Koran states that his tears formed the cherubim. Majestic in appearance, with a tremendous wingspan, Michael is described in the Koran as having "wings the color of green emerald . . . covered with saffron hairs, each of them containing a million faces." He is God's commander-in-chief in the war against the Devil and, in his dramatic confrontation with Satan, defeated an army of 133 million and hurled the fallen Angel down to Hell, bellowing, "I am Michael, Who is like God!" As Guardian Angel of Israel, Michael single-handedly wiped out an Assyrian army of 185,000 men, was responsible for the victory of Judas Maccabaeus, and wrested Moses' dead body from the Devil (who felt the prophet belonged in Hell for killing an Egyptian). In modern times, the Devil, seeking revenge on his old enemy, flew up to earth, terrifying the workers of the church of St. Michael in Cornhill, England, and leaving his claw marks on the bells. Michael became extremely popular after he appeared on battlefields in Italy, France, and England during various world wars, even comandeering a plane during World War II. He defended a convent of nuns in England during the Reformation, protected a party of schoolgirls from robbers, and vanquished the enemies of an Italian town by his use of lightning. After Pope Leo XIII had an out-of-body experience in which he saw Michael victorious over the horrors of Hell, he wrote his famous prayer to the Angel-Saint that is still used at the end of Mass. Michael is so powerful a force in Heaven that he can get people out of Hell and will assist with the judging on Judgment

Day. At the end of the world he will return to earth for his final battle with the AntiChrist. He is depicted in art wearing his shield and carrying his scales, ready to fight or to judge.

Mildburga—February 23
PATRONESS OF BIRDS

Mildburga's aunt, mother, and sisters are Saints; she served as abbess of Wenlock in Shropshire, 670–722. She performed numerous miracles, not the least of which were levitation and restoring dead children to life. During a time of drought, a blow from her horse's hoof caused a spring to flow from a rock—its waters had miraculous properties, as well. At Mildburga's request, the birds of the neighborhood would go easy on the crops until harvest time. Her grave was discovered by accident in the eleventh century, when some boys tumbled into a hole containing sweet-smelling bones. Wonderful cures soon abounded at the site, including the regurgitation by one pilgrim of a record-setting-sized tapeworm.

Modomnoc—February 13
PATRON OF BEES

A member of Ireland's royal O'Neill clan, this sixth-century monk became a student of Saint David of Wales (*whom* SEE). Among his duties as a novice was beekeeping; when it was time for him to return to Ireland, a swarm of bees insisted on accompanying his ship. They were the ancestors of, as his legend has it, "the gifted race of Ireland's bees."

Molaug—June 25
PATRON INVOKED AGAINST HEADACHE AND INSANITY

This Irish-born monk, also known as Molloch and Lugaid, was the first Christian missionary to the Highlands of Scotland and the even more remote Hebrides Islands, where his memory is yet held dear, and where he is invoked against whatever passes for madness in those parts.

Monica—August 27
PATRON OF MARRIED WOMEN AND MOTHERS

Everything we know about this fourth-century Saint we learn from the testimony of her devoted son Saint Augustine of Hippo (*whom* SEE), in his autobiographical *Confessions*. Monica was a member of the Roman-Christian community in Carthage, North Africa, and married a heathen with the unlikely name of Patrick. Her race, and that of her celebrated son, are a matter of some dispute. How did she convert her husband from bad-tempered pagan patriarch to timid True Believer, and her son from a lusty heretic into a Doctor of the Church? She ruthlessly employed a simple mother's method, tried and true. She wept. She sobbed. She sniveled. She bawled. Until, in self-defense, Patrick was baptized and died, and Augustine abandoned his mistress to become a priest. In Southern California, the Spanish explorers found a rock spring that dripped and dribbled ceaselessly. They called it, and the town they founded nearby, Santa Monica.

Morand—June 3
PATRON OF VINTNERS

A German-born Benedictine, Morand had the honor of becoming a trusted counselor to Count Frederick Pferz of Alsace. Because Morand once fasted through Lent, eating nothing but a bunch of grapes, a cluster of that fruit became his emblem, and his Patronage is consequently invoked by the vintners of both France and Germany.

Moses—February 7
PATRON OF THE SARACENS

"Saracen," a word of mysterious origins that the medievals applied to all Arabs, was a name first given to the nomadic tribesmen (Berbers?) inhabiting the Syrian-Palestinian desert on the eastern borders of the Roman empire. Moses was a Christian monk who, in the middle of the fourth century, dwelt among and befriended them; as a condition of a truce arranged with the empire—so the story goes— Mavia, queen of the Saracens, insisted that the humble Moses be appointed their bishop, in which capacity he served until his death in 372.

Moses the Black—August 28

PATRON OF BLACK AFRICANS

Something of a sacred stereotype, unfortunately, Moses is said to have been very large, very strong, and a thief. An unsatisfactory Ethiopian servant in an Egyptian household, he was fired for any number of reasons, and became the leader of a dreadful robber gang. How and why he became a monk in the desert at Skete remains a mystery, but he did; though robed in white, he insisted, "God knows I am still black within." So complete was his conversion to Christian nonviolence that he offered no physical resistance when marauding Berbers attacked his monastery, and he was sent to the Green Pastures by their swords in the year 405.

Nerses—November 19

After the death of his wife, Nerses became a priest and eventually, in 363, bishop (*"katholikos"*) of Armenia. He was obliged to deal with a pair of wicked kings: the first he excommunicated for murdering his wife. The successor, Pap, was worse. Nerses accused him of being possessed by demons. His Majesty, protesting his innocence, invited the bishop to dinner—and poisoned him. Nerses was succeeded as bishop by Isaac, his son and fellow Saint.

Nicetas—June 22

PATRON OF ROMANIA

This fourth-century missionary should not be confused with the five other Saints bearing the same name. He was a poet and composer of sacred music, as well as bishop to the Bessi, Goth, and Dacian people of the area now called Romania, and is generally assumed to be the author of the great Latin hymn *"Te Deum."*

Nicholas—December 6

PATRON OF BAKERS, BARREL MAKERS, BOOTBLACKS, BREWERS, BRIDES, CHILDREN, DOCKWORKERS, FISHERMEN, GREECE, MERCHANTS, PAWNBROKERS, PERFUMERS, PRISONERS, RUSSIA, SAILORS, SPINSTERS, AND TRAVELERS

We know him best by his Dutch name, Santa Claus—this Saint so long and universally beloved by Christians of the East and West. He was a bishop of Myra, a city in southwest Turkey, who may (or may not) have attended the Council of Nicaea in 325. If he did, it was after being martyred in the Diocletian persecution in 305—but, then, Nicholas was a Wonder Worker. He was a singularly holy child—on fast days and Fridays, he would refuse his mother's breast. After his wealthy parents died of plague, he set about doing good deeds. Three young women he knew were about to enter lives of prostitution, for their poor father had no money to provide them with dowries. Secretly, by night, Nicholas threw three bags of gold into their window. (The "three balls," representing financial aid in time of need, became the emblem of the pawnbrokers' guild.) In a time of famine, Nicholas provided the poor with miraculous bread—hence his Patronage of bakers. During that same famine, Our Saint (by now a bishop) visited a local butcher, and was served—to his surprise—meat. Suspecting the worst, Nicholas proceeded to his host's cellar, there to find three barrels containing three murdered boys in brine. Rest as-

sured, the bishop lost no time in restoring them to life, and he has been a Patron of children-in-a-pickle ever since. Since his death, he has often appeared to sailors, to guide their storm-tossed vessels, and to those unjustly imprisoned, to effect their release. When the city of Myra, in which he was enshrined, fell to the Muslims, such Italian cities as Venice and Bari contested possession of his holy relics—for they were the objects of pilgrimage, the lucrative tourist industry of the Middle Ages. In 1087, enterprising sailors from Bari outright *stole* the Saint's bones, which to this day rest in the San Nicola basilica there. A sweet-smelling, myrrh-like substance that oozes from the tomb accounts for Nicholas's Patronage of perfumers.

Nicholas of Tolentino—September 10
PATRON OF SICK ANIMALS, MARINERS, HOLY SOULS, BABIES, MOTHERS, AND THE DYING; INVOKED AGAINST FIRE

Nicholas of Tolentino was born to middle-aged parents after they had made a pilgrimage to the shrine of Saint Nicholas of Myra (*whom* SEE). They dedicated their son to him in gratitude. He joined a friary at eighteen, wore an iron girdle, and at prayer saw angels in white robes chanting "To Tolentino, to Tolentino." Nicholas took off for the town that eventually gave him his surname, Tolentino, and stayed for the next thirty years, until his death in 1305. The town was torn apart by the rival Guelph and Ghibelline factions, and Nicholas set about peacemaking, preaching, visiting the sick, and performing miracles (each followed with a modest "Say nothing of this"). His practice of extreme self-deprivation caused him to have hallucinatory visions of fiendish armies—although the Devil actually did come into his room and beat him with the stick that for centuries afterward was on display in his church. When he was ill, the Blessed Virgin, accompanied by Saint Augustine and his mother, Saint Monica (*both of whom* SEE), appeared to him and told him to eat bread dipped in water and he would recover, which he did. Thus began the custom of "Saint Nicholas's Bread"—rolls soaked in water that are eaten by the sick and by women in labor. A year before his death a star preceded him wherever he went; the same star continued to appear on the anniversary of his death. A record 371 witnesses turned up at his canonization trial. Forty years after his death, a German monk seeking relics for his own country broke into Nicholas's tomb and hacked off the Saint's two arms. The monk fled into the night, only to find himself the next morning back at the tomb—running in place and holding the two bloody arms. Since this incident, the two arms are said to bleed whenever any misfortune befalls the church; the most famous seepage occurred from May 29 to September 1, 1699. Although the rest of Nicholas's body had decomposed, the arms remained fresh, residing in the aptly named Chapel of the Holy Arms. Miracles have been attributed to his statues—a plaster image of Nicholas once bowed down, kissed the feet of a crucifix, and stayed there during the entire length of the Apostles' Creed.

Nicholas von Flüe—March 22
PATRON OF SWITZERLAND

A prosperous fifty-year-old farmer with ten children, Nicholas von Flüe quietly up and left one day to live by himself in a mountain hut and pray. Fortunately, he was stricken on the way with a terrible stomachache, as a result of which he had no need of earthly food for the remaining thirty years of his life. Word soon got around the canton that a wise and holy old geezer was holing up on a mountaintop, living on air, and the locals flocked to his hermitage to talk things over with "Bruder Klaus." He was a man of few words, apparently, but you always came back down the mountain feeling better. In 1481, Switzerland was threatened with civil war. Both sides in the conflict were persuaded to seek Our Saint's counsel, and although history does not relate what he told the would-be combatants, they settled things peacefully.

Nino—December 15
PATRONESS OF GEORGIA

The Georgian Orthodox Church is, says the *Encyclopaedia Britannica,* "one of the most ancient Christian communities in the world. The Georgians adopted Christianity through the ministry of a woman, St. Nino, early in the 4th century." Nino was, according to legend, a beautiful and virtuous Greek (or Italian, or Jewish, or French) girl, transported to Georgia as a slave. A child of the household in which she was employed fell sick, and was restored to health through Nino's prayers. Word of this miracle reached the ears of the queen, who sought out and befriended the slave girl. Nino explained to Her Majesty, as best she could, the Holy Faith. Not long after the queen shared this information with the king, he found himself lost in a misty forest. He invoked the name of Nino's God, and the fog miraculously lifted. The king then petitioned the Emperor Constantine that bishops and priests be sent into his realm, and all Georgia was soon converted. The "female Apostle" herself became a hermitess in the fastnesses of the Caspian mountains, where she died. She is entombed in the ancient capital city of Mtskheta, in the cathedral of Sveti-Tskhoveli, the traditional resting place of the kings of Georgia.

Notburga—September 14
PATRONESS OF PEASANTS AND SERVANTS

Her Tyrolean childhood ended when Notburga was placed as a servant in the castle of the nasty count and countess of Rottenburg, who shamelessly used her as a drudge, mocking her for having only one eye. Still, Notburga grew fat, making "a feast of the affronts heaped on her." When the cruel countess discovered Notburga giving food to the poor instead of to the pigs, she fired her, and the Saint went to work for a farmer. Notburga became upset when the farmer wanted her to work Saturday evening—technically the Sabbath—because he feared the weather would change. She threw her sickle in the air, where it hung suspended, looking like the harvest moon, the

sign of good weather to come. Meanwhile, at the Rottenburgs, the mean countess had died, and her ghost haunted the pigsties, terrifying the pigs. An exorcist had to be called in. Since the ghost lamented the sin of giving the food meant for the poor to the pigs, the count hired Notburga back as housekeeper of the castle. She stayed there until her death in *circa* 1313 and enjoyed a splendid funeral—the waters parted when the funeral cortege approached her former residence. Four hundred years after her death, Notburga's body was dug up by local residents who, in a gesture of questionable taste, dressed the skeleton in a red velvet gown with blue bows. They then placed it in a glass case over the altar of a new church in her name.

Notker Balbulus—April 6
PATRON INVOKED AGAINST STAMMERING

Notker Balbulus's name means, literally, "the stutterer," a defect he overcame through his gifts of music and poetry; he became one of the pioneers of the Gregorian chant. He entered the monastery of Saint Gall in Switzerland in 859, and studied music under the Irish monk Moengel (whom he rechristened Mark because the former name sounded uncouth). Notker was loved by his fellow monks, especially his best friends, Tutilo and Radbert. Together these "three inseparables," who shared a love of music and practical jokes, became friends with the Emperor Charles the Fat, a fellow musician, referring to him as "our Charles." Notker composed his hymn *"Sanctii Spiritus Adsit Nobis Gratia"* to the rhythm of a mill wheel, and rushed it to Charles, who sent back his own hymn by the same messenger. Saint Gall surpassed Rome as the preeminent school of chant after Notker developed the "sequence" to the Liturgy of the Mass and added words to some Gregorian antiphons. He is also believed to have created *Gesta Caroli Magni*, a compilation of folk tales and legends of Charlemagne. When Notker composed a hymn to Saint Stephen, he added a self-effacing inscription: "Sick and stammering and full of evil, I, Notker, unworthy, have sung the triumphs of Stephen with my polluted mouth."

Odilia—December 13
PATRONESS OF ALSACE AND OF THE BLIND; INVOKED AGAINST
BLINDNESS

According to her (eighth-century) legend, Odilia was born blind.
Her father, Adalric, an Alsatian nobleman, wished the child to be "exposed"—that is, left to die (a form of population control often practiced by medieval Christians—see *The Kindness of Strangers* by
historian James Boswell). But her mother gave Odilia into the care of
a peasant woman, who in turn assigned her to a convent. At the age
of twelve, when she was baptized, Odilia was miraculously granted
her sight. Word of this wonder—and of the girl's true identity—
reached her brother. He petitioned his father, Adalric, for his sister's
return—and was slain for his trouble. Then Aldaric waxed contrite.
He welcomed Odilia home, fawned over her, even arranged her engagement to a neighboring German knight. Odilia, who had vowed
to remain a virgin, fled the castle. Once more her dreadful parent
made an attempt on her life, but at length sincerely repented, and financed her foundation of two convents. After his death, Odilia's constant prayers allowed him to be released from Purgatory, and father
and daughter are now united in Heaven.

Odo of Cluny—November 18
PATRON OF MUSIC

Odo was born at Tours in the middle of the ninth century. His
family tried to interest the young man in the frivolous life, but hunting and hawking gave him headaches, so he was permitted to enter a
religious order. When the intense youth dreamed of serpents in an
ancient urn, he interpreted it as a sign from God to give up reading
Virgil and the classics. Odo brought this orthodox viewpoint to the
abbey at Cluny, and his brand of strict monasticism became the stan-
dard for over a century. Odo's Cluniac observance, with its emphasis

on poverty, chastity, abstinence—even his ruling that underwear must be washed only on Saturdays—seemed odd at the time, and the Saint met with initial resistance. One monk, defying Odo's rule against meat and holding that chicken and fish were the same thing, choked on a chicken bone and died. Odo could be a bit of a romantic—when the daughter of a nobleman confessed unhappiness at her upcoming marriage, Odo spirited her away to a convent, and then convinced his horrified superiors that the girl, despite reports of her mental instability, actually had a vocation. Sent to Italy to reconcile two kings, Hugh and Alberic (he succeeded by having Alberic marry Hugh's daughter), on his return he stopped in Tours for the feast of Saint Martin (*whom* SEE) and died a few days later. One of his last acts was to compose a hymn in Martin's honor.

Olaf—July 29
PATRON OF NORWAY

After a long career as a pirate—a "Viking"— this early-eleventh-century Norwegian returned to his native land and seized power, both as king and as a ruthless advocate of Christianity. To encourage his subjects to be baptized in the Faith, he would hack off hands, dig out eyes, and plunder and burn farms of reluctant communicants, afterward justifying his actions by saying, "I had God's honor to defend." Olaf married the illegitimate daughter of the king of Sweden, but was ultimately succeeded by his own illegitimate son by a servant girl. By the end of his bloody twenty-five-year reign, he had managed to alienate all his subjects, who joined forces with King Canute II ("the Great") of England and Denmark to defeat Olaf in battle, thus earning the Saint his dubious "martyrdom." Olaf's military victories—described in numerous ballads, some of them 200 stanzas long—were truly impressive. When coming to the aid of England's King Ethelred the Unready, Olaf was responsible for making London Bridge fall down. During his rampages at the Norwegian frontier, he once tried to convert a band of mercenaries by saying, "It's a great pity that such brave slaughtering fellows as you should not believe in Christ." Olaf died in 1030, and was buried in a riverbank near where he fell in battle. A spring with healing properties sprang from his grave.

Olive of Palermo—June 10

In this sunny seaside southern Italian town lived, eleven centuries ago, a beautiful teenage Christian maiden. Saracen pirates swooped down one night and carried her away to Tunis, where she took up residence in a cave overlooking the city. There she was free to live and pray and work miracles—but when she began, by her holy example, to convert Muslims to the True Faith, she was arrested and cruelly tortured. When she emerged unscathed and singing the Lord's praises from a bath of boiling oil, it was ordered that she be stretched on the rack and—basted as she was—set alight. The very torches with which her pagan tormentors attempted this atrocity refused to cooperate, extinguishing themselves. When she was beheaded, a dove (her soul) was seen ascending to Heaven. The great mosque of Tunis is called Jama as-Zituna, that is, "Temple of Olive."

Onuphrius—June 12

PATRON OF WEAVERS

For sixty years Onuphrius's nakedness was covered only by his long hair and beard (and an apron of leaves), which led this fifth-century hermit of the Egyptian desert to be taken, humorously perhaps, by medieval cloth-making guilds as their Patron.

Osana of Mantua—June 20

PATRONESS OF SCHOOLGIRLS

Osana experienced her first religious ecstasy—a vision of Heaven—in 1454, when she was five years old. She longed to know more about the Faith, and asked her earthly father if she might learn to read. Outraged, that conservative Catholic gentleman forcefully explained his views on the rights of women. But Osana *did* manage to become literate—perhaps by eavesdropping on her brothers' lessons, but more likely, in the opinion of her biographer, through private tutorials conducted by the Blesed Virgin. Her favorite texts were the fire-and-brimstone sermons of the heretical reformist-preacher Savonarola. Although throughout her life she wore an (invisible) wedding ring given her by Christ Himself, and suffered (invisible) Stigmata in sympathy with His Passion, Osana seems to have been an amiable enough character, as female Italian Renaissance mystics went.

Osmund—December 4
PATRON INVOKED AGAINST RUPTURE AND PARALYSIS

This scholarly bishop, who completed the building of an early version of Salisbury Cathedral, was a nephew of William the Conqueror. Osmund died in 1099, but, despite innumerable miracles at his tomb and enormous expenditures by generations of British clergy and royalty, was not officially recognized as a Saint until 1457—and was the last Englishman to be canonized for another 500 years.

Oswald of Worcester—February 29

In the 1930s, this Saint's feast was moved to February 28, but for the preceding centuries—since his death in 992—it was celebrated only in leap years. Of Danish descent, Oswald was both a monk and bishop (of York, 972–92), and apparently a man of political savvy as well as personal piety. The vast tracts of land his order was granted by King Edgar served as buffer zones between His (Danish) Majesty's English realm and the rebellious Saxons to the north and the Welsh to the west. Saint Oswald's lasting achievement was the founding of the great Benedictine abbey at Ramsey.

Owen of Rouen—August 24
PATRON OF INNKEEPERS; INVOKED AGAINST DEAFNESS

This seventh-century Saint, known to the French as Ouen or Dado, remains popular among them—in the city of Saint-Malo, an annual fair is held on his feast. It features the eating of periwinkles and blowing of whistles. Owen was a Frankish courtier until his fortieth year, and a great friend of Saint Eloy (*whom* SEE), when he was ordained a priest and made bishop of Rouen. His holy remains may be found either in that city's cathedral or at Canterbury Cathedral in England—miraculous cures of deafness regularly occur at both sites.

Pachomius—May 9

As a military officer serving in Egypt in the third century, Pachomius was impressed by the selfless character of the local Christians. Demobilized, he resolved to become a monk in the Theban desert—but he was hardly a solitary hermit. Employing his managerial skills, he  founded nine vast religious communities—seven for men, two for women—on the banks of the Nile. Under his centralized command, no fewer than 3,000 devout, hardworking souls, among them his own brother and sister, grew or manufactured products for the markets of Alexandria. The rule under which they all lived, now lost to us, was supposedly dictated to Our Saint by an Angel. Pachomius is depicted in sacred art riding across the Nile on the back of a crocodile, allegedly to visit his sister, but this seems unlikely. His vows forbade him to talk to, or look at, any woman.

Palladius—July 7

In the year 430, this Roman deacon was promoted to the rank of bishop and dispatched by Pope Celestine I to preach the Gospel to the natives of Ireland, who were as yet entirely innocent of the True Faith. Palladius landed (from England) in Wicklow, where he built three churches—into which he had no luck whatsoever in attracting the Celts. He left in what appears to be a huff, sailing to Scotland, where he is remembered fondly around Aberdeen. Two years later, Saint Patrick arrived in Ireland, and the rest is (glorious) history.

Pancras—May 12

PATRON OF CHILDREN, OATHS, AND TREATIES

In the year 309, this fourteen-year-old Syrian orphan was martyred for the Faith in Rome, on the site of the church that now bears his name. Saint Gregory of Tours wrote that oaths taken and treaties signed in that holy place were considered especially binding. The first church founded in England (by Saint Augustine of Canterbury, *whom* SEE) was dedicated to him, as was a church in London where the St. Pancras railroad terminal now stands.

Pantaleon—July 27
PATRON OF DOCTORS AND OF VENICE;
INVOKED AGAINST CONSUMPTION

Although he was raised a Christian, Pantaleon lapsed into apostasy when he became personal physician to Emperor Galerius. When he recovered his Faith, he took to treating poor patients for free, and soon was brutally executed. Because the war cry of Venice was *"Piante Lione!"* ("Plant the lion!"), Pantaleon became the Patron Saint of that city. Its citizens were then known as "pantalons" and the distinctive trousers they wore were called "pantaloons." Thus from the name of a third-century Saint, we derive our English words "pants" and "panties."

Pascal Babylon—May 17
PATRON OF SHEPHERDS

Pascal Babylon was a professional shepherd, living near Aragon in the 1540s. Not a very good one, however—while he prayed, his wandering flock wreaked havoc in the surrounding vineyards. Somewhat reluctantly, the Franciscans allowed the semiliterate Pascal to join their order as a laybrother, but were soon impressed by his prolonged trances of devotion before the Blessed Sacrament.

Patrick—March 17
PATRON OF IRELAND AND NIGERIA; INVOKED AGAINST SNAKES

Patrick wasn't Irish; he was Welsh-Italian. His name wasn't Patrick, it was Succat. He wasn't the first Christian missionary sent to Ireland—that was Saint Palladius (*whom* SEE). And there were never any snakes in the country to begin with. But aside from that, everything you know about Patrick is true. He was declared by the Sacred Congregation of Rites to be the Patron of Nigeria in April 1961.

Paul—June 29

PATRON OF GREECE, MALTA, ROPE MAKERS, TENTMAKERS, AND
UPHOLSTERERS

According to two recently published books, Paul was (1) a self-castrated homosexual, and (2) an anti-Zionist agent of Roman imperialism. He makes his first appearance halfway through the New Testament—and takes over. Courtesy of his fourteen Epistles, we hear more from Paul—verbatim—than we did from Jesus—verbatim—in all the Gospels. He was a convert and, like many converts, "more Catholic than the pope." In Paul's case, the pope was Saint Peter, with whom he frequently disagreed. Paul was God's own CEO, a motivator, an organizer, a hands-on manager, a tireless leader-by-example, a Take-Charge Guy with his eye on the Big Picture. He bought into a tiny Hebrew cult, and personally transformed it into a Multi-National, the biggest and richest in the world. To begin with, he was a Greek-Jewish tentmaker named Saul, violently opposed to the Christian heresy until a vision knocked him, quite literally, off his high horse. His story is told in the Acts of the Apostles: how he traveled continuously, preaching, writing, debating, founding churches, reforming churches, surviving shipwrecks, snakebite, arrests, jailbreaks, hostile and/or adoring mobs. The last we hear of Paul in the official Bible, he is awaiting trial in a Roman prison in A.D. 62. The apocryphal Acts of Paul and Thecla then takes up the tale. The Saint pled his own case, and was acquitted. He proceeded, accompanied by a virgin-convert named Thecla, to Spain. Returning to Ephesus, he was rearrested and thrown to wild beasts in the arena, where he was protected by a lion he had previously baptized. Returning to Rome, he was sentenced to death on the same day as Saint Peter by the dreadful Emperor Nero himself. Peter was crucified upside down, but Paul was beheaded with a sword—a right he claimed as a Roman citizen. Where the Saint's head bounced three times, three fountains, the *Tre Fontane,* sprang up. Although his words have been cited through the centuries by extremists of every Christian and anti-Christian persuasion, Paul appears to have been, theologically, a radical moderate.

Paula—January 26
PATRONESS OF WIDOWS

This aristocratic fourth-century Roman matron (descended from both the Scipios and the Graccis) suffered, in her thirty-second year, the sudden deaths of her husband and eldest daughter, and experienced what today might be called a nervous breakdown. The great Saint Jerome (*whom* SEE) came to her rescue. He persuaded the distraught and wealthy widow, along with her youngest daughter, to accompany him to the Holy Land, give him all her money, and see to his daily needs, such as food and laundry, which he himself was far too spiritual to be bothered with. Jerome was, at the time, laboring on his life's work—translating the New Testament from Greek into Latin—the famous Vulgate. Since he, personally, knew not a word of Greek, and Paula was fluent in that language, there has been some speculation that she may have been of some small assistance to him in that heroic undertaking.

Paul the Hermit—January 15
PATRON OF WEAVERS

In the middle of the second century, young Paul was a man about Thebes; his brother-in-law, covetous for an inheritance, threatened to expose him as a Christian. Paul fled to the wilderness, where he took up residence in a cave convenient to a spring and a palm tree, and stayed there for ninety years. His diet of figs was supplemented by half a loaf of bread a day, delivered by a raven. In the middle of the third century, Saint Anthony the Great (*whom* SEE) was led by a friendly centaur to Paul's cave—as we know on the unimpeachable authority of the great Saint Jerome (*whom* SEE) himself. In honor of the occassion, the raven brought an *entire* loaf for the hermits to share. Paul informed Anthony that he was about to die, and wished to be buried in a cloak that had been given to him—Anthony—back in Thebes, by Saint Athanasius. Much impressed by Paul's miraculous knowledge about the cloak, the younger hermit hastened off to fetch it, but upon upon his return found the Ancient Saint quite dead. A pair of passing lions were kind enough to help Anthony dig a grave.

Pelagia—October 8
PATRONESS OF ACTRESSES

This Pelagia was, in fact, a performer—a glamorous singer-dancer-stripper in decadent old Antioch. Her stage name was Pearl. Bishop Nonnus of Edessa chanced (we know not how) to catch her act, and in a sermon the next day proclaimed, "This girl is a lesson to us bishops! She takes more trouble over her beauty and her dancing than we do about our souls and flocks." Pelagia chanced (again, we know not how) to hear this sermon. She confessed her sins to the bishop, was baptized by him, gave him all her money, and departed for Jerusalem. There, in male-hermit drag, she lived until death as "Pelagius, the beardless monk." This story we have on the authority of Saint John Chrysostom (*whom* SEE), who also tells of *another* Saint Pelagia of Antioch, an equally attractive but chaster young woman who threw herself off a roof to avoid the loss of her virtue. A *third* Saint Pelagia was a Christian maiden of Tarsus who spurned the emperor's son, inspiring him to suicide. The emperor had no luck with her either, and ordered her roasted to death in a brazen bull.

Pelayo—June 26

When the savage Moors occupying Córdoba, Spain, in 922 captured the aged bishop of Asturius and held him for ransom, the local Christians offered them the ten-year-old boy Pelayo as an exchange hostage, just until they could raise the money. The Moors agreed, and for three years the lad languished in prison, until he caught the eye of the emir Abdul Rahman. Offered his freedom in exchange for an act of apostasy (and who knows what other sins), Pelayo refused. He was hung by his wrists and disemboweled, thus adding a soul to Heaven's population and not a penny to the coffers of the perfidious Moors.

Peregrine Laziosi—May 1
PATRON INVOKED AGAINST CANCER

Throughout the medieval period in Italy two factions, the (papal) Guelphs and the (imperial) Ghibellines, struggled for political power.

(The poet Dante, himself a Guelph, consigned a majority of Ghibellines to Hell.) Peregrine was a rowdy young Ghibelline activist in the year 1280, when a papal legate, Philip Benizi, came to town, and Our Saint availed himself of the opportunity to punch Philip in the nose. He was then miraculously converted to the Guelph position and, on the advice of a statue of the Madonna, moved to Siena to join the Servite Order. As a sign of his repentance, Peregrine resolved never again to sit down—which penance became more difficult when he developed, after thirty years, a repulsive and malodorous cancer of the foot. However, the night before the offensive extremity was to be amputated, Christ Himself climbed down from a crucifix on the wall and effected a complete cure.

Peter—June 29
PATRON OF BOATWRIGHTS, CLOCKMAKERS, FISHERMEN, AND NET MAKERS; INVOKED AGAINST FEVER, FOOT TROUBLE, AND WOLVES

Because he is invariably pictured holding keys, Saint Peter is imagined in jokes and folklore to be the gatekeeper of Heaven, in a position to grant or deny entry to the souls of the recently departed. By virtue of those "keys to the kingdom" metaphorically bestowed upon him by Our Lord, Roman Catholics believe him to have been the first pope. In the New Testament, Peter is—except for Christ—the most frequently and fully described character. We learn all about his moods, faults, and virtues, as well as about his deeds. His faith allowed him to walk on water, but his doubt caused him to sink. He bravely drew his sword to defend the Master in the Garden; soon after, he denied Him thrice before cockcrow. (Upon his cheeks, some say, were grooves worn by his tears of guilt.) His name was Simon bar Jonah, but jesting Jesus called him Kephas, which in Latin is "Petrus," or, as we would say, "Rocky." He was the brother of Saint Andrew (*whom* SEE), a married fisherman, when called by Jesus to follow Him. After Pentecost he was the acknowleged leader of the disciples, traveling (in the company of his wife and their daughter Saint Petronilla [*whom* SEE]) first to Antioch and thence to Rome, where the Chair he sat in and the Chains he wore in prison are now venerated on their very own feast days—January 18 and August 1, respectively. It was in Rome that he was martyred, A.D. 64, crucified—at his own request—upside down, near the site of the gargantuan basilica that bears his name. According to his apocryphal *Acts,* he had fled Rome to escape the odious Emperor Nero's persecution of the Christians, but encountered Christ Himself on the road. Our Lord was returning to die again, He replied in answer to Peter's *"Quo vadis?"* And the rest is movie history.

Peter Baptist—February 6
PATRON OF JAPAN

The Japan first discovered in 1548 by Europeans—Portuguese traders and missionary priests—was a divided country, ruled by the lords of many feuding domains. Several of these soon saw fit to take advantage of the political-economic benefits of conversion to Christianity; and the first Jesuit missionaries, following the example of the pioneer Saint Francis Xavier (*whom* SEE), respected local folkways and religious traditions. But traders and Franciscans from Spain, as well as Calvinist merchants and missionaries from Holland, quickly established rival appeals to the self-interest and souls of the leaders and peasants. In 1585 the shogun Hideyosi assumed absolute power and set about unifying his country. All Europeans but Dutch traders were banished, and the corrupting practice of Christianity was outlawed. On this day in 1597, in the port city of Nagasaki, twenty-six Believers, including the Franciscan Spaniard Peter Baptist, the Japanese Jesuit Paul Miki, and Leo Karasuma, a Korean layman, were methodically tortured (their ears were cut off, among other parts) and crucified.

Peter Claver—September 9
PATRON OF AFRICAN AMERICANS, COLOMBIA, RACE RELATIONS, AND SLAVES

Born into Spanish nobility in 1580, Peter fell under the influence of one Alphonsus, the porter at his Jesuit seminary. The porter persuaded him to go to the Americas to succor the slaves in the burgeoning New World slave trade. Peter set out to Cartagena, Colombia, the clearinghouse of the slave industry, where 10,000 Africans, mainly from Angola and the Congo, arrived every year. (A third of them died on the way over.) Working with the holy Father Alonso de Sandoval (whose writings on the evils of the slave trade were the first systematic attack on the system), Peter daily visited the slaves, bringing food and clothing to the disease-infested holds of ships. He learned their dialects and, using pictures, taught them Christianity. He called himself "the slave of the slaves forever." For forty years,

Peter tended to slaves in mines, plantations, holding pens, and hospitals, frequently angering the Christian authorities and clergy. He is credited with baptizing 300,000 slaves and some Protestant dignitaries as well. He was unjustly accused of baptizing some souls twice, and his right to baptize was taken away. But his influence remained so widespread that, once, an African, trying to rebuff a prostitute, cried out, "Look! Here comes Father Claver!" When an arrogant nobleman knocked down a slave and her basket of eggs, Claver touched the broken eggs with his staff and made them whole again. On a mission into the jungle, he contracted the plague, but strapped to his horse, he continued ministering to lepers and slaves. In the final years of Claver's illness, everyone forgot about him, and he was even neglected by his nurse, Manuel, who ate most of his food and would throw the remainder into the Saint's mouth. When he died, he had two funerals: one held by the white hierarchy and the other by slaves and Indians.

Peter Damian—February 21
PATRON INVOKED AGAINST HEADACHES

Peter, who was born to wealthy parents in Ravenna in 1007, was orphaned at a tender age and went to live with his cruel older brother, who made him a swineherd. He was adopted by monks and became deeply religious, wearing a hair shirt, fasting, and praying for long periods of time with his arms outstretched. He would throw himself into a thorn bush at the onset of an impure thought. He eventually became a hermit and founded five other hermitages; he was the first to warn Pope Leo IX about the evils of marriage among the clergy, the "unnatural vice." Peter reasoned that since Christ was a virgin it was only right and proper that He be served by similar virginal souls at the offering of the Mass. When it was pointed out to him that Peter the Apostle was married, he replied quoting Jerome (*whom* SEE) that Peter's martyrdom "washed away the dirt of his marriage." When two popes were elected in 1061, Alexander II and Honorius II, Peter aligned himself with Alexander, attacking Honorius and prophesying his downfall within a year. Pope Alexander sent Our Saint to inform Henry IV of Germany that, despite all that monarch's pleas and

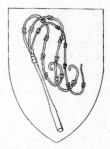

threats, it was not possible for him to obtain a divorce. Peter's austere and rigid behavior continued throughout his life. He once rebuked the bishop of Florence for playing a game of chess—just one—and forbade monks to sit down while chanting. He ate only coarse bread, bran, and stale water, wore an iron girdle, and made wooden spoons for a hobby.

Peter's emblem is a "discipline"—a scourge—which he shares with other self-flagellation enthusiasts such as Aloysius Gonzaga, Ambrose, Boniface, and Dominic (*all of whom* SEE).

Peter Gonzalez—April 14

PATRON OF SAILORS

When he first entered the clergy, Peter's powerful uncle prematurely raised him to the exalted—and simultaneous—titles of canon and deacon. However, when Peter arrived in full regalia at his investiture ceremony, his horse threw him into a dunghill, thereby setting him on a lifetime course of poverty and humility. His zeal as a reformer brought him to King Ferdinand III's court, where the debauched nobles tried to corrupt him by sending a courtesan into his confessional. Not fooled, Peter wrapped his cloak around his body, threw himself into a fire, and asked the woman to join him. Until his death in 1246, he loved sailors and waited at ports for their return, often boarding the ships. The light that appears around masts in storms, often called Saint Elmo's fire, is believed by Portuguese sailors to be sent to them by Peter Gonzalez.

Peter Martyr—April 20

Despite the fact that his parents and uncles subscribed to the Manichaean heresy, Peter entered the Dominicans at fifteen. He soon rose to prominence as a preacher, miracle worker, and "Prince of the Inquisition"; not suprisingly, he specialized in heresies. He was unjustly accused of entertaining women in his cell when the Saints Catherine, Cecilia, and Agnes (*all of whom* SEE) came from Heaven to visit him and their voices were overheard. Ejected from his monastery, he complained bitterly to a crucifix, and the figure of Jesus chastised him, saying, "What have I done to be . . . saturated with opprobrium?" Peter was later vindicated and began preaching in earnest, cutting a very dramatic figure. He traveled on a float decorated with religious paintings, and he dressed in a white tunic with a red cross on the breast and a star in the upper corner. Great things happened when he made the Sign of the Cross: he was able to produce a cloud, make a black charger (actually the Devil) vanish, cure a scorpion bite, and defeat the Cathars in battle. He could be suprisingly mean-tempered, however, and once when some youths were throwing stones from a building, he cursed them, causing the building to collapse and kill them instantly. When a young man confessed to him that he had kicked his mother, Peter told him to cut off his own foot, which he promptly did. (Peter subsequently restored it.) He was assassinated by Cathars on the way to Milan, and in a final dramatic gesture wrote *"Credo Deum"* in his own blood.

Peter Mary Chanel—April 28

PATRON OF OCEANIA

Under the patronage of his parish priest, Peter, a poor French shepherd boy, received a classical education before joining the missionary Priests of the Society of Mary, the Marists. In 1836, Pope Gregory XVI sent him as the True Faith's first ambassador to the South Pacific. Peter landed on the tiny island of Futuna in the New Hebrides, where for three years he made little headway among the local cannibals, until he managed to convert and baptize the son of the chief. That tattooed pagan dignitary lost no time in sending a band of warriors armed with clubs and spears to take care of Father Chanel. Our Saint's dying words to them, which he spoke in the local lingo, were "It is well for me that you do this thing." Suitably impressed, his killers—and indeed the entire population of the island—immediately became devout Roman Catholics.

Peter of Alcántara—October 19

PATRON OF BRAZIL AND NIGHT WATCHMEN

We know on the authority of his friend Saint Teresa of Ávila (*whom* SEE) that this sixteenth-century Franciscan reformer, a genius in the art of self-denial, slept no longer than an hour and a half every night for forty years. His cell was too small to lie down in, so he snoozed in a crouch, with the back of his head pressed against a spike. What's more, the nocturnal spiritual ecstasies he often experienced caused him to howl long and loud, which prevented his fellow monks from sleeping, as well; hence his Patronage of watchmen. While saying Mass, Our Saint was often observed to rise into the air, curl up in a ball, and fly around the church.

Petronilla—May 31
PATRONESS OF FRANCE; INVOKED AGAINST AGUE

She was, says the Roman Martyrology, "the virgin daughter of the Apostle Peter, who refused to wed Flaccus, a nobleman, and asking three days for deliberation, spent them in fasting and prayer and on the third day gave up the ghost." The Carolingian kings of France, who considered themselves the "sons of Saint Peter," took their "sister" Pertronilla as their nation's Patroness. A Mass is offered for France on Petronilla's feast day in her chapel in St. Peter's Basilica. A pious legend relates that Petronilla was a cripple, and that a group of disciples dining at Peter's home once chided him for his inability to cure her. Indignantly, the Prince of Apostles made the Sign of the Cross over his child, so that she rose up hale and hearty and served them all their meal. After which, at another gesture from her father, she collapsed.

Pharaildis—January 4
PATRONESS INVOKED AGAINST CHILDHOOD ILLNESS

This Flemish maiden (who is also the Patroness of the city of Ghent) was the niece of Saint Gertrude of Nivelles (*whom* SEE). Famously compassionate, she caused a miraculous fountain to spring from the earth at Braug (it is there to this day), the waters of which are wondrously effective against a host of childhood diseases. In art, Our Saint is pictured holding a goose, in honor of the famous occasion when she—for reasons unknown—restored a roasted fowl not only to life, but with its original plumage.

Philip—May 3
PATRON OF LUXEMBOURG AND URUGUAY

A Galilean fisherman, married and the father of three, Philip gave up everything to follow Christ. He became the third Apostle. He helped serve the miraculously multiplied loaves and fishes to the multitudes, for which reason a basket of bread is among his emblems. After Pentecost, he traveled to Phrygia, where the Devil, in the form of a hideous dragon, guarded a statue of Mars. Philip performed a public exorcism, in the course of which the fiery breath of the loathsome beast slew several spectators, among them the son of the local pagan priest, who forthwith ordered Our Saint stoned and crucified upside down.

Philip Neri—May 26
PATRON OF ROME

One of the rare Saints (like Francis of Assisi or Thomas More) who seems to have *enjoyed* his Faith, Philip Neri was known in his lifetime as "the Apostle of Rome." He was born in Florence, a notary's son—"Pippo Buono," they called him, "good little Phil." In 1533, at the age of eighteen, penniless, he arrived in Rome. Five years earlier, the Renaissance had ended with a bang—the city had been sacked by imperial troops, thousands of its citizens slain, its art treasures looted. The Vatican, a cesspool of vice and avarice, had begun responding to the Reformation by banning books and burning reformers. Pippo lived in a garret, and to pay his rent, he tutored his landlord's sons. A near-recluse, he wrote poetry and studied philosophy; then one day he took to the streets. He would hail passersby, "Well, my brothers, when shall we begin to do good?" Philip was an eccentric, but a charming one. Young men stopped to talk and listen. And together with him, they began to do actual *good*. They founded, built, and staffed the Santa Trinita dei Pellegrini hospital. The large room where his growing crowd of disciples gathered at night to talk and to pray and to listen to concerts was called their "oratory"; hence they were dubbed "Oratorians," and the type of music they preferred we call, to this day, "oratorios." Philip was determined to remain, with his fellow Oratorians, a layman. But in 1554, while meditating in the catacomb of Saint Sebastian, he underwent a mystical experience. A globe of fire seemed to enter his mouth and dilate his heart. He resolved to become a missionary priest—and Rome would be "his Indies." The sort of sanctity he preached and practiced was not austerity, but affirmation; not hatred of the world, but love of God and man. He was fond of laughter and jokes, even slapstick ones—for instance, he would sometimes appear, deadpan, in public, wearing his clothes inside out, or bearing and sniffing with obvious pleasure a bouquet of whisk brooms. Nuts or not, Philip Neri encouraged and inspired such heroes of the Catholic Counter-Reformation as Ignatius

Loyola, Francis Xavier, and Charles Borromeo (*all of whom* SEE). At age eighty, on the night of May 26, 1595, he observed cheefully, "Last of all, we must die." And he did. The autopsy revealed an extraordinarily large heart.

Philip of Zell—May 3
PATRON OF BABIES AND CHILDREN

We know, on the authority of *Butler's Lives of the Patron Saints,* that this eighth-century hermit "soon after his death . . . came to be regarded as the protector of small children," but we don't know why. Philip, who lived in the woods near the city of Worms, was a friend and spiritual advisor to Pepin, the king of the Franks, as well as to the birds and rabbits of the neighborhood. The place where he and a priest with the unusual name of Horskolf founded a monastery is called "Zell" in honor of their "cells."

Philip the Deacon—June 6
PATRON OF DEACONS

Do not confuse this Philip with the Apostle of the same name. *This* one was a "disciple." When assignments were handed out after the Pentecost, Philip the Deacon was given charge of the spiritual well-being of Jerusalem's Greek-speaking widows, hardly a cabinet-level posting. But he is remembered for having encountered, by chance, the chief eunuch in the service of the visiting queen of Ethiopia, converting him to Christianity—and then performing the first recorded baptism of a Black African.

Phocas—September 22
PATRON OF GARDENERS AND SAILORS

Phocas was a Christian, a gardener by profession, who provided a hospice for travelers on the Black Sea. Soldiers, seeking to execute him during a Christian persecution, unwittingly arrived at his house and were welcomed with his famous hospitality. When the soldiers announced whom they were looking for, the Saint promised to show them Phocas the following morning. That night, he busied himself digging his grave in the garden, and the following morning he told the soldiers: "I myself am the man." The soldiers overcame a momentary attack of scruples, cut off his head, and buried him in the grave he had prepared. He became the Patron of sailors primarily because his name resembles the Breton word for seal, *"phoc."*

Phocas of Antioch—March 5
PATRON INVOKED AGAINST SNAKEBITE

It is flatly asserted in the Roman Martyrology that anyone bitten by a deadly serpent need only touch the doors of a Roman basilica dedicated to *this* Phocas to be immediately cured.

Piran—March 5
PATRON OF MINERS

The tin miners of both Brittany and Cornwall have, since the sixth century, invoked the aid of this holy hermit, who is also called Perran and Pyran. Nothing is known of his life, but experts now believe he probably was *not* the same person as Saint Ciaran, or Kieran, a holy hermit with whom he shares his feast day.

Pirminus—November 3
PATRON INVOKED AGAINST SNAKEBITE AND POISONING

A Spanish bishop, Pirminus escaped the Moorish persecution in Alsace, and in 711 (according to his biographer, Herman the Cripple) was sent to the island of Reichenau by Charles Martel. There Pirminus expelled all the serpents and established the first monastery on German soil. A revisionist theory about his origin suggests that this "shadowy and ubiquitous missionary Saint" may actually have been Irish, and his story about the serpents an echo of Saint Patrick. On a pilgrimage to Rome, after being snubbed by the pope, Pirminus visited the tombs of the Apostles and demonstrated his ability to stand his staff on end, which caused the pope to regret his officious behavior. Pirminus's book *Dicta Pirmini* was a popular study of theology in which he attacked superstition.

Placid—October 5
PATRON INVOKED AGAINST CHILLS AND DROWNING

A young sixth-century monk beloved of Saint Benedict (*whom* SEE), Placid was once saved from drowning by Saint Maurus (*whom* SEE), when, on Benedict's instructions, Maurus dashed across the surface of the lake to rescue Our drowning Saint. Placid's grateful father made a land grant to the Benedictine Order—and there the great abbey of Monte Cassino was erected in A.D. 529. According to a bogus legend, Placid later founded a monastery in Sicily, where he, with his brothers and a sister, was massacred by African pirates.

Porcarius—August 12

On an island off the French Riviera was once a community of more than 500 monks and novices. It was known as Lérins, and its abbot was Porcarius. One night in the year 732, an Angel appeared to that holy man and warned him that pirates, fierce Saracen marauders out of Africa, were approaching. The abbot sent away to safety the students and youngest monks on the only available ship, and then exhorted the remainder to gather around him and with him bravely suffer martyrdom, which, upon the arrival of the pirates, they did.

Porphyry—February 26

Born of noble Macedonian parents in the middle of the fourth century, Porphyry became a monk and traveled to Jerusalem, where he made daily visits to the holy places despite a crippling illness. He sent Mark (his biographer) back to Macedonia to retrieve his (Porphyry's) fortune so he could distribute it to the poor. When Mark returned, he found his friend completely cured. Our Saint explained that on a trip to Calvary he had fainted, and that the Good Thief (Dismas, *whom* SEE) came down from his cross, cured him, and entrusted him with the care of Christ's Holy Cross. Soon after this, Porphyry was made bishop—against his will: he cried bitterly throughout the ceremony. Porphyry befriended the empress of Constantinople, and at his request she ordered the destruction of eight pagan temples. A statue of Venus (prayed to by young girls in their search for husbands) destroyed *itself* when Porphyry walked past it.

Priscilla—January 16
PATRONESS OF WIDOWS

The usefulness of wealthy widows to clergymen—especially in a sect's early stages—can scarcely be exaggerated. After the death of her husband, Mancius Glabrio, this noble matron allowed Saint Peter to use her home on the Via Salaria as his Roman headquarters—the first Vatican, if you will. Beneath its site is a catacomb, named in her honor, in which she is buried.

Prix—February 24

Two totally different stories exist about the political events leading up to Prix's martyrdom. The first maintains that Prix, who was bishop of Clermond *circa* 676, complained to King Chilperic about a certain Hector, who had illegally seized a young woman's estate, which resulted in the king's ordering Hector's execution. Soon afterward, Hector's henchmen split the bishop's head in two. A more convoluted version proposes that because Prix married Merovaeus, the son of King Chilperic, to his aunt, Brunhilde (sister of Chilperic's poisoned first wife), he incurred the wrath of Fredegund, Chilperic's second wife. Fredegund tried to send him into exile, failed, then hired an assassin, who fatally stabbed Our Saint in the armpit.

Processus and **Martinian**—July 2

PATRONS OF PRISON GUARDS; INVOKED AGAINST INFIRMITY, DEMONIC POSSESSION, AND PERJURY

When Nero cast Saints Paul and Peter into prison, Processus and Martinian were their jailers. They soon asked Peter to baptize them. He struck a rock, and a fountain gushed forth, creating an instant baptismal font. Later, when they were escorting a limping Peter from his cell, they beheld a foot bandage descend from Heaven. Thus inspired, they affirmed their Faith by spitting publicly on a statue of Jupiter, and were promptly flogged and decapitated. A pious woman buried the martyrs in a catacomb by the Via Aurelia, over which a church was built in their honor, but in the ninth century their relics were translated to the south altar of St. Peter's Basilica. A fountain still flows in the Mamertine Prison on the site of their baptism.

Procopius—July 14

PATRON OF CZECHOSLOVAKIA

Procopius retreated to a cave near Prague to pursue the life of a hermit, first clearing out the thousand devils who were staying there. He lived undisturbed except for fawns and owls, until the duke of Bohemia came thither a-hunting. As Procopius relates in his autobiography, a stag sought his cave for sanctuary, and the duke, humbled by the hermit, gave him a grant of land. Procopius soon attracted a following and in his later years entered a monastery. He died in the odor of sanctity *circa* 303.

Protus and Hyacinth—September 11

Protus and Hyacinth were two eunuchs who secretly converted to Christianity along with their mistress, Eugenia, the daughter of the Roman consul. The trio, with Eugenia disguised as a boy, escaped to a monastery in the desert. After three years, Eugenia was made abbot, but soon became an object of lust for a local woman, whom she rebuffed. The scorned woman alleged that the abbot had made an attack on her honor. When the abbot/Eugenia appeared at court before her father, her mother instantly recognized her. The parents were reconciled with their child and became instant converts. Protus and Hyacinth got busy baptizing the rest of the nobility, including the famous Basilissa (*whom* SEE), which caused a great commotion in Rome. In the end, all suffered martyrdom except for Eugenia's mother, who flew to Heaven. The *Oxford Dictionary of Saints* gives a less colorful rendition of the lives of these eunuchs, simply maintaining that they were brother martyrs and "teachers of Christian Law."

Pudentiana—May 19
PATRONESS OF THE PHILIPPINES

Saint Pudens was a Roman senator, a contemporary and friend of Saint Peter himself. His daughter Pudentiana is supposed to have died for the Faith in the year 160, at the age of sixteen. The mathematical and/or biological unlikeliness of this caused Pudentiana to be demoted in the Calendar of Saints in 1750, and eliminated from it altogether in 1969. She is venerated now only in the magnificent basilica named for her in Rome, and in the Philippines, of which nation she is Patroness. Her Latin name means "she who ought to be ashamed of herself."

Quentin—October 31

PATRON OF BOMBARDIERS, CHAPLAINS, LOCKSMITHS, TAILORS, AND
PORTERS; INVOKED AGAINST COUGHING AND SNEEZING

An army officer and the son of a
Roman senator, Quentin became a
Christian, and journeyed as a missionary to western Gaul—now Picardy,
France. Sometime after the year 300, he
was martyred with unusual cruelty.
Among other tortures, hot nails were

driven into his head, he was stretched on an elaborate machine of
pulleys and weights, and his mouth was filled with a mixture of
quicklime, vinegar, and mustard. His beheaded body, cast into a
river, surfaced half a century later and cured a blind woman who
stumbled over it. Gratefully, she founded a church dedicated to the
Saint on the site where the city of Saint-Quentin yet stands. It is
slightly ironic that a famous American penitentiary is named for this
Saint; an Angel once descended to the dungeon where he was bound
and released him. One of his first posthumous miracles was to sever
the rope by which a penitent horse thief was being hanged.

Quirinus—June 4

PATRON INVOKED AGAINST HEMORRHOIDS, EARACHE, AND GOUT

A Croatian bishop, Quirinus was arrested in 308, during the Diocletian persecutions. After engaging in some edifying debates on the
subject of religious freedom, first with the local magistrate and then
with the governor of Hungary, he was cast (with the customary stone
around his neck) into the river Raab. His remains were fished out and
sent to be enshrined in Rome, where they continue to work miraculous cures for various unpleasant complaints.

Raphael—October 24

PATRON OF DRUGGISTS, HAPPY MEETINGS, HEALTH INSPECTORS,
LOVERS, TRAVELERS, AND YOUNG PEOPLE LEAVING HOME; INVOKED
AGAINST BLINDNESS

In Hebrew, the name of this Archangel (once described by the poet Milton as "affable") means "the Shining One Who Heals." According to the Old Testament Book of Tobit (which is considered noncanonical, or "apocryphal," by Protestants, who like to take the fun out of everything), Raphael, calling himself Azarias, is of great assistance to the hero Tobias. Together they catch the magic fish that cures the blindness of Tobias's old father, Tobit, and drive out the evil spirit from the beautiful but five-times-widowed Sara. Raphael is also believed to be the Angel who "troubles the waters" of the curative pool Bethesda in Jerusalem.

Raymond Nonnatus—August 31

PATRON OF CATALONIA, CHILDBIRTH, CHILDREN, MIDWIVES,
OBSTETRICIANS, AND PREGNANT WOMEN; INVOKED AGAINST FALSE
ACCUSATIONS

Raymond's surname means "not born," for he was delivered by surgeons after his mother's death in labor—thus his eternal compassion for the pregnant. He became a monk in Barcelona, and succeeded Saint Peter Nolasco as a ransomer of Christian hostages from their Muslim captors. He proceeded to Algeria with a great deal of money for the purpose, and, when it was spent, offered himself as a prisoner in exchange for the freedom of another. The wily pagan authorities, assuming they could demand a high price for the return of this man of God, agreed. Although it was against Islamic law, Raymond persisted in preaching to and even converting the Muslim infidels of Tunis. The penalty for this crime—to which he was duly sentenced—was death by impalement, but Raymond was

granted a reduced sentence. After he "ran the gauntlet," his lips were pierced with a red-hot iron, and a padlock was installed on his mouth. For eight months he languished in a Tunisian dungeon, fed by a jailer who held the key to his lip-lock. Finally, his costly ransom was raised by Saint Peter Nolasco himself, and Raymond, who had been looking forward to martyrdom, was obliged to return home, where he was promoted to cardinal just before his death in 1240.

Raymond of Peñafort—January 7
PATRON OF LAWYERS AND LAW SCHOOLS

This nobleman of Catalonia was already a celebrated lawyer and professor of law when, in 1222 (when he was forty-seven years of age), he joined the Dominican Order in Barcelona. In 1230, Raymond was summoned to Rome, where Pope Gregory IX was in the planning stage of the Inquisition, but needed help researching and gathering ten centuries' accumulation of obscure and contradictory papal decrees—the Immutable Laws of God which the Inquisitors were about to enforce. These "Decretals," as assembled and published by Raymond, formed the basis of Catholic Canon Law until this century. The Saint was made an archbishop for his troubles, and returned to his homeland, where he spent the rest of his life (he lived to be 100) making things plenty hot for heretics, Moors, and Jews. Once he was invited by the king to join him on the island of Majorca, off the Catalan coast. Upon Raymond's arrival, the Saint was shocked to discover that His Majesty was keeping company with a woman not his wife. The outraged Man of God insisted on returning to the mainland, but the Sinful Monarch naughtily denied him the use of a ship—whereupon Raymond laid his cloak upon the surface of the Mediterranean, tied a corner of it to his bishop's staff (for use as a sail), stepped aboard, and wind-surfed home. A church in Barcelona harbor, named in his honor, marks the place where he came ashore.

Reinhold—January 7
PATRON OF STONEMASONS

In 960, Reinhold, a young monk of Cologne, supervised a building project with such zeal that the stonemasons in his charge murdered him.

Remi—October 1
PATRON OF FRANCE

Remi (Latin: Remigius, English: Remy) is known as "the Apostle of the Franks." He was appointed the first bishop of Rheims in 459, when he was only twenty-two, and ministered to the pagan Franks for seventy years. Our Saint had demonstrated his exceptional holiness at an early age, when, as a nursing babe, he cured a passing blind man by anointing him with a squirt of his mother's milk. Clotilda, queen of the Franks, was a devout Christian; however her husband, King Clovis, was anything but. At her urging, the barbaric monarch invoked Christ's aid at a critical juncture in his war against the (dreadful, Germanic) Alemanni tribe, and he won a famous victory. Forthwith, Clovis and 3,000 of his followers were baptized by Bishop Remi on Christmas Day, 496. At that memorable ceremony, Angels descended and replaced the traditional toads (or "frogs") on the Frankish flag with the fleurs-de-lis of France.

René Goupil—October 19
PATRON OF ANESTHETISTS

Born in France in 1606, René was judged too sickly to join the notoriously robust Jesuit Order. Instead, he became a surgeon, and as such voluntarily joined the Jesuit mission to the colony of New France. In the summer of 1642 he accompanied Father Isaac Jogues (SEE Jesuit Martyrs) on a trip through Mohawk country (near what is now Albany, New York). Both priest and doctor were captured and brutally tortured: their hair, beards, and fingernails were torn out, their fingers hacked off with clamshells. On September 29, Goupil was tomahawked for making the Sign of the Cross on the head of a child—thereby becoming the first Christian to die for his Faith in the New World. Jogues escaped with the help of the Dutch; back in France he related the tale of Goupil's heroism. Having received special permission to say Mass with his mutilated hands, he returned to America, and soon succeeded in winning a martyr's crown of his own.

Richard of Chichester—April 3
PATRON OF COACHMEN

Richard de Wyse, who showed early promise as a farmer, chose instead to become a scholar, first at Oxford, then in Paris and Bologna. He returned to England in 1235 to serve as chancellor of his alma mater. When Saint Boniface of Mainz (*whom* SEE) appointed him bishop of Chichester, King Henry III, who had in mind a candidate of his own, objected—but the pope decided for Boniface's man. Richard was revered alike for his clerical reforms and his ability to cultivate figs, and is said to have once dropped the Communion chalice without spilling a drop. He died, while preaching a Crusade, in 1253. Possibly because he drove a farm cart as a boy, the coachmen's guild of Milan took this quintessentially English Saint as their heavenly Patron.

Rita—May 22
PATRONESS OF DESPERATE CASES; INVOKED AGAINST BLEEDING,
INFERTILITY, LONELINESS, TUMORS, AND UNHAPPY MARRIAGE

In modern Italy, devotion to this Saint, particularly among women, rivals that accorded the Blessed Mother Herself. Born in 1381 at Cascia (near Spoleto) to pious, elderly parents, she was married at the age of twelve to Paul di Ferdinando, a local gangster. He was notoriously unfaithful to her. He neglected her. He beat her constantly. They had two sons. One day, after eighteen years of this, she discovered on her doorstep Paul's mutilated body, the victim of vendetta. Rita prayed her sons would not seek to avenge their father, and her prayers were answered: they took sick and died. At last she was free to fulfill her childhood dream to become a holy nun. Twice the Augustinian convent at Cascia rejected her, on the grounds that she

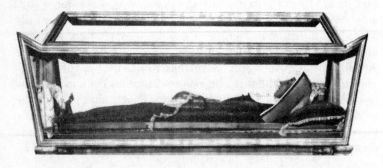

was obviously not a virgin. But after one night when she was miraculously transported into their cloistered midst, they had no choice but to admit her. She soon exceeded the efforts of them all in piety, self-denial, and obedience. Ordered to do so by her superior, she daily watered a dry twig stuck in the ground. Praying before the crucifix, she implored Christ that she might share in His Passion, and in His Mercy He sent one of the thorns from His crown flying into her forehead. There it festered, until the other nuns were obliged to give a wide berth to Rita and the cloud of stench surrounding her. She continued in this life of holy mortification for fifteen years; only after her death in 1457 did her odor become that of roses (which sweet fragrance to this day permeates the atmosphere of the convent, where Rita's incorrupt body is on display under glass).

Robert Bellarmine—September 17
PATRON OF CATECHISTS AND CANONISTS

A Jesuit and Doctor of the Church whose writings, especially *The Controversies*, were the most influential of their day, Bellarmine's intellect was so great that his work was once thought to be that of a team of scholars and his name an anagram. He revised the Vulgate, created a catechism, and as cardinal was prefect of the Vatican library. He became the supreme defender of the papacy (even though he once called Pope John XII "the dregs"). When the megalomaniacal Pope Sixtus V, who hated Bellarmine and wanted him placed on the Index, rewrote the Bible to his own specifications, it was Bellarmine who pulled all copies out of circulation after Sixtus's death, maintaining that a later Bible by Pope Clement VII was actually the Sixtus Bible. Bellarmine perpetrated this forgery so it would not seem that Clement was disputing his infallible fellow Pope Sixtus and his error-laden tome. He fought against heresies, Protestant theologies, anticlerics, and was influential in the recognition of Henry of Navarre as king of France. He disputed Galileo's theory that the earth revolved around the sun, staunchly asserting that the sun "revolves around the earth with great speed," but he was sympathetic to the astronomer (who had dedicated books to him). Bellarmine's promised protection proved useless during Galileo's trial before the Grand Inquisition. During this time the cardinal rather fatefully wrote to a friend that to assert that the earth revolves around the sun "is as erroneous as to claim that Jesus was not born of a virgin." In his later years he withdrew from controversy and wrote books of devotion. His disagreements with Sixtus, who put one of his books about the temporal power of the papacy on the Index, along with his belief that early lives of the Saints were full of incredible embellishments, may explain why Bellarmine's canonization was delayed for 300 years.

Roch—August 17

PATRON OF CATTLE, DOCTORS, DOG LOVERS, AND PRISONERS; INVOKED AGAINST CHOLERA, CONTAGIOUS DISEASES, SKIN DISEASES, AND PLAGUE

This French-born Saint is equally revered in Italy as Rocco, in Spain as Roque, and in England as Rock. Born in 1293, the son of the governor of Montpellier, he enjoyed a wealthy and privileged youth. Orphaned at twenty, he gave all his property to the poor and set out on pilgrimage to Rome. A plague was then ravaging northern Italy, and Roch traveled from town to town nursing its victims. His therapeutic technique consisted of making the Sign of the Cross over the stricken, often with miraculous results. Then, at Piacenza, Roch himself became infected, developing a hideous sore on his thigh. Knowing he was contagious, he selflessly wandered into the forest to die alone—but was soon visited and befriended by a dog. For some time the noble beast daily brought the ailing Saint bread and other food snatched from its master's table. Eventually, Roch recovered and made his way back home to Montpellier. Unrecognized because of his emaciated condition, he was cast into a dungeon as a spy. There he languished for five years, ministered to by an Angel. (The jail must have had a "No Dogs Allowed" policy.) After his death, Roch was recognized by a cross-shaped birthmark on his breast, and much mourned by his relatives. The letters VSR *(Viva Saint Roch)* were once inscribed over most of the doorways of Europe as surefire protection against pestilence. The Saint's cult, which declined as the Black Death abated, was revived during the cholera epidemics of the nineteenth century.

Romanus—February 28
PATRON INVOKED AGAINST DROWNING AND INSANITY

In the year 435, powerfully affected by reading about the early Desert Fathers, Romanus (also known as Romaine) left the monastery at Lyons and took to the hills—specifically, to the cold Alpine slopes of the Jura. There he worked and prayed, his only shelter a large fir tree. He was soon joined by his younger brother Lupicinus, their sister (whose name history does not record), and a number of would-be monks and nuns. All clad themselves in the skins of beasts, and wore wooden shoes. Of the brothers, Lupicinus appears to have been the stricter with regard to dietary regulations, forbidding not just meat and eggs, but milk as well. There are, by the way, seven other Saints named Romanus: two bishops, two martyrs, a hermit, a Russian prince, and a Byzantine hymn-writer.

Rose of Lima—August 23
PATRONESS OF CENTRAL AND SOUTH AMERICA, FLORISTS, GARDENERS, PERU, AND THE PHILIPPINES

Isabel de Santa Maria de Flores y del Oliva, who preferred to be addressed by her confirmation name of Rose, was the first native of the New World to be declared a Roman Catholic Saint. She was born in Lima, Peru, in 1586, a mere fifty years after the Spanish conquest. As befitted her mixed Hispanic and Incan descent, she liked her religion on the flamboyant side, with a good helping of gore— her role model was the devotionally extravagant Saint Catherine of Siena (*whom* SEE). Rose's legendary facial beauty distressed her; she found that rubbing her cheeks with

pepper and her lips with quicklime helped. In public, she invariably wore a crown of roses—and sixty-nine brow-piercing spikes. She lived in a shack in her family garden, whence she was wont to emerge dragging a heavy cross. The Ideal of Catholic Girlhood, she slept on a pile of bricks, wore gloves full of nettles, whipped herself with chains, and gouged hunks out of her flesh with broken glass. She was generally assumed to be loco in the coco until the day she announced that, through her fervid prayers, Lima had been saved from an earthquake. Since there had, indeed, been no earthquake, the populace came to hold her in the highest regard, and rejoiced wildly when she was canonized—in 1671, fifty-three years after her death.

Rose of Viterbo—September 4
PATRONESS OF FLORISTS

A child prodigy of sorts, Rose had her first vision at eight—in 1242—when the Blessed Virgin told her to start wearing the habit of Saint Francis of Assisi (*whom* SEE). Dressed as a male monk, the little girl hit the streets of the Italian town of Viterbo, preaching in her high, childish voice against the excommunicated Emperor Frederick. In denouncing the emperor for taking lands from the pope, Rose placed herself squarely on the side of the anti-German faction (the Guelfs) in the conflict of the city-states. When partisans of the emperor exiled Rose and her family and clamored for her execution, the child predicted (correctly) the emperor's death, earning herself a reputation as a prophetess. Her political activism was described by her biographer as follows: "A child was born . . . destined by providence to be the stone on which the haughty emperor should be broken." When she was ten, Rose challenged an opponent to trial by fire. She jumped into a bonfire, emerged unharmed, and won the debate. She became hysterical when the nuns from the convent of St. Mary of the Roses refused her admission because of her lack of dowry, and threatened "You will not have me now, but perhaps you will be more willing when I'm dead." After her death at seventeen, Rose appeared to Pope Alexander IV in a vision and asked him to have her body moved to that elitist convent, which he immediately did.

Rudolph of Berne—April 17

The local Swiss clergy attested in 1287 that young Rudolph's mutilated body had been discovered in the cellar of a rich Jew, and, following this traditional "blood libel," the traditional pogrom was carried out, accompanied as always by the righteous confiscation of Jewish property. Rudolph was, of course, venerated as a martyr, as were, in similar cases, William of Norwich (1144), Simon of Trent (1475), and "Little Saint Hugh" of Lincoln (1255)—whose story is so movingly told by the Nun's Priest in Chaucer's immortal *Canterbury Tales*.

Rumbald—November 3
PATRON OF FISHERMAN

Rumbald was born in England, of pagan royalty, and lived for a mere three days. He started his brief life by preaching a sermon to his parents, then addressed the public at large, expounding on the Holy Trinity and virtuous living, freely quoting the Scriptures. The prodigy asked for baptism and Holy Communion, ceaselessly repeating his mantra of "I am a Christian." On the third day, he announced his imminent death and dictated his wish to be buried in three consecutive sites. The infant's holy remains finally rested at Buckingham, and as his cult grew, churchs, statues, and streets there were dedicated to him.

Sabas—December 5

In the year 447, when he was eight years old, Sabas ran away from his highly dysfunctional home in Alexandria, Egypt, to join a monastery in Jerusalem. But he longed for the life of a solitary desert hermit, and in his fortieth year took up residence in a cave in the mountains near Jericho. (For a while, the Saint shared the cave with its orginal tenant, a lion—but the two quarreled, as roommates will, and the lion left.) Despite his desire for solitude, hundreds of monks came to join him—thereby forming, willy-nilly, a "laura," that is, a community of hermits. It was called Mar Saba, and to this day Eastern Orthodox monks reside there, making it one of the oldest inhabited monasteries in the world.

Sabina—August 29

PATRON OF HOUSEWIVES; INVOKED AGAINST HEMORRHAGE

There are several Saints by this name, all of them models of domesticity; the lady whose feast we now celebrate was a wealthy Roman widow in whose honor—and at whose expense—a basilica was erected on the Avertine Hill. She was converted to the outlawed Faith by her serving girl Serapia, and due to her lofty social position might well have gone unprosecuted, but she practiced her religion so flagrantly the authorities had no choice but to put her (rejoicing) to the sword.

Sabinus—December 30

Rather than worship a statue of Venus, this Saint of Spoleto—or maybe Assisi—seized and smashed the obscene and idolatrous idol. For punishment, his hands were cut off. In prison with Sabinus was a poor blind boy, whom the Saint cured by blessing him with his stumps. Word of this wonder reached the pagan governor, Venustianus, who himself suffered from eye trouble. He visited the maimed

Saint, was likewise healed, and converted with his entire family to the One True Faith. On December 30, in the year 303, Sabinus, Venustianus, and the wife and child of the latter were put to the sword.

Samson of Dol—July 28

When he was five (around the year 500—just before Britain degenerated into England), Samson's Celtic parents dedicated him to God. After his ordination at fifteen (a dove perched on his shoulder throughout the ceremony), Samson turned around and dedicated *them*—and his brothers as well—to God. He spared his little sister, allowing her "the world's pomps and pleasures." He then became the prototypical wandering Welsh monk, inspired by visions to travel as far as Ireland, Cornwall, and the Scilly Isles, all the while reforming monasteries, intervening in local politics, and naming places after himself. He wound up in Dol, in Celtic France (Brittany), and became that land's first bishop. (He was ordained such in a dream by Saints Peter, James, and John, but recognized by Church authorities in Rome.) In sacred art, Samson is pictured in the act of slaying a dragon, a deed by which he endeared himself to the Bretons.

Sara—May 24
PATRONESS OF GYPSIES

Each year on this day, Gypsies gather in Provence, France, to celebrate the feast of Sara, their highly unofficial Patron Saint. They believe her to have been a servant of the "Three Marys"—Mary, the wife of Cleophas; Mary Salome, the mother of James; and Mary Magdalene (*whom* SEE). Together with Saints Lazarus and Martha (*both of whom* SEE), this company sailed, after Christ's Ascension into Heaven, in a rudderless boat from Palestine to Marseilles. Sara is pictured as swarthy; the Gypsies say she was of Indian descent and also answers to the name of Kali.

Sava—January 14
PATRON OF SERBIA

Until the twelfth century, when Stephen Nemanya told them who they were—and that he was their king—the Serbs thought of them-

selves as just another tribe of Slavs hanging around the Balkans. King
Stephen I of Serbia had three sons. Sava, the youngest and his favorite, was of a religious nature, and in his seventeenth year (it was 1191)
left home to enter the austere Greek monastary on Mount Athos.
Before long, the old king abdicated to join the lad in a life of prayer
and penance. Meanwhile, back in Serbia, the older sons (and their factions) went to war over the crown, establishing the tradition of "bal-
kanization." Sava dutifully returned to his homeland, settled the civil
war, and remained to unify the nation by translating sacred texts into
its language. He also, according to folklore, invented windows. As a
bishop, Sava allied himself and his nation with the Byzantine, or Eastern Orthodox, Church, rather than with the Western ("Roman")
rite—a decision that has had lasting political consequences.

Scholastica—February 10

PATRONESS OF RAIN; INVOKED AGAINST CHILDHOOD CONVULSIONS

   Scholastica was the beloved twin sister of the
founder of Western monasticism, the great Saint
Benedict (*whom* SEE). It was her lifelong conviction
that to become a Saint one had only to "will it."
With her brother's help, she founded, in the year
540 or so, a convent some five miles distant from
his own monastery at Monte Cassino. He visited her one day a year,
and on the last occasion (she knew she was about to die), she begged
him to stay longer. When he refused, she began to pray intently,
flooding the table with her tears, until a tremendous thunderstorm
blew up. "God forgive you, sister," said Benedict, "what have you
done?" "I asked a favor of you and you refused it. I asked it of God
and he granted it," said she, drying her eyes. . . . "And thus they spent
the night together, talking of holy things," as we are told in *The Dialogues* of Saint Gregory the Great (*whom* SEE). Three days later, Scholastica died, and while in his cell praying, Benedict saw his willful
sister's soul ascend to Heaven in the form of a white dove. Their
grave (they were buried together) was discovered shortly after World
War II, in the rubble of the bombed-out abbey at Monte Cassino.

Sebald—August 19

PATRON OF NÜRNBERG; INVOKED AGAINST THE COLD

   In the time of Saint Boniface of Mainz (*whom* SEE), this priest set
out to convert the pagan Franconians—that is, Germans—of Nürn-

berg (of which city he is now the Patron). Once, when preaching to a crowd, Sebald was heckled, and caused the earth to swallow up the mocker. On a famous occasion, Sebald sought shelter one cold winter day in the hut of a peasant couple. He was received with a singular lack of hospitality; the churls refused to add fuel to their low fire, claiming a scarcity of wood. Sebald instructed the stingy hausfrau to gather an armful of icicles from the eaves, and to dump them into the hearth, which (curiously enough) she did. Needless to say, they burst into roaring flames, which made things nice and cozy.

Sebastian—January 20

PATRON OF ARCHERS, ATHLETES, DOCTORS, HARDWARE, PIN MAKERS,
THE POLICE, AND SOLDIERS; INVOKED AGAINST PLAGUE

It was an immensely popular subject of Renaissance painting, rendered by Botticelli, Bernini, and El Greco, among others: a handsome youth, all but naked, bound to a stake, his body pierced with arrows, his eyes lifted to heaven in an almost erotic ecstasy—*The Martyrdom of Saint Sebastian*. Actually, he was beaten to death with sticks. According to his legend, Sebastian was born in Gaul (France), but grew up in Milan. A Christian, and thus a pacifist, he nevertheless joined the Roman army (in 283) as a sort of secret agent. Little did the wicked Emperor Diocletian know that the brave officer he promoted to the elite Praetorian Guard was (on the sly) miraculously curing (gout was his speciality), converting, and baptizing other soldiers and even innocent civilians! As the persecution of the Christians intensified, Sebastian arranged for the pope (Caius) to be hidden in the safest place in Rome—an apartment in the imperial palace. Eventually, Sebastian was betrayed to the authorities, and sentenced to death by a bow-and-arrow firing squad. But after the execution the pious widow who came to claim his martyr's body discovered he was still alive, and nursed him back to health. No sooner had he recovered from his wounds than Sebastian returned to the palace, there to confront Diocletian and castigate him for his pagan policies. The emperor, astonished to encounter a man he believed dead, considered, briefly, becoming a Christian himself. On second thought, he ordered Sebastian cudgeled to death and thrown into a common sewer.

Serf—July 1

PATRON OF THE ORKNEY ISLANDS

Serf, the son of a sixth-century Arabian princess, rejected his Oriental kingdom and even an offer of the papacy to preach to the pagan Scots. Much of his legend involves eating. Once the Devil, trying to lure Serf from his hiding place, possessed a local peasant, causing him to develop a ravenous appetite. The demoniac ate a lamb, a sheep, and a cow, but was still hungry—until Our Saint fed him a flea, causing the screaming Devil to vacate his person. On another occasion, Serf confronted a thief who had stolen a roast sheep, and when the felon tried to protest his innocence, all he could do was bleat. A good Christian once killed, cooked, and fed his only pig to the visiting Saint. Touched, Serf restored the beast to flesh and life. Although he never actually got to visit the Orkney Islands, he remains their Patron Saint.

Sernin—November 29

A Greek who originally followed John the Baptist, Sernin was baptized alongside Christ in the River Jordan. He headed off with Peter through the Middle East, then turned west and preached on both sides of the Pyrenees. He finally landed in Toulouse, where he destroyed idols and cured the emperor's daughter of leprosy. His enemies captured him and tied him to the tail of a bull which dragged him around, causing his brain to fly out. The bull finally trampled Sernin to death where today a church, Taur, marks the spot. With his dying breath the Saint railed against a priest who had deserted him, vowing a hollow curse that no native of Toulouse would ever be made bishop. Two virgins, *les deux pucelles*, took his remains to a town later named after them—Pucelle.

Servais—May 13

PATRON INVOKED AGAINST FOOT TROUBLES, RATS, AND VERMIN

An Armenian-born bishop in fourth-century Belgium, Servais was a mighty warrior in Orthodoxy's battle against the Arian heresy. He clearly foresaw the invasion of the Huns into Gaul, which he attempted to prevent by undertaking a penitential pilgimage to Rome. In Maastricht, where he is invoked against infestations of all kinds, there is a splendid reliquary in

which are preserved Servais's staff and cup, as well as a silver key allegedly bestowed upon him by Saint Peter himself.

Servulus of Rome—December 23
PATRON INVOKED AGAINST PARALYSIS

Afflicted from infancy with a palsy, Servulus could not stand or sit, nor lift his hand to his mouth. Each day his mother and brother would carry him to the porch outside the doors of St. Clement's Church in Rome. Although he was himself a beggar, it is said he shared what little he had with the poor. Servulus would constantly entreat passersby to read Scripture or sing hymns to him—so that he learned them all by heart. He died in the year 590, when Gregory the Great (*whom* SEE) became pope; it was he who conducted the paralyzed beggar's funeral Mass, and we have it on papal authority that the corpse "smelled fragrant."

Seven Brothers—July 10

Buried in seven cemeteries in Rome are seven martyrs who may (or may not) have been brothers. Their names were Alexander, Felix, Januarius, Martial, Philip, Silvanus, and Vitalis. Their story, and that of their mother, Felicity, is a Christianization of the Jewish saga of the Six Maccabees. She was allegedly a rich Roman widow; with her sons, she refused to deny her Faith, and was obliged to watch as they were individually tortured to death. According to Saint Augustine, who knew a thing or two about nagging mothers, she shouted encouragement to them throughout their ordeal, and went proudly to her own beheading. Their feast has been celebrated on this date since the earliest times; their relics were widely distributed and venerated in medieval Europe.

Seven Sleepers of Ephesus—July 27
PATRONS INVOKED AGAINST INSOMNIA

In this Christian version of Rip Van Winkle, seven boys from Ephesus (Maximian, Malchus, Marcian, Denis, John, Scrapian, Constantine), escaping persecution from the Emperor Decius, hid in a cave that was walled up, and proceeded to sleep for either 208 or 363 years. When they awoke, one of the boys furtively entered Ephesus, now thoroughly Christian, looking to buy bread. The boy paid for

the bread with coins that the locals thought were part of a stolen treasure. They followed him to the cave and found the rest of the boys stretching and yawning, their complexions still rosy. The sleepers became quite famous and are even mentioned in the Koran, along with their dog, Katmir. He stayed with them the whole time, and is one of the nine animals permitted to enter Paradise. King Edward the Confessor, who saw them in a vision, divined that when the sleepers turned from their right side to their left, sorrows—war, pestilence, and famine—fell on the world.

Severus—February 1
PATRON OF HATTERS AND MILLINERS

The child of poor, sixth-century French peasants, Severus was hired by Corbican, a rich pagan, to tend his mares. When his new employee, on his first trip to town, gave all his clothes to the poor and returned to the farm naked, Corbican banished Severus to the barn, where the mares' breath kept him warm. Seeing this, Corbican was converted. Severus went on to become a priest, and later, much against his will, a bishop. According to a mystifying legend, one of his flock once went to the baths and neglected to pay. The forgetful bather dropped dead at home, and the proprietor of the baths arrived, demanding a huge sum of money from the grieving widow. She sought the aid of Bishop Severus, who led an expedition to the graveyard, where he inquired of the dead man how much he owed for his bath. The corpse sat up and replied, "One egg," which apparently settled the matter. Severus died a hermit in the forest, but nothing in his biography explains his traditional Patronage of the hat trade.

Sidwell—August 2
PATRONESS OF FARMERS

The name "Sidwell" combines the words "scythe" and "well"—and wouldn't you know it? this maiden of (pre-Saxon) Exeter is pictured (in a stained-glass window at All Souls College, Oxford) standing beside a well, with a scythe in her hand. In her other hand she holds her head—for this Saint was decapitated by reapers in the pay of her wicked, jealous stepmother. An even worse fate befell Sidwell's equally beautiful and innocent sister, Jutwara. When that virgin complained of chest pains, the stepmother recommended she apply two cream cheeses to her breasts—and then informed her own dastardly son Bana that Jutwara was pregnant. He confronted the chaste maiden, confirmed his suspicions by observing her moist and swollen condition, and struck off her head.

Sigfrid—February 15
PATRON OF SWEDEN

This eleventh-century Englishman (bishop of York), was sent by King Ethelred (at the pleading of the Swedes) to renew Christianity among them. Arriving in the company of three nephews, Sigfrid immediately converted and baptized the Swedish king, Olaf, receiving from that monarch a palace as a gift. Sigfrid's nephews were soon murdered and thrown into a deep well, but he was led to their bodies by a heavenly light. He forgave the killers, declining Olaf's offer to execute them, or to fine them heavily. Sigfrid's memory is still esteemed in Scandinavia, where he is invoked against hunger. (In art he is shown holding his nephews' heads, which have sometimes been mistaken for loaves.)

Simeon Stylites—January 5
PATRON OF SHEPHERDS

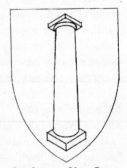

Simeon, the most famous of the desert ascetics also known as anchorites, was born the son of a Syrian shepherd in the year 390. He entered a local monastery at age thirteen, but because of the extreme austerities and mortifications he practiced (such as winding his body with chains until his flesh was raw, and delicately replacing the maggots when they emerged from his stinking wounds for a breath of air), he was expelled. He next became a solitary hermit on a mountaintop, but the fame of his flamboyant holiness (he dressed in the skins of wild beasts, slept very little, and was especially proficient at fasting—he could totally abstain from food for the full forty days of Lent) inspired crowds to seek him out for their edification, or possibly for entertainment. To escape their unwanted attentions, he erected a ten-foot-high pillar and took up residence atop it. Curiously enough, this attracted even greater crowds, and for the remaining thirty-five years of his life he lived on higher and higher pillars—his final earthly home was a six-foot-square platform on a pillar sixty feet tall.

Simon Stock—May 16
PATRON OF TANNERS

Born in Kent, England, in 1165, Simon traveled to Jerusalem on pilgrimage and there joined the Order of Carmelite hermits. Driven from the Holy Land by heathen Muslim hordes, he returned home, there to become the first prior general of the English Carmelite Friars. In the vision for which he is famous, the Mother of God assured him that no one who wears the "scapular," that is, the brown felt, poncholike garment affected by Carmelites, will burn in Hell. This Afterlife Insurance Policy (if you will) has had an understandable appeal to generations of sinners, and "scapular medals" are still available in Roman Catholic church boutiques for a surprisingly reasonable price.

Sithney—August 4
PATRON OF MAD DOGS

A sixth-century Cornish monk and nephew of Saint David (*whom* SEE), Sithney was known for his holy misogyny. He once roundly cursed a housewife for doing her wash in his well—and the woman's brat promptly disappeared. It was widely assumed the child had plunged from a nearby cliff, and Sithney heard some criticism about it, but he himself soon discovered the toddler quite unharmed, playing on the beach below. For reasons of His own, God once offered Sithney the post of Patron of girls. The Saint objected that the flighty creatures would be forever pestering him to supply them with fine clothes and/or husbands. He protested that he'd rather be Patron of mad dogs. And so he is.

Solangia—May 10
PATRONESS OF LITTLE CHILDREN, SHEPHERDS, AND RAIN

The innocent and beautiful daughter of a worker in the local vineyards, Solange, as the French call her, tended sheep in the meadows near Bourges. The little peasant girl caught the eye of Bernard, son of the count of Poitiers, but she rejected his salacious advances, whereupon he stabbed her to death. The crime did much to raise class consciousness among the ninth-century French.

Spiridon—December 14
PATRON OF CORFU AND DALMATIA

Spiridon, a rough-and-ready sheep farmer, lived on the island of Cyprus with his wife and family. He was also a stalwart Christian, and had suffered the loss of an eye rather than take part in an idolatrous ceremony. The Cyprians elected him bishop, and sent him as their delegate to the Council of Nicaea in 325. The bishops and deacons from surrounding lands with whom Spiridon set out for the council were all learned and dignified churchmen, and somewhat embarrassed by the company of this one-eyed rustic. One night they conspired to prevent his accompanying them further, by cutting off the heads of the two mules—a brown one and a white one—on which he and his servant rode. Before dawn, Spiridon awoke and discovered the decapitations. In the dark, he restored the animals' heads. And that is why Bishop Spiridon came to Nicaea riding a white mule with a brown head.

Stanislaus—April 11
PATRON OF POLAND

Stanislaus Szczepanow, the eleventh-century bishop of Cracow, was so devout that once, when he was ill, the great second-century Saint Barbara (*whom* SEE) appeared to serve him the Eucharist. He is sometimes called the Thomas à Becket (*whom* SEE) of Poland, because of his long-standing (and finally lethal) feud with his king. Stanislaus objected strenuously when His Royal Highness Boleslaus ran off with a nobleman's wife. The king in turn haled the bishop into court, on the charge of stealing land from a citizen named Peter, then deceased. Our Saint, after three days of prayer and fasting, made his way to Peter's grave and summoned forth the corpse, who, in his moldy burial clothes, accompanied Stanislaus to the courthouse, where Peter testified that he had been paid in full, before returning to his tomb. Next, Boleslaus, under threat of excommunication, boldly entered the cathedral in Cracow, causing Stanislaus to halt in the middle of the High Mass he was celebrating. The enraged monarch drew his sword and chased the prelate out into the streets, where he hacked him to pieces (which sacred relics three eagles from Heaven instantly descended to protect). For years thereafter, a delicate fragrance wafted from the coffin of the Saint. Crude, atheistic, and revisionist historians have recently suggested that Stanislaus was martyred for his part in a plot to overthrow the king.

Stanislaus Kostka—November 13

PATRON OF POLAND AND OF YOUNG PEOPLE; INVOKED
AGAINST BROKEN LIMBS, DOUBT, AND PALPITATIONS

The child of sixteenth-century Polish nobility, Stanislaus was tormented by a bullying older brother and a vulgar tutor. Delicate in sensibility as well as health, he was accused of being a prig by his worldly relatives, the standing family joke being, "Don't tell that story in front of Stanislaus, he would faint." At school in Vienna, his brother continued to taunt him, once sending a prostitute to his room, and even forcing him to live with Protestants. When this shabby  treatment caused the Saint to fall deathly ill, his Lutheran landlord refused to let a priest bring him Holy Communion. Saint Barbara, ever helpful in these situations (SEE Saint Benedict the Black), sent two Angels to Stanislaus with Holy Communion; eventually, even the Blessed Virgin and the Holy Infant came to visit his sickroom. The Virgin let him play with the Baby and suggested Stan join the Jesuits. The Jesuits of Vienna, afraid of alienating Stanislaus's father, rejected him, forcing the Saint to walk 350 miles to Rome, where he entered the order at the age of seventeen. His poor health returned, due to a combination of fasting, mortification, and the Roman summer, and he died nine months later. In his final moments, he whispered to those present that the Blessed Virgin was in the room. Meanwhile, his father, fuming that Stanislaus had entered the Jesuits, sent his guilt-ridden brother to bring him back. When the brother arrived in Rome, he learned that Stanislaus was dead and that all Rome was flocking to his tomb, calling him the new Polish saint. His brother and tutor were witnesses at his beatification (blaming each other) and later both entered the Jesuits.

Stephen—December 26
PATRON OF BRICKLAYERS, BUILDERS, HORSES, AND MASONS

Stephen is called "the protomartyr," for he was the first Christian to die for the Faith (not including the Holy Innocents and John the Baptist, *whom* SEE). Although not an Apostle, Stephen was one of the seventy-two original disciples, and after Pentecost was appointed one of Jerusalem's seven deacons. Accused by pious Jews of preaching blasphemy, he was arrested, tried before the high priest, Caiphas, and condemned to death by stoning. The rocks and bricks employed by his executioners are treasured relics of Christendom; there is an astonishing number of them. In Poland (where his is a popular name), parishioners shower the priest with oats after Mass on Saint Stephen's Day, for the sake of their horses. In England and Ireland, children remember the Saint today by hurling rocks at wrens.

Stephen of Hungary—August 16
PATRON OF HUNGARY

As the first millennium (the year 1000) approached, the end of the world—that is, of Christendom—seemed, verily, to be at hand. From the north, heathen Viking raids continued. Infidel Muslims from the south occupied Spain. And now from the east, from Hungary, of all places, came merciless hordes of pagan Magyar horsemen, overrunning Moravia and Burgundy and advancing on Paris. Their very name in French, *ogres*, became a byword for super- (or sub-) human Evil. Then, providentially, the Hungarians received the Gift of Faith, which happened to include the gift of a splendid crown for their king, sent to him personally by the pope in 1001. The king, Vaik, son of Geza, was baptized Stephen. An economic progressive by the standards of the age, Stephen vigorously imposed both feudalism (a system of tax collection) and Christianity (a system of tithe collection) upon his grateful subjects. He was, unfortunately, predeceased by his beloved son and designated heir, Saint Americus (*whom* SEE).

Swithbert—March 1
PATRON INVOKED AGAINST ANGINA

This eighth-century Englishman's holy mission was to save from perdition those savage heathens, the Frisians—natives of what is now southern Holland. His patronage of angina sufferers is traditional, but of unknown origin.

Swithin—July 15

PATRON OF AND INVOKED AGAINST RAIN

Every Britisher knows that if it rains on Saint Swithin's Day, it will keep raining for the next forty days. Swithin (or Swithun) was a bishop of Winchester, renowned for his financial acumen and good deeds. His most celebrated miracle, while living, was the putting-together-again of a peasant woman's basketful of broken eggs. He is said to have enjoyed the rain, and wished to be buried in the church-yard, where it would fall upon his grave. He died in 862. In honor of his canonization in 971, his bones were dug up and enshrined inside the cathedral, on July 15 . . . whereupon a forty-day deluge ensued, as it may again at the height of any English summer.

Sylvester—December 31

New Year's Eve is Saint Sylvester's Night, and if an east wind occurs then it is said that it betokens a calamitous twelve months in the offing. According to one legend, Pope Sylvester cured the Emperor Constantine of leprosy and baptized him; in turn, the grateful ruler made Christianity the state religion of the Roman empire, and bestowed upon the bishop of Rome enormous and perpetual temporal powers. Another tells how Constantine summoned Sylvester to a conclave of magicians, pagan priests, and rabbis to debate "the Name of God." A wizard whispered into an ox's ear, and the animal dropped dead. But Sylvester called that the Devil's work, and restored the beast to life in Christ's name—thus converting the emperor and all his subjects.

Symphorian—August 22

PATRON OF CHILDREN AND STUDENTS

In the third century, in the town of Autun, France (then the Roman province of Gaul), this Christian schoolboy bravely refused to participate in the pagan rites honoring the harvest goddess Cybele. Symphorian carried on an edifying theological debate with the local magistrate while being flogged, and was then escorted outside the town and beheaded, while his proud mother stood on the walls and shouted encouragement to her brave son.

Tammany—May 1

PATRON OF DEMOCRACY

St. Tammany is the name of a town in Louisiana, whose patron is Tammanend, a wise and respected chief of the Delaware tribe in colonial America. Because their enemies, the British-Loyalist Tories, belonged to political clubs named "St. George" and "St. Andrew," the freedom-loving "Sons of Liberty" decided (somewhat blasphemously) to call their club "St. Tammany." Once the Revolution was won, members of the Tammany Society continued to oppose Federalist privilege and aristocracy—from New York City's Tammany Hall. For the next century, Tammany was the "machine" through which immigrants and the working class were able to participate in the (otherwise exclusive) American political system known as patronage (in the non-Saintly sense of the word).

Tarcisius—August 15

PATRON OF ALTAR BOYS AND FIRST COMMUNICANTS

The cult of "Little Saint Tarcisius" arose after his appearance in a Victorian historical-romance-Catholic-propaganda novel entitled *Fabiola* (1854). A comely (but manly) lad of noble birth, born in the early fourth century, Tarcisius volunteered to carry the Blessed Sacrament from the hands of Pope Sylvester (*whom* SEE), then hiding in the catacombs, to imprisoned Christians awaiting martyrdom. Set upon by a gang of street toughs, Tarcisius steadfastly refused to reveal his Holy Mission, or surrender into their profane hands the Sacred Host. So they stoned him to death. His shining example of piety and courage suitably intimidated generations of parochial school first-graders.

Teresa of Ávila—October 15

PATRONESS OF SPAIN; INVOKED AGAINST HEADACHES AND HEART
DISEASE

The first woman to be honored by the Church with the title of Doctor (by Pope Paul VI, in 1970), Teresa, who was born in 1515, was controversial, charming, stubborn, and witty—a practical and energetic reformer as well as a passionate mystic. In her were combined, a poet wrote, "the eagle and the dove." As a very young child in her native Castile, Teresa read the *Lives of the Saints* and ran away from home, resolved to be gloriously martyred by the Moors. As a teenager, she enjoyed racy novels, and (to her everlasting shame) took an interest in perfume and fashion. At twenty, she entered the large and wealthy Carmelite convent at Ávila, which was a sort of easygoing society nunnery, where an episode of malaria left her virtually paralyzed for three years. It was not until 1555, when she was forty years of age, that Saints Mary Magdalene and Augustine of Hippo (*both of whom* SEE) appeared to her and granted her a vision of the especially nasty place prepared for her in Hell. When her confessor, Saint Peter of Alcántara (*whom also* SEE), confirmed that the voices she continued to hear and her mystical experiences (which included levitations in ecstasy) were of Divine, not demonic or psychotic, origin, Teresa undertook to save not only her own soul, but that of the Carmelite Order, which until the end of her life she strove to restore to its austere and penitential Primitive Rule. Her efforts at reform got her rather disliked, and ultimately divided the Carmelites into shod (calced) and barefooted (discalced) branches. She founded seventeen small, poor, contemplative convents. ("God preserve us from stupid nuns!" was one of her own prayers.) Influenced by her, Carmelite friars also undertook reforms (SEE Saint John of the Cross). Somehow, she found time to write her autobiography as well as a classic of mystical literature, *The Interior Castle*. The mental distress her visions caused her—she said to God, "If this is how you treat your friends, no wonder you don't have many!"—entitles Teresa to be a Patroness invoked against headaches. She once experienced God's love "like a lance driven into her heart"—and on that organ, to this day displayed under glass in the convent in Ávila (it wears a little crown), deep wounds may be observed. A slice of this heart is venerated in Milan. Because the Saint's body remained miraculously incorrupt, it, like all her relics—including an arm in Lisbon and a breast at St. Pancras's Church in Rome—has remained juicy.

Teresa of Jesus—August 26
PATRON OF OLD PEOPLE

Mother Teresa of Jesus Jornet e Ibars (1843–97) founded the Order of the Abandoned Old. She devoted her life to caring for the elderly poor people of Spain. She (and they) are now in Heaven, and so may it be said of all of us.

Teresa of Lisieux—October 1
PATRONESS OF FLORISTS, FOREIGN MISSIONS, PILOTS, AND FRANCE; INVOKED AGAINST TUBERCULOSIS

The youngest of five sisters, all Sisters—that is to say, all nuns—this member of an obscure French Carmelite cloister, born in 1873, became, soon after her early demise in 1897, the center of a modern-day worldwide cult devoted to venerating her as "The Little Flower." Their sacred text is her artless, not to say simpleminded, autobiography, titled in English *The Story of a Soul.* So sheltered and uneventful was her life that the Vatican, with an irony approaching sarcasm, has appointed her Patroness of airline pilots as well as foreign missions. (She had, in fact, once expressed a desire to be sent as a missionary to French Indochina, i.e., Vietnam—but her delicate health precluded travel.) The secret of her sanctity was what she called her "little way." Forbidden because of her fragility to starve, whip, or mutilate herself as the Great Virgin-Martyr-Saints of the past had done, Theresa discovered she could make herself beatifically miserable by enduring the *little* things. She would not brush away a fly, or scratch an itch. She would sleep under a heavy blanket in the summer heat, and without it in winter. She would piously and smilingly endure the irritating faults of others (while keeping careful count). Imagine her delight—and that of all who knew her—when she came down with lethal, blood-spitting tuberculosis.

Thaïs—October 8
PATRONESS OF FALLEN WOMEN

A beautiful and wealthy harlot of fourth-century Alexandria, Egypt, Thaïs had been raised as a Christian, and when reminded of this fact by Paphnutius, a visiting desert monk, she burned her wardrobe, gave away her jewelry, and entered a convent. To atone for her sins, Thaïs was lodged in a low, narrow room furnished with a small hole through which she was occasionally fed bread and water. When she inquired about waste disposal, she was assured that conditions would surely be worse in Hell. After three years, Paphnutius was informed in a vision that Thaïs had completed her penance. Released from her cell, she died fifteen days later, and went straight to Heaven. Nevertheless, the naughty French novelist Anatole France eventually wrote a naughty French novel about her, and the naughty French composer Massenet, an opera.

Theneva—July 18
PATRONESS OF GLASGOW

In the sixth century, Theneva was a princess of the Picts, the aboriginal people of Scotland. Although a heathen, she had taken a vow of virginity, and so defied her father, King Loth, by refusing to marry Owen, a prince of neighboring Cumbria. Her enraged parent drove her from his door, and Theneva took shelter with a Christian swineherd, who not only respected her vow, but taught her the rudiments of the True Faith. But somehow, Theneva turned up pregnant; her seducer, identified in the legend as "a beardless youth," may have been Eugenius, king of the Scots. Berserk with rage, her royal father ordered that she be thrown off a cliff into the sea. Miraculously, she was unharmed, and escaped in a waiting boat. Guided by a shoal of fishes, she landed at Culrose, and there gave birth to her son. A nearby hermit bishop, Saint Servan by name, heard her singing a lullaby and made haste to rescue and baptize both mother and child. Theneva reformed her life and moved to Glasgow. Her son (named Mungo) grew up to be a famous Saint as well, and is co-Patron of the city with his mother.

Theobald of Alba—June 2
PATRON OF PORTERS AND SHOEMAKERS

Born into a noble family in Piedmont, Theobald was moved by his reading of the Gospel to adopt a simple life, and apprenticed himself to a cobbler. He became so skilled at the trade that it was his master's dying wish that Our Saint marry his daughter. Theobald, bound as he was by a vow of chastity, departed on a pilgrimage to Spain. Upon his return to Alba, he sought even more menial employment, carrying sacks of grain and giving away his meager salary to the poor until his death in 1150.

Theobald of Provins—June 30
PATRON OF CHARCOAL BURNERS

Theobald was born, in 1017, into the nobility of Champagne, but influenced by his reading of the *Lives of the Desert Fathers* refused a splendid military career. Over his parents' strong objections, Theobald clad himself in rags, and set out for the vicinity of Luxembourg, where he lived in a hovel, supporting himself and his close personal friend William by working at the lowliest of tasks, such as stable mucking and charcoal burning. After many years, his old parents back home heard tales of "the holy hermit of Salingo" and made a pilgrimage there. Imagine their joy and surprise at being thus reunited with their long-lost son!

Theodard—September 10
PATRON OF CATTLE DEALERS

Theodard was the head of a large bishopric in Flanders who, in 668, set out to complain to the king about land being appropriated by nobles. On his return he was waylaid by robbers, to whom he addressed a long speech. They countered with a philosophical speech of their own, quoting Horace to the effect that death is common to all, and finishing with a fatal hatchet blow.

Theodore of Sykeon—April 22
PATRON OF RAIN

Theodore's father, a typical fifth-century circus acrobat and bareback rider, abandoned him at birth, and Theodore was raised by his mother, aunt, and grandmother, all of whom were prostitutes. One day, Saint George (*whom* SEE) appeared to his mother, instructing her to educate Theodore and providing her with a chef, which allowed her to transform her brothel into a restaurant. In appreciation, Theodore propagated the cult of Saint George his entire life. A poor student, he was able to learn his psalter only after tasting some honey that came from the mouth of an Icon of Christ. Theodore became a priest, then a hermit so devout that he stayed in a wooden cage from Christmas to Palm Sunday with an iron girdle around his waist. Later he graduated to life in an iron cage suspended in midair over the face of a rock, with his hands and feet encased in iron rings. He was a famous exorcist, specializing in driving unclean spirits out of young girls. Once, when he appeared before a possessed girl, the demon became visible under her skin, running up and down her limbs like a mouse. Another time, when a possessed women entered his church, he led the congregation in chanting the *"Kyrie Eleison,"* which caused her to fly up and out of the church. A clairvoyant, he was able to divine that a chalice was the former chamber pot of a prostitute and to predict that a general, Maurice, would ascend to the throne. In gratitude for his confidence, Maurice encouraged Theodore, whose health had been damaged by his hermit years (his biographer said he smelled like a corpse), to become bishop. As bishop, Theodore received as a kindred spirit the African monk Antiochus, who had hair and a beard down to his loins and hadn't eaten bread in thirty years, living only on uncooked vegetables and water. Our Saint had little tolerance for men of property, however, and when the wealthy Theodosus kicked the chair from under him, Theodore resigned as bishop. He returned to the monastery, performing miracles such as curing the emperor's son of elephantiasis, delivering crops from pests, and reconciling unhappily married couples.

Theodotus—May 18

PATRON OF INNKEEPERS

The romantic (third-century) tale of Theodotus, an innkeeper by trade, and of his pious foster mother, Thecusa, is long, elaborate, and historically worthless. It concerns the recovery of martyrs' holy relics, a corpse identified by a ring on its finger, a wine-selling priest getting cruel Roman soldiers drunk, and naked Christian virgins drowned for refusing to participate in an orgy. You don't want to know.

Thomas—July 3

PATRON OF ARCHITECTS, BUILDERS, CONSTRUCTION WORKERS,
CARPENTERS, GEOMETRICIANS, MASONS, SURVEYORS, THE EAST INDIES,
INDIA, AND PAKISTAN; INVOKED AGAINST BLINDNESS AND DOUBT

A Jew and a Galilean, Thomas was one of the original twelve Apostles, and was called Didymus ("twin"), since he was the twin brother of Saint James. He is characterized in the Gospels by his incredulous nature, hence his nickname: "Doubting Thomas." He refused to believe in the Resurrection until he had put his fingers into the wounds of the risen Christ, and similarly doubted the Assumption of Mary until She lowered Her girdle to him from Heaven. Gnostic Gospels have been attributed to him, not surprisingly one in which Christ says, "The Kingdom of the Father is spread upon the earth and men do not see it." When the Apostles drew lots to see who would go to India, Thomas lost; he balked at going, and so Christ appeared to an Indian merchant named Abban and sold Thomas to him as a slave/ carpenter. Abban took Thomas with him to India. When they arrived, the king gave Thomas money to build a palace, but Thomas gave the money to the poor instead. This so angered the king that he sentenced Thomas to death. In the meantime, the king's brother Gad died and went to Heaven, where he saw the palace Thomas had built with the king's money. Gad told the king about this in a dream, so Thomas was released—only to be killed soon after by a local prince who thought the Saint had bewitched his wife. The prince murdered him with a spear sometime around A.D. 53, and five hundred years later the site of his martyrdom started oozing blood. An Eastern sect called Nestorians, along with a a large group of people from the Malabar Coast region, call themselves "the Christians of Saint Thomas." The women there wear their saris in a distinctive way that makes them easily recognizable. In sacred art, Thomas is usually shown holding a spear or a T square. A bowl in the British Museum depicts seven scenes from his life, in most of which he is shown expressing disbelief. Popes would grant indulgences to those who visited his remains in Ortona, Italy.

Thomas à Becket—December 29

PATRON INVOKED AGAINST BLINDNESS

Chaucer's pilgrims, who tell the *Canterbury Tales,* are on their way to the site of this Saint's martyrdom and tomb; his popularity extends to our own time—the poet T. S. Eliot wrote him up in a verse drama *(Murder in the Cathedral)* and Richard Burton played him in a Hollywood movie *(Becket).* Thomas was a drinking buddy, companion in arms, and lord chancellor to England's King Henry II. But when His Majesty arranged to have him made archbishop of Canterbury, Thomas got religion. The ex-friends were equally bad-tempered and stubborn, and commenced to quarrel over the separation of Church and State. Finally, a group of overzealous soldiers heard Henry mumble something about wishing he were rid of Thomas. They stormed into the cathedral and bashed out the archbishop's brains. The pope was appalled at the sort of example this might set, and within three years, even though the king apologized, Thomas was declared a Saint. For centuries, the lame, the halt, and particularly the blind were cured in great numbers at his elaborate tomb in the cathedral, until King Henry VIII, who had his own problems with the pope, outlawed all veneration—or mention—of Our Saint.

Thomas Aquinas—January 28

PATRON OF SCHOLARS, THEOLOGIANS, AND PENCIL MAKERS

When Thomas died, in 1274, his fellow monks showed their recognition of his sanctity by decapitating the corpse and boiling it, the better to preserve his sacred (and valuable) relics. Known to posterity as "the Angelic Doctor" and "the Light of the Church"—and to his fellow students as "the Dumb Ox"—Thomas of Aquino remains the most influential theologian/philosopher in all Christendom. In his two great works, the *Summa contra gentiles* and the *Summa theologica,* he "cast greater light within the Church than all the other Doctors taken together," asserted Pope John XXII when canonizing him, in 1323 . . . and they remain enshrined among the Great Books of the Western World to this day. His prohibition (based on "Natural Law") of abortion, and indeed of any and all forms of contraception, is still the granite cornerstone of Roman Catholic doctrine. And it must be admitted that Thomas had a somewhat negative attitude toward the Fair Sex and sex in general. He says in his *Summa theologica:* "Because there is a higher water content in women, they are more easliy seduced by sexual pleasure," and "Nothing drags the mind of man down from its elevation so much as the caresses of woman and the bodily contacts without which a man cannot possess his wife." But he had his reasons. When he was a bookish seventeen-year-old, Thomas wrote to his aristocratic, if somewhat raffish, family that he wished to become a monk. His mother (Countess Theodora) had him kidnapped from the monastery, and locked in the tower of the family castle. His brothers (both military men) then sent a beautiful naked prostitute up to his room. The young Saint had the presence of mind to seize a firebrand and drive the shameless hussy from his chamber—whereupon he had a vision. Two Angels appeared, carrying a glowing girdle, with which they seemed to gird his loins; and never afterward was he troubled with any temptation against holy purity. (All this Thomas revealed to his confessor, Father Reynolds, thirty years after the event. Reynolds marveled that "at forty-eight he was as pure as a child of five years old.") Who better, then, to serve as the Ultimate Authority on sex, marriage, and procreation for the next seven centuries?

Thomas More—June 22
PATRON OF CIVIL SERVANTS AND LAWYERS

If you have seen the film *A Man for All Seasons* (1966), you know all about this remarkable Saint. If you have not seen the film, you really should. Better still, see the play. Best of all, read More's own *Utopia*.

Thorlac—December 23
PATRON OF ICELAND

This native of Iceland, who died in 1193, was five years later declared to be a Saint by the Icelandic parliament, the Althing. Rome has yet to officially confirm their decision. As a young man, Thorlac went abroad to study in Norway and England—and he returned to Iceland as a bishop, full of crusading zeal for such newfangled ideas as clerical celibacy and a Church financially independent of civil authorities. For a while he was heartily disliked, but, wielding bulls of excommunication like a berserker's battle-ax, he soon achieved his reforms.

Timothy—January 26
PATRON INVOKED AGAINST STOMACHACHE

On this day, the feast of the great Saint Paul's own miraculous conversion, we celebrate the life and death of his longtime companion Timothy. This son of a Greek father and a Jewish mother was instructed in the True Faith by Paul, who personally circumcised the youth, for complicated theological reasons. In an epistle to him, Paul advised his disciple to "use a little wine for thy stomach's sake" (I Timothy 5:23)—hence Our Saint's traditional Patronage of those suffering from digestive problems. In his old age, as bishop of Ephesus, Timothy allegedly took strenuous exception to the lewd dancing in the streets on the feast of the pagan goddess Diana, for which he was beaten to death with sticks by the pagan merrymakers.

Titus—January 26
PATRON OF CRETE; INVOKED AGAINST FREETHINKERS

Paul, at the Council of Jerusalem in the year 49, insisted that his friend, disciple, and personal secretary Titus be allowed to retain his foreskin. He then appointed Titus bishop of Crete, whose natives Paul characterized as "always liars, evil beasts, slow bellies" (Titus 1:12).

Toribio—March 23
PATRON OF LATIN AMERICAN BISHOPS

By 1580, twenty-five years after Pizarro had claimed the land for the Spanish crown, Peru was a mess. Negligent of their duties as emissaries of Christian civilization, the conquistadores were warring among themselves, and enslaving and slaughtering the natives. Toribio Alfonso de Magroveja was a devout, middle-aged layman, chief judge of the Inquisition at Granada, when he was summarily ordained a priest, consecrated a bishop, and dispatched to Lima to straighten things out. His new parish consisted of 18,000 square miles of forests, mountains, Spanish landlords crazy with greed, Spanish soldiers crazy with bloodlust, and Spanish clergy just plain crazy—as well as countless oppressed pagan souls. He personally baptized 500,-000 of the latter, and labored to vitiate the worst excesses of his fellow Europeans. He even—at the risk of being accused of "liberation theology"—attempted to learn the language of the natives.

Triduana—October 8
PATRONESS INVOKED AGAINST DISEASES OF THE EYES

This holy Benedictine abbess accompanied the treasured relics of Saint Andrew (*whom* SEE) to Scotland. The abbey she founded at Restalrig, together with its miraculous well, was destroyed by devout Presbyterians in 1560. She is invoked against eye troubles in honor of an edifying incident from her life—after a local clan chieftain fell in love with her because of her beautiful eyes, Our Saint plucked out the offending organs and sent them to him on a plate.

Tropez—December 29
PATRON OF CHILDREN; INVOKED AGAINST GOUT

The notoriously decadent Mediterranean resort city of Saint-Tropez was named for Trophimus, the legendary first bishop of Arles. The medieval French took great pains to demonstrate that they were Europe's first Christian nation, brought to the True Faith by the missionary labors of Jesus' own disciples (SEE Lazarus, Mary Magdalene, etc.). Tropez, they maintained, was an Ephesian gentile, the convert and friend of Saint Paul mentioned in Acts 20:4.

Tryphena—January 31
PATRONESS OF NURSING MOTHERS

In the town of Czyicus on the Hellespont, this virtuous Christian matron, the mother of a newborn infant, had the child torn from her arms and was martyred publicly in the arena, cheerfully suffering unspeakable torments before being gored to death by a wild bull. On the spot where she fell, a miraculous fountain of milk gushed up.

Tychon—June 16
PATRON OF VINTNERS; INVOKED AGAINST INSECTS

A bishop on Cyprus around 450, Tychon is revered there as "Tikhon the Wonderworker" for his efforts at suppressing the local cult of Aphrodite. A poor man, he is said to have once planted a dead vine discarded by a neighbor in his own barren vineyard and prayed earnestly over it, thereby achieving a miraculously early vintage. To this day his feast is celebrated on Cyprus with the ceremonial drinking of a singularly nasty beverage made from unripe grapes.

Ubald—May 16
PATRON INVOKED AGAINST DOG BITES AND RABIES

Born in 1100, this bishop of Gubbio (Italy) talked the ferocious Emperor Frederick Barbarossa out of sacking the town, which was much appreciated by his flock. Ubald was strongly opposed to the marriage of priests, banning the practice in his diocese and refusing personally to "pollute himself with the pleasures of women." We may assume that the many expert exorcisms he performed account for his effectiveness when invoked against dog bites—in his day, no nice distinctions were made between hydrophobia and demonic possession.

Ulfrid—January 18

An eleventh-century English missionary to the idolatrous Scandinavians, Ulfrid was inspired in his zeal to take an ax to a statue of the god Thor, and was immediately lynched by a mob of angry Swedes.

Ulric—July 4
PATRON INVOKED AGAINST DIFFICULT BIRTHS, DIZZINESS, MICE, AND MOLES

Ulric was the first Saint officially declared by papal canonization (in 993). Thenceforth, the power of "making Saints" was the pope's alone. A Swiss bishop, Ulric made a practice of visiting a hospital every afternoon and washing the feet of twelve paupers. He argued against clerical celibacy on the basis of the Bible and common sense, accusing some prelates of "pressing the breasts of Scripture to yield blood, not milk." He himself shunned female company, however, saying, "Take away the fuel and you take away the fire." He was justly accused of nepotism for attempting to have his nephew succeed him in office, but Our Saint repented before his death. His pastoral cross was used to heal those bitten by mad dogs, and pregnant women drank from his chalice to obtain easy labor. The earth in which Ulric is buried (at Augsburg) is a powerful rodent repellent, and has often been carried off for that purpose.

Uncumber—July 20
PATRONESS INVOKED AGAINST MEN

She was named Wilgefortis ("strong virgin"), and was one of the septuplet daughters of the cruel pagan king of Portugal. He wished her to marry his ally, the king of Sicily, despite her vow of chastity. But her fervent prayers to become unattractive were answered when she sprouted, overnight, a full beard and mustache. Her irate father had her crucified, and from the cross she promised to all who invoked her aid that she would free them from male encumbrances—hence her name in English, "Uncumber." The custom of unhappy British brides leaving sacks of oats at her shrines was roundly denounced by Saint Thomas More (*whom* SEE). The oats were intended to inspire horses to carry their riders, cruel or troublesome husbands all, to the Devil. The most famous depiction of Our Saint, at Lucca—a bearded figure in regal robes on a cross—is believed by some art historians to be merely a figure of Christ. Yet there is no denying that a minstrel who prayed to her at that very crucifix was rewarded by the Saint with the gift of her silver foot.

Urban of Langres—April 12
PATRON OF BARREL MAKERS AND VINTNERS; INVOKED AGAINST BLIGHT AND FROST

The ancient cathedral city of Langres in Burgundy is not far from the great wine-producing areas of the Côte-d'Or and Champagne, but it is further to the north and east, and its vineyards are threatened by cold Swiss weather. The protection of Urban, a popular fourth-century bishop, is still annually invoked by everyone engaged in the wine industry of the Haute-Marne district.

Ursula—October 21
PATRONESS OF ORPHANS, SCHOOLGIRLS, TAILORS, TEACHERS, AND UNIVERSITIES; INVOKED AGAINST PLAGUE

A cryptic inscription on a basilica at Cologne gave rise to the story of the martyrdom of Ursula and her 11,000 maidens. According to

The Golden Legend, she was a famously beautiful British (that is to say, Breton) princess engaged against her will to marry a pagan prince of England. Ursula sought to prevent or at least delay the nuptials by insisting that ten English virgins, each accompanied by a thousand chaste handmaids, convert to Christianity and join her on a pilgrimage to Rome. To her astonishment, the prince agreed. Once this holy sorority was gathered and aboard ship, an Angel descended to act as pilot. In one day they had sailed as far as Cologne (where the Angel secretly informed Ursula she would be martyred on the return voyage), and on the second day they reached the Eternal City. There they were warmly greeted by Pope Ciriacus. Ursula told the pontiff of their impending martydom, and His Holiness decided to join them on the return voyage. Because of this act of impetuosity (says the author) his name was stricken from the official list of popes. The company was made complete by the sudden arrival of Ursula's English fiancé, newly baptized and eager to die for his Faith. Sure enough, when their vessel docked at Cologne, the city was under siege by the Huns. The pope, the prince, and all 11,000 virgins joyously disembarked, and were methodically slaughtered. For the beautiful Ursula, however, the Hun chieftain had other plans. When the Saint repulsed his odious advances, he shot her with an arrow. The literal ("historical") truth of this tale was long doubted—*The Golden Legend* itself dated the events as either 258 or 452. But in 1155 many thousands of bones were unearthed on the site of the alleged massacre. They have all since become highly efficacious relics. Because of the excellent care she took of the young women placed in her charge, Ursula is the traditional patroness of parochial school girls and their devoted teachers (SEE Saint Angela Merici).

Ursus of Aosta—April 13
PATRON INVOKED AGAINST FAINTNESS AND KIDNEY DISEASE

When Ursus became a Christian, this Sicilian native was forced to flee the wrath of his pagan gangster father. He journeyed north to Ravenna, where he became bishop in 378, and did much to revive the local celebrations of Saints' feast days.

Valentine—February 14
PATRON OF LOVERS

The martyrdoms of three different Saints named Valentine are celebrated on this day; in various Roman churches eight complete bodies (and one head) of Valentine are venerated. One of these, a priest and/or physician beheaded in 269, is traditionally invoked against blindness and epilepsy. The association of this date with courtship may arise from the mid-February pagan fertility feast of Lupercalia, and/or from the medieval belief that the birds chose their mates on this day. "Valentines" were originally cards boys drew by lot, inscribed with the names of girls to be courted. An attempt to improve this custom by substituting the names of Saints to be emulated was once made, without much success, by Saint Francis de Sales (*whom* SEE).

Valerian—December 15
PATRON INVOKED AGAINST EXPOSURE AND SNOWSTORMS

It is somewhat ironic that the Saint traditionally invoked against the vicissitudes of winter was African. Valerian was the eighty-year-old bishop of Tunis (mid-fifth century) who defied Hunneric, king of the Vandals, by refusing to surrender the precious treasures of his church. The punishment he endured was exile—*within* his own city. The old clergyman was evicted from his home and obliged to wander the streets—to offer him shelter, food, or care was forbidden. And in the streets, on a winter night, he died.

Venantius—May 18
PATRON OF LEAPING; INVOKED AGAINST DANGER FROM FALLING

The story of this interesting early martyr has been redeemed from obscurity by Maurice Walsh, editor of *Butler's Lives of the Patron Saints*

(1990). Apparently Venantius not only endured—and survived—the usual tortures of scourging, burning, beating, and being fed to wild beasts . . . but was also thrown from a cliff (or off the city walls; accounts vary), only to bounce up, praising the Lord until his head was cut off.

Venerius—September 13

PATRON OF LIGHTHOUSE KEEPERS

Venerius left the monastery seeking a life of greater austerity and became a hermit on the Italian isle of Tino. After his death in the year 600, a strong cult sprang up around him as his body was moved from place to place. In 1962, Pope John XXIII declared Venerius the Patron of lighthouse keepers "because the radiance of his life shone out."

Verana—September 1

PATRONESS OF MILLERS

Until the Reformation, this hermit-maiden was much venerated by millers among the Alpine Swiss in the region of Saint-Moritz. The city itself is named in honor of Saint Maurice (*whom* SEE), the martyred leader of the Theban Legion. Verana was a cousin of Maurice's fellow officer Saint Victor (*whom* SEE). She traveled to Agaunum, as the Romans called the town where the massacre took place, hoping to gather holy relics of her relative. She took up residence in a mountain hermitage, and undertook to care for the local peasants. Her concern apparently extended to their personal hygiene, for her emblems in art are a basin and a brush.

Veronica—July 12

PATRONESS OF LAUNDRESSES

In Catholic tradition, Veronica is the middle-aged woman who took pity on Christ and wiped His bloody and perspiring brow when He was on the way to His crucifixion. Our Lord left the imprint of His Face on her handkerchief, which important relic is known as the "Sudarium," or sweat cloth. St. Peter's in Rome claims possession of this cloth, which bears the true image, or *"vera icon"*—hence her name. Veronica did not assume an important role in the story of the Passion until the fourth century, when her good deed was immortal-

ized as the fourth Station of the Cross. The Greeks call her "Berinike" and identify her as the woman cured by Christ in the Gospels of a mysterious "issue of blood." Her veil or handkerchief—sometimes called the "vernicle"—has had, like the Holy Grail and the Shroud of Turin, a long and miraculous history. From time to time it glows with a supernatural light, and the Holy Face printed on it assumes a tinge of lifelike color. In its owner's honor, the pious Spaniards have named the bullfighting pass in which the toreador draws his cape across the bull's face a "veronica."

Veronica Giuliani—July 9

When her dying mother assigned each of her five children a wound of Christ, Veronica received the one in His side, indicating to her that her heart was one with Christ's. An irritable child and adolescent, she started having heart pains, which she carefully diagrammed. After her death in 1727, an autopsy revealed the marks of incisions on her heart that corresponded to her diagram. In the convent, Veronica was favored with visions, ecstasies, the marriage ring of Christ (this time it was adorned with a raised, reddish stone), and finally, one Good Friday, the Stigmata. The bishop (who had earlier predicted her Sainthood) had her strictly monitored. Her hands were tightly wrapped, and she was even denied Holy Communion. After her phenomena were declared genuine, she rose to become mistress of her convent, where she improved the water supply by installing pipes. She resented those who did not share her enthusiasm for strict religious disciplines until she had a vision in which she saw her heart—and it was made of steel. She wrote a forty-four-volume autobiography, detailing her mystical experiences. Her emblem, not surprisingly, is a heart.

Victor—October 10
PATRON OF SOLDIERS

In hagiographic circles, there remains some understandable confusion about this soldier-Saint Victor and the soldier-Saints Maurice and

Victor of Marseilles (*both of whom* SEE). Perhaps they were all one person. Perhaps he was black. In some versions of the legend of the Theban Legion, *this* Saint Victor, a pagan, was delayed en route, and arrived to discover his fellow 6,659 legionaries in the process of being slaughtered for their Faith. Moved by a combination of the Holy Spirit and esprit de corps, he joined them.

Victor of Marseilles—July 21
PATRON INVOKED AGAINST FOOT TROUBLE AND LIGHTNING

A third-century Christian soldier in the Roman army, Victor was captured and subjected to a variety of tortures, including being fed poisoned meat while hanging in chains, and then spending three days in a furnace. He was consoled by Christ and a host of Angels who visited him in his cell, filling it with light. When asked to worship at a pagan shrine, Victor defiantly kicked over the idols, for which crime the heretic governor ordered his foot chopped off. He was finally decapitated and thrown into the sea. In art he is, for some reason, shown with a windmill. His shrine at Marseilles has enjoyed a long period of popularity as a pilgrimage center.

Vincent de Paul—September 27
PATRON OF CHARITABLE SOCIETIES, HOSPITAL WORKERS, MADAGASCAR, AND PRISONERS

The son of a swineherd, Vincent was ordained a priest in the year 1600, when he was just nineteen. In his heady early years in Paris, he was unjustly accused of theft by his roommate. The story that he was then captured by African pirates and lived in Tunisia for some years is no longer believed. Upon his return, he landed a cushy job as chaplain to a noble family at Folleville, and began to visit the impoverished peasants of the countryside. Realizing the deplorable physical and moral state of the poor (he heard some shocking confessions), he founded the Vincentians, an order of priests dedicated to ministering to the oppressed. With the help of Saint Louise de Marillac (*whom* SEE), he next established the Sisters of Charity. The compassion of "Monsieur Vincent" was legendary—he set up a sort of welfare system for the French proletariat; like their founder, the Vincentians were devoted to invalids, orphans, war victims, convicts, and galley slaves. Vincent himself once traded places with a convict in the galleys, having heard the man despair of ever again seeing his wife and children. The Saint slaved for weeks until his followers bought his freedom; his ankles were permanently swollen from the shackles he had worn. Vincent had a gift for persuading the wealthy, especially women, to be charitable. He was an influential advisor to Queen Anne of Austria, but could never convince her to fire the infamous Cardinal Mazarin (who enjoyed ridiculing Vincent's homely face and frumpy dress).

Vincent Ferrer—April 5
PATRON OF BUILDERS

A Spaniard born in Valencia of noble parents around 1350, Vincent joined the Dominican Order to study philosophy, but in a heavenly vision he was implored by Saint Dominic and Saint Francis (*both of whom* SEE)—a pair of Saints who hardly ever agreed about anything— to employ his gift of eloquence to preach penance and salvation. It was his custom to prepare his sermons by staring for hours at a crucifix and meditating on Christ's wounds; when he hit the pulpit his remarkable good looks and powerful baritone voice often caused his female listeners to swoon. His career, as he traveled throughout all of western Europe, was not uneventful. Although he spoke only Spanish, his words were understood by all nations, and he converted 8,000 Moors and 25,000 Jews, including a rabbi who later became a bishop. Once an audience doubted Vincent's somewhat grandiose claim to be "the Angel of Judgment," and Our Saint was obliged to halt a passing funeral cortege and raise the recently deceased from the dead to corroborate his testimony. On another occasion, his statement that Judas Iscariot had repented his betrayal of Christ and was now in Heaven resulted in Vincent's being placed on the Inquisition's blacklist—but his good friend the antipope Benedict XIII, one of three contending claimants to the Chair of Peter at the time—had Vincent's Inquisition dossier burned. Vincent, somewhat ungratefully, then withdrew his support for Benedict's papacy, which forced Benedict to resign—thus bringing about (God's ways are not our ways) the reunification of Holy Mother Church.

Vincent of Saragossa—January 22
PATRON OF ROOFERS, SCHOOLGIRLS, VINEGAR MAKERS, AND VINTNERS

Still a boy when he was ordained a deacon by Bishop Valerius, Vincent was arrested with his mentor in the year 300, by order of Dacian, the cruel Roman governor of Spain. Because the elderly bishop stammered, it was up to young Vincent to argue their case in court, and he was fearless and forthright in declaring his readiness to suffer for the Faith. Impressed, Dacian dismissed all charges against Valerius, but  prescribed a course of tortures for Vincent unique in the gory annals of martyrdom. (Both the poet Prudentius and Saint Augustine [*whom* SEE] have described them in wonderful detail.) He was stretched on the rack, and torn with iron hooks. He was forced upon a bed of iron spikes set over a fire, and salt was rubbed into his wounds. He was finally rolled in broken pottery, then locked up and left to starve. (The faithful would visit his cell, and dip cloths in his blood, many of which precious relics are still venerated in Valencia.) Vincent has long been considered the patron of vintners in France because his name begins with *vin*. Really.

Vitalis of Gaza—January 11

In the year 500, this sixty-year-old hermit left his lonely desert cell and traveled to Alexandria with a mission—to save the souls of the innumerable harlots of that sinful city. With the money he earned each day as a laborer, Vitalis would each night buy the company of a fallen woman—and spend the hours until dawn crouched in her room, praying for her. His nightly arrivals at, and daily departures from, houses of ill repute caused a scandal in the Christian community, but the Saint refused to either desist or explain himself—until one angry prude punched him in the head at a whorehouse door, killing him. A weeping (and newly saved) prostitute rushed into the street, bewailing the death of the Saint—and told all to a gathering crowd. Vitalis's funeral was a spectacular event, graced by the presence of many grief-stricken and apparently respectable matrons who, over the years, he had redeemed from lives of shame.

Vitus—June 15

PATRON OF ACTORS, COMEDIANS, DANCERS, AND SICILY; INVOKED AGAINST CHOREA, EPILEPSY, SNAKEBITE, STORMS, WILD ANIMALS, AND OVERSLEEPING

The cult of Vitus is very old, but credible details about his life are few; nor can we be certain of his connection with the debilitating

medical condition of rheumatic chorea
called Saint Vitus's dance. They say that
while still a child in southern Italy (perhaps Sicily), he became a Christian under
the influence of his tutor Modestus and
his nurse Crescentia, two martyrs who
are likewise honored on his feast day. His
father, the pagan senator Hylas, was outraged, and turned the lot over to the
proper authorities for a beneficial scourging. Angels came to dance for them in
prison, causing somewhat of a distrac-
tion, during which the trio escaped and
fled to Rome. There young Vitus exor-

cised an evil spirit from the son of the Emperor Diocletian, for which
good deed he was accused of sorcery and, with his companions, condemned to death. Lions refused to maul them, but immersion in a
cauldron of boiling oil did the trick. At the moment of their deaths, a
tremendous storm destroyed numerous pagan temples. Vitus's relics
were translated to Saxony in the mid-ninth century, and throughout
Germany it was long believed that good health for a year was assured
to anyone who danced before his statue on his feast; perhaps such
dancing to excess became identified with the spasms of one suffering
from chorea. Because a rooster was tossed into the pot with him, it is
among his emblems; Vitus also became known as Patron against
oversleeping.

Vladimir—July 15
PATRON OF RUSSIA

Vladimir was an idolatrous tenth-century prince of Kiev, who had
five wives and three times that number of mistresses when he converted to Christianity. Although he was courted by the Muslims,
their religion held little appeal to him, largely because of his affinity
for wine and pork. Byzantine Christianity and its attendant political
advantages caught the eye of the pagan prince, who loved the ritual
and the fluttery white robes of the deacons (which he mistook for Angels' wings.) His Christian marriage to Ann, sister of the Byzantine
emperor, while hardly a love match, sealed the alliance between their
two empires. The new convert forced the entire city of Kiev—start-

ing with the nobles—to be baptized. Thousands filled the river, while a priest stood on the shore yelling out patronyms, in a mass baptism. His new religion must have had some effect, because Vladimir did step up his almsgiving and reduced the number of robbers sentenced to death.

Walburga—February 25

PATRONESS OF CROPS; INVOKED AGAINST COUGHS, FRENZY, AND THE PLAGUE

An English nun from Dorset and a niece of Saint Boniface of Mainz (*whom* SEE), Walburga joined her uncle and brothers Winebald and Willibald on their mission to heathen Germany. There, at Heidenheim in 761, she established an ecclesiastical precedent, taking charge of an order of monks as well as nuns. Walburga was a Woman of Power, skilled in the practice of medicine and a bit of an herbalist. She once cured a girl possessed of a ravenous appetite by feeding her three ears of grain—with which she is depicted in sacred art. At Eichstätt in Germany, miraculous cures are still ascribed to a fluid flowing from a rock near her relics. Walburga's name underwent a change in northern Germany, becoming Walpurgis, and on the eve of her feast, Walpurgisnacht, witches hold their revels in the Hartz Mountains. Possibly they are confusing our Holy Saint with the Teutonic goddess Walburg, who, coincidentally, also had ears of grain as her emblem.

Walstan—May 30

PATRON OF CATTLE AND FARMERS; INVOKED AGAINST BLINDNESS, FEVER, LAMENESS, AND PALSY

Walstan was a simple farm hand in Norfolk, England, so gracious in his manner that it was rumored he was really a king, come to live piously among the common people. According to his legend, a rich farmer offered to make Walstan his heir; Our Saint demurred, asking rather the gift of two calves. When he died in 1016 praying in a field "for all the sick, and for cattle," those animals brought his body to the church at Bawburgh. On his feast, for centuries, the farmers and laborers of Norfolk used to gather in the church to honor one of their own, a worker with a scythe who had achieved True Holiness; the Reformation put an end to such nonsense.

Walter of Pontnoise—April 8
PATRON OF PRISONERS AND VINTNERS

When Walter came to the defense of a peasant who was locked up in the monastery for some wrongdoing, his fellow monks beat him unmercifully, but later made him abbot anyway. At his investiture he knocked away King Philip I's hand, saying, "It's not from you but from God that I accept governance of this abbey." Nevertheless, he ran away from the abbey several times, only to be retrieved by his fellow monks, until he was forced to remain by order of the pope. Even in extreme old age he would stand all night at prayer and be found unconscious the next morning. Considered sanctimonius by some, his denouncement of married priests saying Mass and the general easy living among the clergy caused a bishop to spit in his face. He died in 1099.

Wenceslaus—September 28
PATRON OF CZECHOSLOVAKIA, BOHEMIA, BREWERS, AND SHEEP

Wenceslaus was taken from his pagan mother, Drahomira ("the disheveled one") and given to his saintly grandmother Ludmila for upbringing. Ludmila urged Wenceslaus to take the throne away from his mother and enforce Christianity, but, in 921, the evil queen had the old lady killed. At the age of twenty, Wenceslaus was recognized as king and set out to enforce his own boorish brand of Christianity. At royal banquets he would pressure guests to recite the Our Father, unmercifully beating those who refused. He was hated by his mother, whom he banished, and by his brother, who wanted to seize control of the kingdom. Wenceslaus, indifferent to the rage at court, pursued his devotion to the Holy Mass, personally making the wine and grinding the wheat to make the wafers for the ceremony. He built churches, did good deeds at night, and worked tirelessly for the conversion of his subjects. To the horror of his enemies, Wenceslaus established relations with the rest of the Christian world, allying his country with Emperor Henry of Germany (who gave him the arm of Saint Vitus as tribute). He ignored warnings of treason, and was murdered by his brother Boleslaus on the feast of Saints Cosmas and Damian, crying, "God forgive thee, brother." His mother, returned from exile, flung herself on the dead body of her son, but quickly fled when she learned Boleslaus wanted her murdered as well. Wenceslaus's relics became the site of a pilgrimage, and his face on coins a

symbol of Czech nationalism. He was unknown in England, a country he never visited, until it was discovered that his name could be
fitted to a traditional melody. He became the subject of a Christmas
carol, "Good King Wenceslaus," and soon, thereby, a folk hero.

Wendel—October 21
PATRON OF PEASANTS AND SHEPHERDS;
INVOKED AGAINST SICKNESS IN CATTLE

In 1417, a great fire in the German city of
Saabrücken was miraculously extinguished
through the intercession of this Saint, who
had died in the vicinity in 607. According to
his legend, Wendel was the son of a Scottish
king, who, because of his excessive piety, was
condemned to herd swine. How he ended up tending sheep in southwest Germany is not known, but he is still venerated there for his
simple sanctity and heavenly veterinary skills.

Werenfrid—August 14
PATRON OF VEGETABLE GARDENS; INVOKED AGAINST GOUT

The Christian Anglo-Saxons were tireless in their attempts to save
the heathens of Holland; seemingly, everyone whose name began
with W became an English missionary to the (all-too-appropriately
named) "Low" countries—e.g., Saints Walburga, Wigbert, Willehad,
Willibald, Willibrord, Wilfrid, Winnebald, Winfrith, Wiro (most of
whom SEE), and Werenfrid. The latter is venerated in the Netherlands,
where he harvested souls and vegetables until his death in the year
760.

Wilfrid of York—October 12

Throughout the seventh century in England, two Catholic theo-
logical/political parties, the Celtic (Irish) and Roman (Saxon), struggled for supremacy. At issue were such weighty topics as the date of
Easter and whether priests should shave their heads in the back or the
front. There was also a lot of real estate at stake. Wilfrid was (the
Saxon) bishop of York, appointed by (the Saxon) King Alcfrid, and
confirmed by Rome, in 663. Over the next forty-six years, Wilfrid was
deposed, traveled to Rome, was vindicated by Pope Agatho, re-

instated, deposed again, imprisoned, and exiled. He traveled again to Rome, and was once more papally vindicated and reinstated to his English episcopate. His death in 709 doubtless came as a great relief to all concerned. For his first posthumous miracle, he cured the arthritis in the hands of the old woman washing his corpse.

William of Fenoli—December 19

The extreme sanctity of the cloistered Carthusian monks of thirteenth-century Lombardy could only be assumed by the local laity—but of Brother William's holiness there was no doubt. His duties obliged him to leave the monastery each week to buy, sell, and trade in the town market. One day while riding home on his mule, Brother William was set upon by a band of brigands. The man of God dismounted, removed the mule's leg, and brandished it as a weapon, which soon put the thieves to flight. He then calmly restored its limb to the animal, and they continued on their way.

Willibrord—November 7
PATRON OF HOLLAND; INVOKED AGAINST CONVULSIONS

Willibrord is, not surprisingly, confused with his brothers Willibald and Winebald—fellow English monks and missionaries. He was born in 658, and was only five when his father, Wilgris, became a hermit and shipped his youngest son off to a monastery. A priest at twenty, Willibrord took twelve companions and went to Friesland, preceding Boniface of Mainz (*whom* SEE), as the first missionary to Germany. When Willibrord was made bishop, the Sicilian pope, Sergius I, unable to pronounce his name, changed it to Clement. After baptizing the ubiquitous Charles Martel, Willibrord took his work to Holland and Denmark, where he earned the enmity of the pagan king, Rodbod. Rodbod banished the Saint and burned his churches, only to have Willibrord retaliate by desecrating sacred cows and publicly baptizing Danes in a loud voice. The Saint almost succeeded, finally, in converting his old enemy, but when Rodbod stepped into his baptismal waters he asked Our Saint where his own royal Danish ancestors were. Told "in Hell," Rodbod replied that he would rather be in Hell "with a pack of heroes than in Heaven with a pack of beggars." (Ironically, his grandson and namesake Saint Rodbod succeeded Willibrord as bishop of Utrecht.) Willibrord patterned his monastery on that at Canterbury, thereby extending England's spiritual influence on the Continent. His shrine at Luxembourg became famous because clergy and pilgrims there perform a sacred, early-day conga-line dance on his feast—taking three steps forward and two steps back. The procession jumps and dances until it circles Willibrord's tomb, and then snakes out of the church. This queer ritual is supposed to help cure everything from convulsions or epilepsy to lumbago. In art, Willibrord is shown with a church in his hand and, because of his ability to multiply wine, a barrel of wine at his feet.

Willigis—February 23
PATRON OF CARTERS

Willigis was born in 1011, of peasant stock—his father drove a cart. When he became archbishop of Mainz, he asked that the emblem on his coat of arms be a simple cartwheel (and a cartwheel is the emblem of the city of Mainz today). Willigis was a statesman, the chaplain to Emperor Otto II, and regent of the boy-emperor Otto III, upon whose death Our Saint contrived to have Saint Henry of Bavaria (*whom* SEE) achieve the imperial throne. Henry was his cousin.

Wiro—May 8
PATRON OF HOLLAND

Missionary bishops from Northumbria, England, Wiro and his companion, Plechelm, devoted themselves to Christianizing the pagan Frisians and building churches among them in the early eighth century. They were encouraged by King Pepin of the Franks, who desired to include the people of the Low Countries in his Holy Empire; Wiro himself was Pepin's favorite confessor.

Wolfgang—October 31
PATRON OF CARPENTERS, SHEPHERDS, AND WOODSMEN; INVOKED AGAINST STOMACH TROUBLE AND WOLVES

Wolfgang was a figure of some importance in the Holy Roman (German) Empire of the tenth century. He founded schools, reformed disorderly nunneries, and served as tutor to Emperor (and Saint) Henry II (*whom* SEE). His mission to bring the Gospel to the savage Magyars of Pannonia (Hungary) was less than fruitful, but as bishop of Regensburg he was renowned as both just and generous. All his life he had wished to be a simple hermit, and as such he died, in the year 994.

Wolfhard—April 30
PATRON OF SADDLERS; INVOKED AGAINST GALLSTONES

Wolfhard was a German merchant and saddler who moved to Verona in 1096, gave everything he earned to the poor, and was revered as a living Saint. This made him uncomfortable, so he went to live as a hermit on the river Adige until a boatman encouraged him to join a local monastery. For the remainder of his life, he kept a stone coffin beside him in his cell. Wolfhard once stated that he wished to be buried under a porch, so that his grave would be trampled underfoot.

Woolos—March 29

His real name was Gwynllyw, but everyone called him Woolos. He was a fiery Celtic chieftain in fifth-century Wales, who enlisted (they say) the aid of King Arthur himself in the raid he staged to kidnap his true love, Gladys, from her fierce Celtic clan. For years, Woolos and Gladys lived a less-than-edifying life, devoted to banditry and random acts of violence, until the birth of their son Saint Cadoc (*whom* SEE). Under the relentless influence of his piety, they abandoned first their criminal life-style and, in the end, each other, becoming holy hermits.

Zeno—April 12
PATRON OF ANGLERS

Zeno, born in Africa, moved to Verona, where he was made bishop, with leisure to indulge his passion for fishing in the river Adige. Two hundred years after his death, when this river overflowed its banks, people came to the church of St. Zeno for refuge. The water, rising many feet, didn't enter the church, even though the doors and windows were open: "It was as though the thin liquid element had been transformed into a solid wall." While living Zeno saved the city of Pistoria (now Pistoia) from destruction by flood by making a canal between the Arno and Ombrone rivers. During his lifetime he campaigned against the abuses of love feasts and the practice of loud lamenting during funeral Masses. In art, he is shown with a fish hanging from his bishop's crozier.

Zita—April 27
PATRONESS OF HOUSEMAIDS AND DOMESTIC SERVANTS; INVOKED IN THE SEARCH FOR LOST KEYS

This thirteenth-century domestic servant worked for two generations of the wealthy Fatinelli family in Italy, who were often irritated by her Saintly ways. Once when the senior Fatinelli correctly suspected she had bread in her apron that she intended for beggars, his inspection revealed only a bounty of flowers. Innocent and somewhat dotty, she received the constant ministrations of Angels: when she was caught in the rain, Angels kept her dry with their wings, and when Zita gave her master's fur cloak to a beggar, an Angel brought it to her door the following day. (In Lucca, that door is still called "the Angel's door.") They helped her with her household chores as well, doing her housework and baking bread when she was in ecstasy. Even the Blessed Virgin Mary came to her assistance to revive her and lead her home when she became lost after a long pilgrimage. The night she died, a bright star shone from her attic window illuminating all of Lucca, and when her coffin was opened in 1446, 1581, and 1652, her body was found to have remained incorrupt. Zita's vast iconography includes a rosary, keys, bread/flowers in an apron, praying at a well, giving alms to the poor, and a basket of fruit.

Zoe—May 2

She and her husband, Hesperus, were slaves and Christians—although not especially devout ones. Their two young sons, however, were zealous believers, and refused to partake in their master Catullus's pagan household rituals. The lads were cruelly tortured before their parents' eyes, which inspired Zoe and Hesperus to remain steadfast. Zoe was hanged from a tree by her hair—after which the whole family was roasted. Together the family received their heavenly crowns on this day in the year 135.

PART II

Calendar of Saints

JANUARY

1   Clarus (invoked against myopia)
2   Adelard (of gardeners)
    Basil the Great (of hospital administrators, Russia)
    Macarius (of pastry cooks)
3   Geneviève (of Paris; invoked against drought, fever, floods, plague)
4   Pharaildis (invoked against childhood illness)
5   Simeon Stylites (of shepherds)
6   Balthazar, Caspar, and Melchior (of travelers)
    Macra (invoked against breast disease)
7   Aldric (invoked against asthma)
    Raymond of Peñafort (of lawyers)
    Reinhold (of stone masons)
8   Amalburga (invoked against bruises)
    Gudula (of Brussels; invoked against toothache)
9   Basilissa (invoked against breast-feeding problems, chilblains)
10 Agatho
11 Vitalis of Gaza
12 Allan
    Benet Biscop (of architects, glass workers, musicians, painters)
13 Hilary of Poitiers (of backward children, lawyers; invoked against
        insanity, snakebite)
14 Felix of Nola (invoked against perjury)
    Sava (of Serbia)
15 Maurus (invoked against colds)
    Paul the Hermit (of weavers)
16 Priscilla (of widows)
17 Anthony the Great (of basket weavers, brush makers, butchers, do-
        mestic animals, grave diggers, herdsmen, swine; invoked against
        eczema, ergotism)
    Devota (of Corsica, Monaco)
18 Ulfrid
19 Canute IV (of Denmark)
    Henry of Uppsala (of Finland)
    Fillian (invoked against insanity)

20 Fabian (of lead founders, potters)
    Sebastian (of archers, athletes, hardware, lace makers, the military, pin makers, potters, police officers; invoked against plague)
21 Agnes (of Girl Scouts, virgins)
22 Vincent of Saragossa (of roofers, schoolgirls, vinegar makers, vintners)
23 Emerentiana (invoked against stomachache)
24 Francis de Sales (of editors, journalists, writers; invoked against deafness)
25 Dwyn (of lovers; invoked against sickness in animals)
26 Paula (of widows)
    Timothy (invoked against stomachache)
    Titus (of Crete; invoked against freethinking)
27 Angela Merici
28 Thomas Aquinas (of pencil makers, students, theologians)
29 Gildas the Wise (invoked against dog bites, rabies)
30 Adelelm (of menservants)
    Aldegund (invoked against cancer, childhood illness, fever, eye disease, sudden death, wounds)
    Bathild (of children)
    Martina (of nursing mothers)
31 John Bosco (of apprentices, editors)
    Tryphena (of nursing mothers)

FEBRUARY

1 Brigid (of dairy maids, fugitives, Ireland, newborns, New Zealand, nuns, poultry raisers)
   Severus (of hatters, milliners)
2 Joan de Lestonnac
3 Anskar (of Denmark, Iceland, Norway)
   Blaise (of sick cattle, wool combers; invoked against throat disease, wild animals)
4 Andrew Corsini (invoked against quarrels, sudden death)
   John de Brito (of Portugal)
5 Agatha (of bell makers, bell ringers, jewelers, nurses, wet nurses; invoked against breast disease, fire, volcanos)
6 Amand (of brewers, hotel workers, wine and beer merchants)
   Dorothy (of brides, florists, gardeners, newlyweds; against fire, lightning, thieves)
   Peter Baptist (of Japan)
7 Moses (of Saracens)
8 Jerome Emiliani (of orphans)
   Meingold (of bakers, bankers, millers, miners)

9   Apollonia (of dentists; invoked against toothache)
10   Scholastica (for rain; of nuns; invoked against convulsions in children)
11   Caedmon (of poets)
12   Julian the Hospitaler (of boatmen, circus performers, innkeepers, travelers)
13   Agabus (of fortune-tellers)
     Modomnoc (of bees)
14   Cyril and Methodius (of Czechoslovakia, Europe, the Slavs)
     Valentine (of lovers)
15   Euseus (of shoemakers)
     Sigfrid (of Sweden)
16   Juliana
17   Fintan
18   Fra Angelico (of artists)
19   Conrad (invoked against famine, hernia)
20   Eleutheris of Tournai
21   Peter Damian (invoked against headache)
22   Margaret of Cortona (of fallen women)
23   Mildburga (of birds)
     Willigis (of carters)
24   Prix
25   Walburga (of crops; invoked against coughs, frenzy, plague)
26   Porphyry
27   Gabriel Possenti (of college students)
     Galmier (of locksmiths)
28   Romanus (invoked against drowning, insanity)
29   Oswald of Worcester

MARCH

1   David (of poets, Wales)
     Swithbert (invoked against angina)
2   Agnes of Bohemia
3   Cunegund (of Lithuania, Luxembourg)
     Guignolé (invoked against impotence, infertility)
4   Casimir (of Lithuania, Poland; invoked against plague)
5   Phocas of Antioch (invoked against snakebite)
     Piran (of miners)
6   Fridolin (of optometrists)
7   Drausius (of champions)
     Felicity (of mothers; invoked against infertility)
8   John of God (of booksellers, hospitals, nurses, printers; invoked against alcoholism, heart disease)

9   Catherine of Bologna (of artists)
    Dominic Savio (of choirboys, juvenile delinquents)
    Frances of Rome (of motorists, widows)
10 Kessog (of Scotland)
11 Eulogius of Córdova (of carpenters, coppersmiths)
12 Fina
13 Ansovinus (of harvests)
14 Lubin (invoked against rheumatism)
15 Louise de Marillac (of orphans, social workers, widows)
    Matrona (invoked against dysentery)
16 Herbert (for rain)
17 Gertrude of Nivelles (of cats, gardeners, travelers; invoked against
        mice)
    Joseph of Arimathaea (of cemetery keepers, pallbearers, tin miners)
    Patrick (of Ireland, Nigeria; invoked against snakes)
18 Edward the Martyr
19 Joseph (of Austria, Belgium, Canada, carpenters, fathers, house
        hunting, Mexico, Peru, Vietnam, workers; for a happy death; in-
        voked against communism, doubt)
20 Cuthbert (of sailors)
21 Enda
22 Nicholas von Flüe (of Switzerland)
23 Toribio (of Latin American bishops)
24 Catherine of Sweden (invoked against abortion, miscarriage)
    Gabriel (of childbirth, diplomats, messengers, postal workers,
        stamp collectors, telephone workers)
25 Dismas (of criminals, thieves, undertakers)
26 Ludger (of Saxons)
27 Alkelda (invoked against eye disease)
28 Gontran
29 Woolos
30 John Climacus
31 Balbina (invoked against diseases of the lymph glands, scrofula)

APRIL

1   Catherine of Palma
2   Francis of Paolo (of naval officers, sailors, seafarers)
    Urban of Langres (of barrel makers, drunkards, vintners; invoked
        against blight, frost)
3   Irene (of peace)
    Richard (of coachmen)
4   Benedict the Black (of African Americans)

5   Vincent Ferrer (of builders)
6   Notker Balbulus (invoked against stammering)
7   John-Baptist de la Salle (of teachers)
8   Walter of Pontnoise (of prisoners, vintners)
9   Casilda (invoked against bad luck, sterility)
10 Hedda
11 Gemma Galgani (of hospital pharmacists)
    Godberta (invoked against drought, plague)
    Stanislaus (of Poland)
12 Zeno (of anglers)
13 Ursus of Aosta (invoked against faintness, kidney disease)
14 Lydwina (of skaters)
    Peter Gonzalez (of sailors)
15 Hunna (of laundresses)
16 Benedict Labre (of beggars, the homeless, pilgrims)
    Bernadette (of shepherds)
    Magnus of Orkney (of fishmongers, Norway)
    Drogo (of coffeehouse owners, shepherds; invoked against hernia,
        gravel in the urine)
17 Rudolph of Berne
18 Aya (against lawsuits)
19 Expiditus (of emergencies; invoked against procrastination)
20 Peter Martyr (of Inquisitors)
21 Bueno (invoked against cattle diseases)
22 Theodore of Sykeon (for/against rain)
23 Adalbert (of Prussia)
    George (of Boy Scouts, cavalry, England, equestrians, farmers,
        horses, Portugal; invoked against leprosy, syphilis)
24 Fidelis
25 Mark (of cattle breeders, Egypt, notaries; invoked against fly
        bites)
26 Marcellinus
27 Zita (of housemaids, servants; invoked in the search for lost keys)
28 Peter Mary Chanel (of Oceania)
29 Catherine of Siena (of Italy; invoked against fire)
30 Adjutor (of swimmers, yachtsmen; invoked against drowning)
    Wolfhard (of saddlers; invoked against gallstones)

MAY

1   Brioc (of purse makers)
    Marculf (invoked against scrofula)
    Peregrine Laziosi (against cancer)

2 Zoe
3 James the Lesser (of the dying, hatters, Uruguay)
  Philip (of Luxembourg, Uruguay)
  Philip of Zell (of babies)
4 Florian (of Austria, brewers, chimney sweeps, fire fighters, Poland,
      soap boilers; against fire, flood)
5 Avertine (invoked against dizziness)
  Judith (of Prussia)
6 Ava (of children learning to walk)
7 Domitian (invoked against fever)
  John of Beverley
8 Wiro (of Holland)
9 Pachomius
10 Cathal (invoked against drought, hernia, storms)
   Job (invoked against depression, ulcers)
   Solangia (of children, shepherds; for/against rain)
11 Gengulf (invoked against unhappy marriage)
12 Francis Patrizi (of reconciliations)
   Pancras (of children, oaths, treaties)
   Tammany (of democracy)
13 Imelda (of first communicants)
   Servais (invoked against foot troubles, rats, vermin)
14 Matthias (invoked against alcoholism)
15 Dymphna (of asylums, mental-health workers; invoked against epi-
       lepsy, insanity, sleepwalking)
   Hallvard (of Oslo, and in defense of innocence)
   Isidore (of farmers, farm workers, ranchers)
16 Brendan (of Ireland, sailors)
   Honoratus (of bakers, millers)
   John of Nepomuk (of Bohemia, bridges, bridge builders,
       Czechoslovakia; invoked against detraction)
   Simon Stock (of tanners)
   Ubald (invoked against dog bites, rabies)
17 Madern (invoked against lameness)
   Pascal Babylon (of shepherds)
18 Eric IX (of Sweden)
   Theodotus (of innkeepers)
   Venantius (of leaping; invoked against danger from falling)
19 Celestine V (of bookbinders)
   Dunstan (of armorers, blacksmiths, goldsmiths, jewelers,
       locksmiths)
   Ivo of Kermartin (of Brittany, judges, lawyers, notaries, orphans)
   Pudentiana (of the Philippines)

20   Bernardino of Siena (of advertising, public relations; invoked against
        hoarseness)
     Ethelbert (invoked against thieves)
21   Andrew Bobola
22   Julia (of Corsica, Portugal)
     Rita (of desperate cases; invoked against bleeding, infertility,
        loneliness, tumors, unhappy marriage)
23   Didier (invoked against perjury)
24   Sara (of Gypsies)
25   Bede (of scholars)
26   Philip Neri (of Rome)
27   Augustine of Canterbury (of England)
28   Bernard of Montjoux (of mountain climbers, skiers)
29   Bona (of flight attendants)
30   Ferdinand (of engineers, governors, magistrates, rulers)
     Joan of Arc (of France, the military)
     Walstan (of farmers)
31   Petronilla (invoked against ague)

JUNE

 1   Gwen (of infants, nursing mothers; invoked against cradle cap)
     Justin (of philosophers)
     Theobald of Alba (of porters, shoemakers)
 2   Blandina (of girls)
     Elmo (of childbirth, sailors; invoked against seasickness,
        stomachache)
 3   Charles Lwanga (of young Africans)
     Kevin (of Ireland)
     Morand (of vintners)
 4   Quirinus (invoked against earache, gout, hemorrhoids)
 5   Boniface of Mainz (of brewers, Germany, Prussia)
     James Salomonelli (invoked against cancer)
 6   Claude (of linseed growers, toy makers; invoked against bad luck,
        twitching)
     Philip the Deacon (of deacons)
 7   Meriadoc (invoked against deafness)
 8   Médard (of harvests; invoked against rain, toothache)
 9   Columba (of Ireland, poets)
     Ephraem (of Syria)
10   Olive of Palermo
11   Barnabus (of Cyprus, harvests)
12   Onuphrius (of weavers)
13   Antony of Padua (of harvests, the poor, Portugal, spinsters; invoked
        against infertility; to find lost objects)

14   Dogmael (of babies learning to walk)
15   Alice
     Vitus (of comedians, dancers, Sicily; invoked against chorea, epilepsy, lightning, snakebite, oversleeping, wild animals)
16   Benno (of weavers)
     Cyricus (of children)
     John-Francis Regis (of illegitimate children, lace makers, marriage, social workers)
     Tychon (of vintners; invoked against insects)
17   Harvey (invoked against blindness, demons, foxes, wolves)
18   Alena (invoked against eye disease, toothache)
19   Boniface of Querfurt (of Prussia)
     Gervase and Protase (of haymakers; invoked against rain)
20   Osana of Mantua (of schoolgirls)
21   Alban (of refugees)
     Albinus of Mainz (invoked against gallstones, kidney disease, sore throat)
     Aloysius Gonzaga (of young men)
     Leufredus (invoked against flies)
     Méen (invoked against skin diseases)
22   Acacius (invoked against headache)
     Thomas More (of civil servants, lawyers)
     Nicetas (of Romania)
23   Agrippina (invoked against evil spirits, leprosy, thunder)
     Audrey (invoked against neck pain, throat disease)
     Joseph Cafasso (of prisoners)
24   John the Baptist (of auto routes, candlemakers, farriers, health spas, Jordan, leather workers, Quebec, road workers, wool workers)
25   Eurosia (of crops; invoked against storms)
     Molaug (invoked against headache, insanity)
26   Pelayo
27   Lazlo (of Hungary)
28   Basildes (of prison guards)
29   Paul (of Greece, Malta, rope makers, tentmakers, upholsterers)
     Peter (of boatwrights, clock makers, fishermen, net makers; invoked against fever, foot trouble, wolves)
30   Theobald of Provins (of charcoal burners)

July

1   Serf (of the Orkneys)
2   Processus and Martinian (of prison guards; invoked against demonic possession, infirmity, perjury)
3   Thomas (of architects, builders, carpenters, construction workers,

the East Indies, geometricians, India, masons, Pakistan, surveyors; invoked against blindness, doubt)

4   Elizabeth of Portugal (of Portugal)

     Ulric (invoked against difficult birth, dizziness, mice, moles)

5   Athanasius of Athos

6   Fermin (of Pamploma)

     Goar (of potters; invoked against whirlpools)

     Godeleva (of Flanders, for/against rain; invoked against throat disease)

     Maria Goretti (of teenage girls)

7   Palladius

8   Kilian (of Austria, whitewashers)

9   Veronica Giuliani

10   Seven Brothers

11   Benedict (of of architects, coppersmiths, the dying, Europe, farm workers, monks, spelunkers, servants who break things; invoked against gallstones, kidney disease, poison, witchcraft)

12   John Gualbert (of foresters, park keepers)

     Veronica (of laundresses)

13   Henry the Emperor (of Finland)

14   Camillus de Lellis (of hospitals, nurses, the sick; invoked against compulsive gambling)

     Procopius (of Czechoslovakia)

15   Swithin (for/against rain)

     Vladimir (of Russia)

16   Helier (of Jersey)

17   Alexis (of beggars)

18   Arnulf of Metz (of millers, music; to find lost articles)

     Theneva (of Glasgow)

19   Justina and Rufina (of potters, Seville)

20   Elias (invoked against drought, earthquakes)

     Margaret (of childbirth)

     Uncumber (invoked against men's lust)

21   Victor of Marseilles (invoked against foot trouble)

22   Mary Magdalene (of glovers, hairdressers, fallen women, perfumers)

23   Bridget (of scholars, Sweden)

     Liborius (invoked against gallstones)

24   Boris (of Moscow, Russia)

     Christina the Astonishing (of psychiatrists)

25   James the Greater (of furriers, Guatemala, Spain, Nicaragua, veterinarians; invoked against arthritis)

     Christopher (of bachelors, bus drivers, ferryboat men, police officers, soldiers, skiers, truck drivers, travelers; invoked against nightmares, perils from water, tempests)

26 Anne (of Canada, housewives, cabinetmakers, miners, grandmothers; invoked against infertility)

27 Pantaleon (of Venice, doctors; invoked against consumption)
Seven Sleepers (invoked against insomnia)

28 Samson of Dol

29 Lupus (invoked against stomachache)
Martha (of dieticians, housewives, waitresses)
Olaf (of Norway)

30 Abdon (of barrel makers)

31 Ignatius Loyola (of the military, religious retreats; invoked against scruples)

AUGUST

1 Alphonsus Mary de' Ligouri (of moral theologians)

2 Sidwell (of farmers)

3 Lydia (of cloth dyers)

4 John-Baptist-Marie Vianney, the Curé of Ars (of parish priests)
Sithney (of mad dogs)

5 Addai and Mari (of Iran, Syria)
Afra (of fallen women)

6 Justus and Pastor

7 Albert of Trapani (invoked against demonic possession, earthquakes, fever, jaundice, sterility, stiff neck)
Dometius the Persian (invoked against sciatica)

8 Cyriacus (invoked against demonic possession, eye disease)
Dominic (of astronomers, the Dominican Republic)
The Fourteen Holy Helpers
Hormisdas (of stableboys)

9 Emygdius (invoked against earthquakes)

10 Besse (of draft dodgers)
Lawrence (of Ceylon, cooks, librarians, the poor; invoked against fire, lumbago)

11 Alexander the Charcoal Burner (of charcoal burners)
Clare (of embroiderers, television; invoked against eye disease)

12 Porcarius

13 Cassian (of teachers)
Concordia (of nannies)
Hippolytus (of horses, prison guards)

14 Maximilian Kolbe (of drug addicts; invoked against drug addiction)
Werenfrid (of vegetable gardens; invoked against gout)

15   Arnulph of Soissons (of brewers)
     Tarsicius (of first communicants)
16   Armel (invoked against headache, gout, fever, rheumatism)
     Stephen of Hungary (of Hungary)
17   Hyacinth (of Lithuania)
     Mamas (of nurses, shepherds; invoked against colic)
     Roch (of doctors, dog lovers, cattle, prisoners; invoked against
        cholera, contagious diseases, skin diseases, plague)
18   Agapitus (invoked against colic)
     Helena (of archaeologists)
19   Sebald (invoked against freezing)
20   Bernard of Clairvaux (of bees, beekeepers, candle makers, Gibralter,
        wax melters)
21   Bernard Tolomei (of olive growers)
22   Symphorian (of children, students; invoked against syphilis)
23   Rose of Lima (of Peru, Central and South America, the Philippines,
        florists, gardeners)
24   Bartholemew (of Armenia, cheese merchants, plasterers, tanners;
        invoked against nervous tics)
     Owen of Rouen (of innkeepers; invoked against deafness)
25   Genesius (of actors, comedians, lawyers, secretaries; invoked
        against freezing, epilepsy)
     Louis of France (of button makers, marble workers, masons,
        sculptors, tertiaries, wig makers)
26   Teresa of Jesus (of old people)
27   Monica (of married women, mothers)
28   Augustine of Hippo (of brewers, printers)
     Hermes (invoked against insanity)
     Moses the Black (of black Africans)
29   Sabina (of housewives)
30   John Roche (of boatmen)
31   Raymond Nonnatus (of Catalonia, childbirth, midwives, obstetri-
        cians, pregnant women; invoked against perjury)

SEPTEMBER

1   Fiacre (of gardeners, cabdrivers; against hemorrhoids, venereal dis-
        ease)
     Giles (of beggars, nursing mothers; invoked against breast-feeding
        problems, lameness, leprosy, sterility)
     Verana (of millers)
2   Agricola of Avignon (invoked against bad luck; for/against rain)
3   Gregory the Great (of music, popes, singers, teachers, schoolchil-
        dren; invoked against plague)

4 Rose of Viterbo (of florists)
5 Laurence Gustiani (of Venice)
6 Athanasius (of fullers)
   Bega (Bee) (of laborers)
   Magnus of Füssen (of crops; invoked against caterpillars, hail, reptiles, vermin)
7 Cloud (of nail makers; invoked against carbuncles)
8 Adrian (of arms dealers, butchers, prison guards)
9 Peter Claver (of African Americans, Colombia, race relations, slaves)
10 Nicholas of Tolentino (of sick animals, mariners, holy souls, babies, mothers, the dying; invoked against fire)
   Theodard (of cattle dealers)
11 Protus and Hyacinth
12 Ailbe (of wolves)
   Guy (of horses)
13 John Chrysostom (of orators)
   Venerius (of lighthouse keepers)
14 Notburga (of peasants, servants)
15 Catherine of Genoa (of nurses)
16 Cornelius (invoked against earache, twitching, cattle disease)
   Cyprian (of Algeria, North Africa)
   Ludmila (of Czechoslovakia)
17 Lambert (of children, dentists, nannies, truss makers)
   Robert Bellarmine (of catechists)
18 Ferreolus (of sick poultry; invoked against rheumatism)
   Joseph of Cupertino (of the Air Force, astronauts, pilots)
19 Januarius (of blood banks; invoked against the evil eye)
20 Eustace (of hunters, difficult Madrid situations; invoked against family troubles)
21 Matthew (of accountants, customs officials, security guards, stock-brokers, tax collectors)
22 Maurice (of Austria, dyers, hatters, infantrymen, knife grinders, Sardinia, weavers; invoked against arthritis, cramps, gout)
   Phocas (of gardeners, sailors)
23 Cadoc (invoked against cramps, deafness, glandular disorders)
24 Gerard (of Hungary)
25 Finnbar
   Joseph Calasanctius (of Christian schools)
26 Cosmas and Damian (of barbers, druggists, chemical workers, doctors; invoked against bladder disease, blindness)
27 Elzear (of Christian gentlemen)

Vincent de Paul (of Madagascar, hospital workers, prisoners)
28   Bernardino of Feltre (of bankers, pawnbrokers)
Wenceslaus (of brewers, Bohemia, Czechoslovakia, sheep)
29   Michael (of bankers, the Basques, Brussels, Germany, grocers, Papua New Guinea, radiologists, paratroopers, policemen; invoked against peril at sea)
30   Jerome (of librarians, students)
Gregory the Enlightener (of Armenia)

OCTOBER

1   Remi (of France)
Teresa of Lisieux (of florists, foreign missions, France, pilots; against tuberculosis)
2   Guardian Angels (of police)
Leger (invoked against blindness)
3   Gerard of Brogne (invoked against jaundice, scrofula)
4   Francis Assisi (of animals, ecology, Italy, merchants, needle workers, tapestry makers; invoked against fire)
5   Placid (invoked against chills, drowning)
6   Bruno (invoked against demonic possession)
Faith of Agen (of prisoners, soldiers)
7   Justina (of Padua, Venice)
8   Demetrius (of Bulgaria, Serbia, Macedonia)
Pelagia (of actresses)
Thaïs (of fallen women)
Triduana (invoked against eye disease)
9   Andronicus (of silversmiths)
Denis (of France; invoked against headaches, frenzy)
Ghislain (invoked against twitching)
Louis Bertrand (of Colombia)
10   Francis Borgia (of Portugal; invoked against earthquakes)
Gereon (invoked against headaches)
Victor (of soldiers)
11   Gomer (of unhappy husbands, woodcutters; invoked against hernia)
James Grissinger (of glass painters)
12   Wilfrid of York
13   Colman (of Austria, cattle, hanged men, horses)
14   Callistus I
15   Andeol (of Switzerland)
Teresa of Ávila (of lace makers, Spain; invoked against headaches, heart attacks)

16   Gall (of birds, Switzerland)
      Gerard Majella (of childbirth, mothers)
      Hedwig (of Bavaria, Silesia)
      Margaret-Mary (invoked against polio)
17   John the Dwarf
18   Luke (of doctors, artists, butchers, glass-industry workers, lace makers, notaries, painters, sculptors)
19   Jesuit Martyrs (of Canada)
      René Goupil (of anesthesiologists)
      Peter of Alcántara (of Brazil, watchmen)
20   Contard Ferrini (of universities)
21   John of Bridlington (invoked against complications in childbirth)
      Ursula (of orphans, schoolgirls, tailors, teachers, universities; invoked against plague)
22   Donatus
23   John of Capistrano (of military chaplains)
24   Raphael (of health inspectors, druggists, happy meetings, leaving home, travelers; invoked against blindness)
      Anthony Claret (of weavers, savings banks)
25   Crispin and Crispinian (of shoemakers)
26   Bonaventura of Potenza (invoked against disease of the bowels)
27   Frumentius (of Ethiopia)
28   Jude (of hopeless cases)
29   Baldus (of cattle; invoked against family problems)
30   Dorothy of Montau (of Prussia)
31   Quentin (of bombardiers, locksmiths, porters, tailors; invoked against coughs, sneezes)
      Wolfgang (of carpenters, shepherds; invoked against apoplexy, gout, hemorrhage, stomach trouble, wolves)

NOVEMBER

 1   Marcel of Paris (invoked against vampires)
      Mathurin (of fools)
 2   All Souls
 3   Hubert (of hunters, mathematicians, machinists, metalworkers; invoked against dog bites, rabies)
      Pirminus (invoked against snakebite, poisoning)
      Rumbald (of fishermen)
      Martin de Porres (of hairdressers, persons of mixed race, public-health workers, race relations, television—in Peru)
 4   Americus (of America)
      Charles Borromeo (of apple orchards, catechists, seminarians, starch makers; invoked against stomachache, ulcers)

5   Elizabeth (of pregnant women)
6   Leonard (of childbirth, horses, prisoners of war; invoked against robbery)
7   Florentius (invoked against gallstones, rupture)
     Willibrord (of Holland; invoked against convulsions)
8   Four Crowned Martyrs (of stonemasons, Freemasons)
9   Benen (invoked against worms)
     Theodore the Recruit (of the military)
10   Aedh Mac Breic (invoked against headaches)
     Andrew Avellino (of Sicily; invoked against apoplexy, sudden death)
     Leo the Great (of choirs, musicians)
11   Martin of Tours (of beggars, drunkards, equestrians, harvests, horses, innkeepers, the military, new wine, tailors)
     Menas (of caravans, merchants)
12   Emillion (of Spain; to find lost objects)
     Josaphat (of Ukraine)
     Lebuin (of the dying)
13   Diego Alacalá (of cooks)
     Frances Xavier Cabrini (of hospital administrators, emigrants, immigrants)
     Homobonus (of garment workers, tailors)
     Stanislaus Kostka (of Poland, young people; invoked against broken limbs, doubt, palpitations)
14   Lawrence O'Toole (of Dublin)
15   Leopold (of Austria)
     Albert (of medical technologists, science students, scientists)
16   Gertrude the Great (of the West Indies)
     Margaret (of Scotland)
17   Elizabeth of Hungary (of bakers; invoked against plague)
     Gregory the Wonderworker (of desperate situations; against floods, earthquakes)
     Hugh of Lincoln (of sick children)
18   Odo of Cluny (of music)
19   Nerses
20   Bernward (of architects, goldsmiths, painters, sculptors)
     Edmund (invoked against plague)
21   Gelasius I
22   Cecilia (of composers, music, musicians)
23   Clement (of blacksmiths, farriers, stonecutters, tanners)
     Columban (aginst depression, floods)
24   Colman of Cloyne

25   Catherine of Alexandria (of lawyers, librarians, millers, nurses, phi-
          losophers, rope makers, secretaries, schoolgirls, spinsters, teach-
          ers, universities, wheelwrights; invoked against tongue disease)
       Mercury (of the military)
26   John Berchmans (of altar boys, teenage boys)
27   Maximus (of babies, the dying)
28   Catherine Labouré
29   Sernin
30   Andrew (of fishermen, Greece, Russia, sailors, Scotland, spinsters;
          invoked against gout, neck problems)

DECEMBER

1   Edmund Campion (of printers)
      Eloy (of coin collectors, garage and gas-station workers, horses,
          metalworkers, smiths, jewelers, jockeys, veterinarians)
2   Bibiana (invoked against hangovers)
3   Cassian of Tangier (of shorthand writers, stenographers)
      Francis Xavier (of Australia, Borneo, China, Goa, India,
          missionaries, Outer Mongolia, tourism)
4   Barbara (of architects, the artillery, fire fighters, fireworks, miners,
          sailors; invoked against lightning, fire, explosions, sudden death)
      Maruthas (of Iran)
      Osmund (invoked against paralysis, rupture)
5   Sabas
6   Emilian (of druggists)
      Nicholas (of bakers, barrel makers, bootblacks, brides, brewers,
          children, dockworkers, fishermen, Greece, pawnbrokers,
          perfumers, Russia, sailors, Sicily, spinsters, thieves, travelers)
7   Ambrose (of beekeepers, geese, orators)
8   Mary, the Immaculate Conception (of the USA)
9   Leocadia (of Toledo; invoked against plague)
10   Eulalia (of Barcelona, childbirth, sailors, travelers; invoked against
          miscarriage; for calm waters)
11   Damasus (of archaeologists)
      Gentian (of innkeepers)
12   Cury (invoked against blindness, deafness, demonic possession)
13   Josse (of harvests, ships; invoked against fire, fever, storms)
      Lucy (of glass workers, gondoliers, lamplighters; invoked against
          dysentery, eye disease, hemorrhage, throat disease)
      Odilia (of Alsace, the blind; invoked against blindness)
14   John of the Cross (of poets)
      Spiridon (of Corfu, Dalmatia)

15 Nino (of Georgia)
    Valerian (invoked against cold, exposure)
16 Adelaide
17 Lazarus (of housewives, lepers, sextons)
18 Flannan
19 William of Fenoli
20 Dominic of Silos (of shepherds, captives; invoked against insects, mad dogs)
21 Peter Canisius (of Germany)
22 Chaeremon
23 John of Kanti (of Lithuania, Poland)
    Servulus (invoked against paralysis)
    Thorlac (of Iceland)
24 Adam (of gardeners)
    Levan (of malformed children)
25 Eugenia
26 Stephen (of bricklayers, builders, horses, stonemasons)
27 John the Divine (of Turkey, writers; invoked against poison)
28 The Holy Innocents (of babies, choirboys)
29 Thomas à Becket (of the blind)
    Tropez (of children; invoked against gout)
30 Sabinus
31 Sylvester

PART III

Appendices

Name Saints

At their baptism, when they were "born again," early Christians naturally assumed new personal names—invariably the names of exemplary Saints who had gone before them. Thereafter, throughout the Middle Ages in Europe, an infant was customarily named at baptism—"christened"—after the Saint upon whose feast he or she had been born. In 1556, the Council of Trent made this traditional practice mandatory. (In France, even today, only official Saints' names are recognized by the government as legal.) And the practice spread, as missionaries to pagan Asia, Africa, and the New World invariably bestowed upon their native converts the (however incongruous) names of European Saints. (Apache chief Geronimo was named for Saint Jerome.)

After 2000 years of this, the chances are that right now, simply by virtue of your own first or "given" name (known in some times and places as your "Christian name"), you have at least one of your very own "Name Saints"—personal heavenly Patrons. (If your name is John or Mary, you have hundreds, but there are, as yet, no official Saints Ashley, Dylan, Kyle, or Whitney.)

Many but not all of the popular Name Saints listed below are profiled in our biographical section—however, each of their edifying stories may be found in such reference books as Butler's definitive four-volume *Lives of the Saints*. What's more, his or her feast day is your "Name Day," which you are encouraged to celebrate.

NAME SAINTS, FEMALE:

Alexandra, Allie—December 12
Alice, Allison—June 15
Amanda, Mandy—February 6
Aimee, Amy—September 13

Andrea—November 30
Angela—January 27
Ann, Anna, Anne, Annette—July 26

Barbara—December 4

Bess, Beth, Betsy, Betty = Elizabeth

Beverly—May 7 (the feast of John of Beverley)

Bonnie—May 29

Brittany—May 19 (the feast of Saint Ivo [Yves], Patron of Brittany)

Brenda—May 16

Caitlin, Cathy, Catherine—November 5

Carrie, Carol, Caroline, Cheryl—November 4

Christina, Christine—July 24

Clare, Claire—August 11

Connie, Constance—September 19

Crystal (Chrysa)—August 24

Daisy = Margaret

Danielle—January 3

Dawn (Alba)—June 17

Denise—December 6

Desiree—February 10

Diana, Diane, Dianna—June 9

Dora, Dorothy, Dot—February 6

Elaine, Eleanor, Eileen, Ellen = Helen

Elizabeth—November 5

Emily—June 17

Erin—February 1 (the feast of Saint Brigid, Patroness of Erin)

Frances—March 9

Grace—July 5

Gwen—June 1

Helen, Helena—August 18

Hilary—January 13

Hope—August 1

Jacqueline—July 25

Jane, Janet—December 12

Jennifer, Jenny—January 3

Jean, Joan, Jodie—May 30

Jessica, Jessie, Joanne, Joanna—May 24

Judith, Judy—June 29

Jill, Julia, Julie—May 22

Karen, Kate, Kathleen, Katy, Kathy, Kitty = Catherine

Kelly—May 1

Kristin = Christina

Laura, Lauren—October 19

Linda, Lynne—February 13

Lily, Lisa, Liz = Elizabeth

Louise—March 15

Lucy—December 13

Maggie, Margaret, Megan—June 10

Maria, Marie, Marissa, Mary, Molly—August 15

Marian, Marianne—May 26

Martha—July 29

Melanie—December 31

Melissa (Mella)—March 9

Michaela, Michelle—August 26

Nancy = Anne

Natalie—September 8

Nell (Cornella)—March 31

Nicole—December 6

Pat, Patricia—August 25

Phoebe—September 3

Priscilla—January 16

Rachel—November 23

Rebecca—September 24

Renee—September 7

Roberta, Robin—September 17

Rose, Rosie, Rosemary—August 22

Ruth—September 1

Sandra, Sandy, Sacha = Alexandra

Sally, Sara, Sarah—May 24

Sharon—September 8 (the birthday of the Blessed Virgin Mary, known as the "the Rose of Sharon")

Sophia, Sophie—August 1

Stephanie—December 26

Susan, Susanna—August 11

Terry, Tracy, Teresa—October 15

Theresa—October 1
Tiffany—January 6 (the feast of the Epiphany, of which the word "Tiffany" is a French corruption)

Tricia, Trish = Patricia
Valerie—December 9
Victoria, Vickie—November 17
Wendy—November 3
Zoe—May 2

Name Saints: Male

Aaron—July 3
Adam—December 24
Alexander—December 12
Albert—October 15
Allan—January 12
Andrew—November 30
Anthony—January 17
Arnold—July 18
Arthur—December 11
Barry—September 27
Benedict—July 11
Benjamin—March 31
Brandon, Brendan—May 16
Brian—March 22
Bruce (Brice)—November 13
Carl, Charles—November 4
Christopher—July 25
Daniel—October 10
David—March 1
Donald—July 15
Edward—October 31
Eric—May 18
Ernest—November 2
Francis, Frank—October 4
Fred, Frederick—July 18
Gary, Gerald, Gerry—October 13
Gene (Eugene)—August 23
George—April 23
Gregory—September 3
Harold—November 1
Henry—July 13
Jacob, Jake, James—July 25
Jason—July 12
Jeffrey—November 8
Jeremy—February 16

John—June 24
Joseph—March 19
Jordan—February 15
Joshua—September 1
Justin—June 1
Kenneth—October 11
Kevin—June 3
Kurt (Constantine)—July 27
Larry, Lawrence—July 21
Lewis, Louis—August 25
Luke—October 18
Mark—May 3
Martin—November 11
Matthew—September 21
Max, Maximillian—March 12
Michael—September 29
Nicholas—December 6
Oliver—July 1
Patrick—March 17
Paul—June 9
Peter—June 29
Philip—May 3
Raymond—January 7
Richard—February 7
Robert—September 17
Ronald—August 20
Sean = John
Stanislaus, Stanley—April 11
Stephen, Steven—December 26
Thomas—July 3
Timothy—January 26
Vincent—January 22
Walter—April 8
William—May 23
Zack—November 5

APPENDIX II
Patron Saints

Of Ecology
Of Ethnicity
Of Illness
Of Life-Styles and the Life Cycle
Of Occupations
Of Personal Problems
Of Recreations
Miscellaneous Patrons

OF ECOLOGY:

of Animals	Francis of Assisi
of Animals (domestic)	Anthony the Great
of Animals (sick)	Dwyn, Nicholas of Tolentino
invoked against Animals (wild)	Blaise, Vitus
of Bees	Bernard, Modomnoc
of Birds	Gall, Mildburga
of Apple Orchards	Charles Borromeo
invoked against Blight	Urban of Langres
invoked against Caterpillars	Magnus of Füssen
of Cattle	Baldus, Colman, Roch
of Cattle (sick)	Blaise, Bueno, Cornelius, Sebastian
invoked against Cold	Valerian
of Crops	Eurosia, Magnus of Füssen, Walburga
of Dogs (mad)	Sithney
invoked against Dogs (mad)	Dominic of Silos
invoked against Drought	Cathal, Elias, Geneviève, Godberta, Eulalia
invoked against Earthquakes	Albert of Trapini, Elias, Emygdius, Francis Borgia, Gregory the Wonderworker
of Ecology	Francis of Assisi
invoked against Fire (danger of)	Agatha, Barbara, Dorothy, Josse, Nicholas of Tolentino

invoked against Fire (actual)	Catherine of Siena, Florian, Francis of Assisi, Lawrence
invoked against Flies	Leufredus
invoked against Floods	Columban, Geneviève, Gregory the Wonderworker
invoked against Foxes	Harvey
invoked against Frost	Urban of Langres
of Geese	Ambrose, Martin of Tours
invoked against Hail	Magnus of Füssen
of Harvests	Ansovinus, Antony of Padua, Barnabus, Josse, Martin, Médard
of Horses	Colman, Eloy, George, Guy, Hippolytus, Leonard, Martin, Stephen
invoked against Insects	Dominic of Silos, Tychon
invoked against Lightning	Agrippina, Barbara, Dorothy, Vitus
invoked against Mice	Gertrude of Nivelles, Ulric
invoked against Moles	Ulric
of Poultry (sick)	Ferreolus
invoked against Rats	Servais
for/against Rain	Agricola, Geneviève, Gervase and Protase, Godleva, Herbert, Médard, Scholastica, Solangia, Swithin, Theodore of Sykeon
invoked against Reptiles	Magnus of Füssen
of Sheep	Wenceslaus
invoked against Snakes	Patrick
invoked against Storms	Cathal, Christopher, Eurosia, Josse, Theodore of Sykeon
invoked against Thunder	Agrippina
of Swine	Anthony the Great
invoked against Vermin	Magnus of Füssen, Servais
invoked in peril from Water	Christopher
invoked for calm Waters	Eulalia
invoked against Volcanic Eruptions	Agatha

invoked against Whirlpools	Goar
invoked against Wolves	Harvey, Peter, Wolfgang
of Wolves	Ailbe

OF ETHNICITY:

African American	Benedict the Black, Peter Claver
Africa	Moses the Black
African Youth	Charles Lwanga
Algeria	Cyprian
Alsace	Odilia
America	Americus
Armenia	Bartholemew, Gregory the Enlightener
Australia	Francis Xavier
Austria	Colman, Florian, Joseph, Maurice, Stephen, Leopold
Barcelona	Eulalia
Basque	Michael
Bavaria	Hedwig, Kilian
Belgium	Joseph
Bohemia	Cyril and Methodius, John of Nepomuk, Wenceslaus
Borneo	Francis Xavier
Brazil	Peter of Alcántara
Brittany	Ivo
Brussels	Gudula, Michael
Bulgaria	Demetrius
Canada	Anne, the Jesuit Martyrs, Joseph
Catalonia	Raymond Nonnatus
Central and South America	Rose of Lima
Ceylon	Lawrence
Chile	James
China	Francis Xavier
Colombia	Louis Bertrand, Peter Claver
Corfu	Spiridon
Corsica	Julia, Devota
Crete	Titus

Cyprus	Barnabus
Czechoslovakia	Cyril and Methodius, John of Nepomuk, Ludmila, Procopius, Wenceslaus
Dalmatia	Spiridon
Denmark	Anskar, Canute IV
Dominican Republic	Dominic
Dublin	Lawrence O'Toole
East Indies	Thomas
Egypt	Mark
England	Augustine of Canterbury, George
Ethiopia	Frumentius
Europe	Benedict, Cyril and Methodius
Finland	Henry of Uppsala, Henry the Emperor
Flanders	Godleva
France	Denis, Joan of Arc, Martin of Tours, Remi, Teresa of Lisieux
Georgia	Nino
Germany	Boniface of Mainz, Michael, Peter Canisius
Gibraltar	Bernard of Clairvaux
Glasgow	Theneva
Goa	Francis Xavier
Greece	Andrew, Paul
Guatemala	James the Greater
Gypsies	Sara
Holland	Willibrord, Wiro
Hungary	Gerard, Lazlo, Stephen of Hungary
Iceland	Anskar, Thorlac
India	Thomas
Iran (Persia)	Addai and Mari, Maruthus
Ireland	Brigid, Columba, Kevin, Patrick
Italy	Catherine of Siena, Francis of Assisi
Japan	Peter Baptist
Jersey	Helier
Jordan	John the Baptist
Latin America	Rose of Lima
Lithuania	Casimir, Cunegund, Hyacinth, John of Kanti
Luxembourg	Cunegund, Philip
Macedonia	Demetrius
Madagascar	Vincent de Paul

Malta	Agatha, Paul
Mexico	Joseph
Monaco	Devota
Moravia	Cyril and Methodius
Nicaragua	James the Greater
Nigeria	Patrick
New Zealand	Brigid
North Africa	Cyprian
Norway	Anskar, Olaf, Magnus of Orkney
Oceania	Peter Mary Chanel
The Orkneys	Serf
Outer Mongolia	Francis Xavier
Padua	Justina
Pakistan	Thomas
Pamplona	Firmin
Papua New Guinea	Michael
Paris	Geneviève
Peru	Joseph, Rose of Lima
Philippines	Pudentiana, Rose of Lima
Poland	Casimir, Florian, John of Kanti, Stanislaus, Stanislaus Kostka
Portugal	Antony of Padua, Elizabeth of Portugal, Francis Borgia, George, John de Brito, Julia, Vincent of Saragossa
Prussia	Adalbert, Boniface of Mainz, Boniface of Querfurt, Dorothy of Prussia, Judith
Quebec	John the Baptist
Romania	Nicetas
Rome	Philip Neri
Russia	Andrew, Basil the Great, Boris, Nicholas, Vladimir
Saracens	Moses
Saxons	Ludger
Sardinia	Maurice
Sicily	Andrew Avellino, Nicholas, Vitus
Scotland	Andrew, Kessog, Margaret of Scotland
Serbia	Demetrius, Sava
Seville	Justina and Rufina
Silesia	Hedwig
Slavs	Cyril and Methodius

Spain	Emillion, James the Greater, Teresa of Ávila
Switzerland	Andeol, Gall, Nicholas von Flüe
Sweden	Bridget, Eric, Sigfrid
Syria	Addai and Mari, Ephraem
Toledo	Leocadia
Turkey	John the Divine
Ukraine	Josaphat
Uruguay	James the Lesser, Philip
USA	Mary, the Immaculate Conception
Venice	Justina, Laurence Gustiani
Vietnam	Joseph
Wales	David
West Indies	Gertrude the Great
Yugoslavia	Cyril and Methodius
Persons of mixed race	Martin de Porres

OF ILLNESS:

Abortion	Catherine of Sweden
Ague	Petronilla
Alcoholism	John of God, Matthias
Angina	Swithbert
Apoplexy	Andrew Avellino, Wolfgang
Arthritis	James the Greater, Maurice
Asthma	Aldric
Bladder disease	Cosmas and Damian
Bleeding	Rita
Blindness	Odilia, Cosmas and Damian, Cury, Harvey, Leger, Raphael, Thomas, Thomas à Becket
Bowel disease	Bonaventure of Potenza
Breast disease	Agatha, Macra
Breast-feeding problems	Basilissa, Giles
Broken limbs	Stanislaus Kostka
Bruises	Amalburga
Cancer	Aldegund, James Salomonelli, Peregrine Laziosi
Carbuncles	Cloud
Childbirth	Elmo, Eulalia, Gabriel, Gerard Majella, Leonard, Margaret, Raymond Nonnatus

Childbirth complications	Ulric, John of Bridlington
Childhood illnesses	Aldegund, Hugh of Lincoln, Pharaildis
Chilblains	Basilissa
Chills	Placid
Cholera	Roch
Chorea	Vitus
Coughs	Quentin, Walburga
Colds	Maurus
Colic	Agapitus, Baldus, Elmo, Mamas
Consumption	Pantaleon
Contagious diseases	Roch
Convulsions	Willibrord
Convulsions in children	Scholastica
Cradle cap	Gwen
Cramps	Cadoc, Maurice
Deafness	Cadoc, Cury, Francis de Sales, Meriadoc, Owen of Rouen
Depression	Columban, Job
Dizziness	Avertin, Ulric
Dog bites	Gildas, Hubert, Ubald
Drug addiction	Maximilian Kolbe
Drowning	Adjutor, Placid, Romanus
Dysentery	Lucy, Matrona
Earache	Cornelius, Quirinus
Eczema	Anthony the Great
Epidemics	Godberta
Epilepsy	Dymphna, Genesius, Vitus
Ergotism	Anthony the Great
Exposure	Valerian
Eye disease	Aldegund, Alena, Alkelda, Clare, Cyriacus, Harvey, Lucy, Triduana
Faintness	Ursus of Aosta
Fever	Albert of Trapani, Aldegund, Armel, Domitian, Geneviève, George, Peter, Josse
Fly bites	Mark
Foot trouble	Peter, Servais, Victor

Freezing	Genesius, Sebald
Frenzy	Denis, Walburga
Gallstones	Albinus, Benedict, Florentius, Liborius, Wolfhard
Glandular disorders	Cadoc
Gout	Andrew, Armel, Baldus, Maurice, Quirinus, Werenfrid, Wolfgang
Gravel in the urine	Drogo
Headache	Acacius, Aedh Mac Breic, Armel, Denis, Gereon, Peter Damian, Teresa of Ávila, Molaug
Hangover	Bibiana
Heart attack	Teresa of Ávila
Heart disease	John of God
Hemorrhage	Lucy, Wolfgang
Hemorrhoids	Fiacre, Quirinus
Hernia	Cathal, Conrad, Drogo, Gomer
Hoarsness	Bernardino of Siena
Impotence	Guignolé
Infertility	Anne, Antony of Padua, Guignolé, Felicity, Rita
Insanity	Dymphna, Fillian, Hermes, Hilary of Poitiers, Molaug, Romanus
Jaundice	Albert of Trapani, Gerard of Brogne
Kidney disease	Albinus, Benedict, Ursus of Aosta
Lameness	Giles, Madern
Leprosy	Agrippina, George, Giles, Lazarus, Vincent de Paul
Lumbago	Lawrence
Lymph-gland disease	Balbina
Miscarriage	Bridget of Sweden, Eulalia
Myopia	Clarus
Neck disease	Audrey
Neck problems	Andrew
Neck stiffness	Albert of Trapani
Nervous tics	Bartholomew
Nightmares	Christopher
Palpitations	Stanislaus Kostka
Paralysis	Osmund, Servulus

Plague	Casimir, Edmund, Elizabeth of Hungary, Geneviève, Godberta, Gregory the Great, Leocadia, Roch, Sebastian, Ursula, Walburga
Poisoning	Benedict, John the Divine, Pirminus
Polio	Margaret-Mary
Rabies	Gildas, Hubert, Ubald
Rheumatism	Armel, Ferreolus, James the Greater, Lubin
Rupture	Florentius, Osmund
Sciatica	Dometius the Persian
Scrofula	Balbina, Gerard of Brogne, Marculf
Seasickness	Elmo
Skin disease	Méen, Peregrine Laziosi, Roch
Sleepwalking	Dymphna
Snakebite	Hilary of Poitiers, Patrick, Phocas of Antioch, Pirminus, Vitus
Sneezing	Quentin
Sore throat	Albinus
Stammering	Notker Balbulus
Sterility	Albert of Trapini, Casilda, Giles
Stomachache	Charles Borromeo, Elmo, Emerentiana, Lupus, Timothy, Wolfgang
Syphillis	George, Symphorian
Throat disease	Audrey, Blaise, Godeleva, Lucy
Tongue disease	Catherine of Alexandria
Toothache	Alena, Apollonia, Gudula, Médard
Tuberculosis	Teresa of Lisieux
Tumors	Rita
Twitching	Claude, Cornelius, Ghislain
Ulcers	Charles Borromeo, Job
Venereal disease	Fiacre
Wounds	Aldegund
Worms	Benen

OF LIFE-STYLES AND THE LIFE CYCLE

Newborns	Brigid, Maximus
Infants	Gwen
Babies	Holy Innocents, Maximus, Philip of Zell
Toddlers	Ava, Dogmael

Children	Bathild, Cyricus, Lambert, Nicholas, Pancras, Philip of Zell, Solangia, Symphorian, Tropez
Backward children	Hilary of Poitiers
Malformed children	Levan
Illegitimate children	John-Francis Regis
Orphans	Jerome Emiliani, Louise de Marillac, Ivo of Kermartin, Ursula
Girls	Agnes, Blandina
Boys	Aloysius Gonzaga
Schoolchildren	Gregory the Great
Schoolboys	Symphorian
Schoolgirls	Osana of Mantua, Ursula, Vincent of Saragossa
Teenage girls	Maria Goretti
Teenage boys	John Berchmans
Young people	Stanislaus Kostka
Juvenile delinquents	Dominic Savio
College students	Gabriel Possenti
Virgins	Agnes
Christian gentlemen	Elzear
Bachelors	Christopher
Spinsters	Andrew, Antony of Padua, Catherine of Alexandria, Nicholas
Lovers	Dwyn, Valentine
Drunkards	Martin of Tours, Urban of Langres
Fallen women	Afra, Margaret of Cortona, Mary Magdalene
Pregnant women	Elizabeth, Raymond Nonnatus
Brides	Dorothy, Nicholas
Newlyweds	Dorothy
Married women	Monica
Unhappy husbands	Gomer
Unhappy wives	Uncumber
Fathers	Joseph
Nursing mothers	Gwen, Martina, Tryphena
Mothers	Felicity, Monica, Nicholas of Tolentino
Troubled families	Eustace
Widows	Frances of Rome, Louise de Marillac, Paula, Priscilla

Grandmothers	Ann
Old people	Teresa of Jesus
The Homeless	Benedict Labre
The Dying	Benedict, James the Lesser, Lebuin, Maximus, Nicholas of Tolentino
Against sudden death	Aldegund, Andrew Avellino, Andrew Corsini, Barbara
For a happy death	Joseph

OF OCCUPATIONS

Accountants	Matthew
Actors	Genesius
Actresses	Pelagia
Advertising	Bernardino of Siena
Ammunition workers	Barbara
Apprentices	John Bosco
Archaeologists	Damasus, Helena
Architects	Barbara, Benet Biscop, Benedict, Thomas
Armorers	Dunstan
Arms dealers	Adrian
Art dealers	John the Divine
Artists	Benet Biscop, Bernward, Catherine of Bologna, Fra Angelico, Luke
Astronauts	Joseph of Cupertino
Astronomers	Dominic
Athletes	Sebastian
Authors	Francis de Sales
Bakers	Elizabeth of Hungary, Honoratus, Meingold, Nicholas
Bankers	Bernardino of Feltre, Michael, Meingold
Barbers	Cosmas and Damian
Barrel makers	Abdon, Nicholas, Urban of Langres
Basket makers	Anthony the Great
Beekeepers	Ambrose
Beer merchants	Amand
Beggars	Alexis, Benedict Labre, Giles, Martin of Tours
Bell makers	Agatha
Bell ringers	Agatha
Belt makers	Alexis
Blacksmiths	Clement, Dunstan, Eloy

Boatmen	Julian the Hospitaler, John Roche
Boatwrights	Peter
Bookbinders	Celestine V
Booksellers	John of God
Bootblacks	Nicholas
Brass workers	Barbara
Bridge builders	John of Nepomuk
Brewers	Amand, Arnulph of Soissons, Augustine of Hippo, Boniface of Mainz, Nicholas, Wenceslaus
Bricklayers	Stephen
Brush makers	Anthony the Great
Builders	Vincent Ferrer, Stephen, Thomas
Bus drivers	Christopher
Butchers	Adrian, Anthony the Great, Luke
Button makers	Louis of France
Cabdrivers	Fiacre
Cabinetmakers	Anne
Candle makers	Ambrose, Bernard of Clairvaux, John the Baptist
Carpenters	Eulogius of Córdova, Joseph, Thomas, Wolfgang
Cattle breeders	Mark
Cattle dealers	Theodard
Cemetery keepers	Joseph of Arimathaea
Charcoal burners	Alexander, Theobald of Provins
Cheese merchants	Bartholomew
Chemical workers	Cosmas and Damian
Circus performers	Julian the Hospitaler
Civil servants	Thomas More
Clockmakers	Peter
Cloth dyers	Lydia, Maurice
Cloth workers	Homobonus
Coachmen	Richard
Coffee house owners	Drogo
Comedians	Genesius, Vitus
Composers	Cecilia
Construction workers	Thomas
Cooks	Diego Alcalá, Lawrence, Martha
Coppersmiths	Benedict, Eulogius of Córdova, Maurus

Criminals	Dismas
Customs officials	Matthew
Cutlers	Lucy
Dairy maids	Brigid
Dancers	Vitus
Diplomats	Gabriel
Dockworkers	Nicholas
Editors	Francis de Sales, John Bosco
Embroiderers	Clare
Engineers	Ferdinand
Farmers	Isidore, George, Sidwell, Walstan
Farm workers	Benedict, Isidore
Farriers	Clement, Eloy, John the Baptist
Ferryboat men	Christopher, Julian the Hospitaler
Fire fighters	Florian
Fishermen	Andrew, Nicholas, Peter, Rumbald
Fishmongers	Magnus of Orkney
Flight attendants	Bona
Florists	Dorothy, Rose of Lima, Rose of Viterbo, Teresa of Lisieux
Foresters	John Gualbert
Fortune-tellers	Agabus
Fullers	Athanasius the Fuller
Furriers	James the Greater
Garage workers	Eloy
Garment workers	Homobonus
Geometricians	Thomas
Glovers	Mary Magdalene
Goldsmiths	Bernward, Dunstan
Glass painters	James Grissinger
Glaziers	Benet Biscop, Lucy, Luke
Gondoliers	Lucy
Governors	Ferdinand
Grave diggers	Anthony the Great
Grocers	Michael
Hairdressers	Martin de Porres, Mary Magdalene
Hardware workers	Sebastian
Hatters	James the Lesser, Maurice, Severus
Haymakers	Barnabus, Gervase and Protase
Health inspectors	Raphael

Health workers	Martin de Porres
Herdsmen	Anthony the Great
Housemaids	Zita
Housewives	Anne, Lazarus, Martha, Sabina
Innkeepers (and hotel workers)	Amand, Gentian, Julian the Hospitaler, Martin of Tours, Owen of Rouen, Theodotus
Jewelers	Agatha, Dunstan, Eloy
Jockeys	Eloy
Journalists	Francis de Sales
Judges	Ivo of Kermartin
Knife grinders	Maurice
Laborers	Bee, Isidore
Lace makers	John-Francis Regis, Luke, Sebastian
Lamplighters	Lucy
Laundresses	Hunna, Veronica
Lawyers	Catherine of Alexandria, Genesius, Ivo of Kermartin, Raymond of Peñafort, Thomas More
Lead founders	Fabian
Leather workers	John the Baptist
Librarians	Catherine of Alexandria, Jerome, Lawrence
Lighthouse keepers	Venerius
Linseed growers	Claude
Locksmiths	Dunstan, Galmier, Quentin
Machinists	Hubert
Magistrates	Ferdinand
Marble workers	Clement I, Louis of France
Maritime pilots	Nicholas
Masons	Louis of France, Reinhold, Stephen, Thomas
Mathematicians	Hubert

MEDICAL

Anesthetists	René Goupil
Blood-bank workers	Januarius
Dentists	Apollonia, Lambert
Dieticians	Martha
Doctors	Cosmas and Damian, Luke, Pantaleon, Roch
Druggists	Cosmas and Damian, Emilian, Raphael

Hospital pharmacists	Gemma Galgani
Hospital administrators	Basil the Great, Frances Xavier Cabrini
Hospital workers	Vincent de Paul
Medical technologists	Albert
Mental-health workers	Dymphna
Midwives	Raymond Nonnatus
Nurses	Agatha, Camillus of Lellis, Catherine of Genoa, John of God, Mamas
Obstetricians	Raymond Nonnatus
Optometrists	Fridolin
Psychiatrists	Christina the Astonishing
Radiologists	Michael
Truss makers	Lambert
Menservants	Adelelm
Merchants	Francis of Assisi, Menas
Messengers	Gabriel
Metalworkers	Eloy, Hubert

THE MILITARY

General	Adrian, Faith of Agen, Ignatius Loyola, Martin of Tours, Mercury, Sebastian, Theodore the Recruit
Air Force	Joseph of Cupertino
Artillery	Barbara
Chaplains	John of Capistrano
Cavalry	George
Draft dodgers	Besse
Infantry	Maurice
Naval officers	Francis of Paolo
Paratroopers	Michael
Prisoners of war	Dominic of Silos, Leonard
WACS and WAVES	Joan of Arc
Millers	Arnulf of Metz, Catherine of Alexandria, Honoratus, Meingold, Verana

Milliners	Severus
Miners	Anne, Barbara, Meingold, Piran
Musicians	Benet Biscop, Cecilia, Leo the Great, Odo of Cluny
Nail makers	Cloud
Nannies	Concordia, Lambert
Needleworkers	Francis of Assisi
Net makers	Peter
Notaries	Ivo of Kermartin, Luke, Mark
Olive growers	Bernard Tolomei
Orators	Ambrose, John Chrysostom
Pallbearers	Joseph of Arimathaea
Paper makers	John
Park keepers	John Gualbert
Pastry cooks	Macarius
Pawnbrokers	Bernardino of Feltre, Nicholas
Peddlers	Lucy
Pencil makers	Thomas Aquinas
Perfumers	Mary Magdalene, Nicholas
Philosophers	Catherine of Alexandria, Justin, Thomas Aquinas
Pilots	Joseph of Cupertino, Teresa of Lisieux
Pin makers	Sebastian
Plasterers	Bartholomew
Poets	Caedmon, Columba, David, John of the Cross
Police officers	Christopher, Guardian Angels, Michael, Sebastian
Poultry raisers	Brigid
Postal workers	Gabriel
Porters	Theobald of Alba, Quentin
Potters	Fabian, Goar, Justina and Rufina, Sebastian
Printers	Augustine of Hippo, Edmund Campion, John of God
Prison Guards	Adrian, Basildes, Hippolytus, Processus and Martinian
Prisoners	Barbara, Faith of Agen, Joseph Cafasso, Leonard, Roch, Vincent de Paul, Walter of Pontnoise
Public-Relations workers	Bernardino of Siena

Publishers	Paul
Ranchers	Isidore

RELIGIOUS

Altar boys	John Berchmans
Bishops (Latin American)	Toribio
Catechists	Robert Bellarmine, Charles Borromeo
Choirboys	Dominic Savio, The Holy Innocents
Choirs	Leo the Great
Clergy	Gabriel Possenti
Confessors	Francis de Sales
Deacons	Philip the Deacon, Stephen
First communicants	Imelda, Tarcisius
Foreign Missionaries	Francis Xavier, Teresa of Lisieux
Monks	Benedict
Nuns	Brigid, Scholastica
Parish priests	John-Baptist-Marie Vianney
Pilgrims	Benedict Labre
Popes	Gregory the Great
Seminarians	Charles Borromeo
Sextons	Lazarus
Tertiaries	Elizabeth of Hungary, Louis of France
Theologians	Augustine, Thomas Aquinas
Theologians (moral)	Alphonsus Mary de' Liguori
Road workers	John the Baptist
Roofers	Vincent of Saragossa
Rope makers	Catherine of Alexandria
Rulers	Ferdinand
Saddlers	Lucy, Wolfhard
Sailors	Andrew, Barbara, Brendan, Cuthbert, Elmo, Eulalia, Francis of Paolo, Nicholas, Peter Gonzalez, Phocas
Salespersons	Lucy
Scholars	Bede, Bridget of Sweden, Thomas Aquinas
Science students	Albert the Great

Scientists	Albert the Great
Sculptors	Bernward, Claude, Louis of France, Luke
Security guards	Matthew
Secretaries	Genesius, Cassian of Tangier, Catherine of Alexandria
Servants	Notburga, Zita
Shepherds	Bernadette, Dominic of Silos, Drogo, Mamas, Pascal Babylon, Simeon Stylites, Solangia, Wolfgang
Shoemakers	Crispin and Crispinian, Euseus, Theobald of Alba
Silversmiths	Andronicus
Singers	Gregory the Great
Slaves	Peter Claver
Stableboys	Hormisdas
Starch makers	Charles Borromeo
Soap boilers	Florian
Social workers	John-Francis Regis, Louise de Marillac
Steel workers	Eloy
Stenographers	Cassian of Tangier
Stockbrokers	Matthew
Stonecutters	Clement
Stonemasons	Four Crowned Martyrs, Reinhold
Students	Gabriel Possenti, Gregory the Great, Jerome, Thomas Aquinas
Surveyors	Thomas
Tailors	Boniface of Crediton, Homobonus, Martin of Tours, Quentin, Ursula
Tanners	Bartholomew, Clement, Simon Stock
Tapestry makers	Francis of Assisi
Tax collectors	Matthew
Teachers	Cassian of Imola, Catherine of Alexandria, Gregory the Great, John-Baptist de la Salle, Ursula
Telephone workers	Gabriel
Television workers	Clare, Gabriel
Tentmakers	Paul
Thieves	Dismas, Nicholas
Tin miners	Joseph of Arimathaea

Truck drivers	Christopher
Toy makers	Claude
Undertakers	Dismas, Joseph of Arimathaea
Vegetable gardeners	Werenfrid
Upholsterers	Paul
Veterinarians	Eloy, James the Greater
Vinegar makers	Vincent of Saragossa
Vintners	Morand, Tychon, Urban of Langres, Walter of Pontnoise, Vincent of Saragossa
Watchmen	Peter of Alcántara
Waitresses	Martha
Wax melters	Bernard of Clairvaux
Weavers	Anthony Claret, Barnabas, Benno, Onuphrius, Maurice, Paul the Hermit
Wet nurses	Agatha
Wheelwrights	Catherine of Alexandria
Woodcutters	Gomer
Wine merchants	Amand
Wool combers	Blaise
Wool workers	John the Baptist
Writers	Francis de Sales, John the Divine

OF PERSONAL PROBLEMS

invoked against Bad Luck	Agricola of Avignon, Casilda
invoked against Communism	Joseph
in Defense of Innocence	Hallvard
invoked against Demons	Agrippina, Albert of Trapani, Bruno, Cury, Cyriacus, Harvey, Processus and Martinian
in Desperate Situations	Gregory the Wonderworker, Rita
invoked against Detraction	John of Nepomuk
in Difficult Situations	Eustace
invoked against Doubt	Joseph, Stanislaus Kostka, Thomas
in Emergencies	Expiditus
invoked against the Evil Eye	Januarius

when Falsely Accused	Raymond Nonnatus
invoked against Family Troubles	Baldus, Eustace
invoked against Free-thinking	Titus
invoked against Gambling	Bernardino of Siena, Camillus de Lellis
in Hopeless Cases	Jude
when House Hunting	Joseph
when Leaving Home	Raphael
invoked against Loneliness	Rita
to find Lost Articles	Antony of Padua, Arnulf of Metz, Emillion
to find Lost Keys	Zita
invoked against Oversleeping	Vitus
in Peril at Sea	Michael
invoked against Perjury	Didier, Felix of Nola, Processus and Martinian
invoked against Procrastination	Expiditus
invoked against Quarrels	Andrew Corsini
of Reconciliations	Francis Patrizi
invoked against Robbery	Dismas, Ethelbert, Leonard
invoked against Scruples	Ignatius Loyola
of Servants Who Break Things	Benedict
invoked against Unhappy Marriage	Gengulf
invoked against Vampires	Marcel of Paris
invoked against Witchcraft	Benedict

OF RECREATIONS:

Anglers	Zeno
Archers	Sebastian

Athletes	Sebastian
Boy Scouts	George
Cat lovers	Gertrude of Nivelles
Coin collectors	Eloy
Dog lovers	Roch
Equestrians	George, Martin of Tours
Fireworks	Barbara
Gardeners	Adam, Adelard, Dorothy, Fiacre, Gertrude of Nivelles, Phocas
Girl Scouts	Agnes
Hunters	Eustace, Hubert
Leapers	Venantius
Mountain climbers	Bernard of Montjoux
Philatelists	Gabriel
Skaters	Lydwina
Skiers	Bernard of Montjoux, Christopher
Spelunkers	Benedict
Swimmers	Adjutor
Tourists	Francis Xavier
Yachtsmen	Adjutor

MISCELLANEOUS PATRONAGES

Asylums	Dymphna
Auto routes	John the Baptist
Bridges	John of Nepomuk
Caravans	Menas
Champions	Drausius
Christian schools	Joseph Calsanctius
Emigrants	Frances Xavier Cabrini
invoked against Explosions	Barbara
invoked against Famine	Conrad
Fools	Maruthin
Freemasons	Four Crowned Martyrs
Fugitives	Brigid
Hanged men	Colman
Happy meetings	Raphael
Health spas	John the Baptist

Hospitals	Camillus de Lellis, Jude
Immigrants	Frances Xavier Cabrini
Motorists	Frances of Rome
New wine	Martin of Tours
Peace	Irene
Peasants	Notburga
The Poor	Antony of Padua, Lawrence
Race relations	Martin de Porres
Refugees	Alban
Savings Banks	Anthony Claret
Seafarers	Francis of Paola
Ships	Josse
Travelers	Christopher, Eulalia, Gertrude of Nivelles, Joseph, Julian the Hospitaler, The Magi (Balthazar, etc.), Nicholas, Raphael
Universities	Contard Ferrini, Ursula
Workers	Joseph

Bibliography

Attwater, Donald. *The Penguin Dictionary of Saints*. New York: Penguin Books, 1976.

Baring-Gould, Sabine. *Lives of the Saints* (14 volumes). Edinburgh: John Grant, 1914.

Bede, The Venerable. *A History of the English Church and People*. New York: Hippocrene Books, 1985.

Bentley, James. *A Calendar of Saints*. New York: Facts on File, 1986.

Broderick, Robert C. *Catholic Encyclopedia*. New York: Nelson, 1987.

Cruz, Joan Carroll. *Relics*. Indiana: Our Sunday Visitor, 1984

Delaney, John J. *Dictionary of Saints*. New York: Doubleday, 1980.

Delehaye, H. *The Legends of the Saints*. London: Folcroft, 1907.

DeVoraigne, Jacobus. (Trans Caxton) *The Golden Legend*. London: Ayer Publishing Co., 1973.

Dooley, Kate R. *The Saints Book*. New Jersey: Paulist Press, 1981.

Drake, Maurice and Wilfred. *Saints and Their Emblems*. New York: B. Franklin, 1971.

Elliot, Alison G. *Roads to Paradise*. Hanover and London: Cambridge University Press, 1987.

The Encyclopedia of Catholic Saints (12 volumes). Pennsylvania: Dimension Books, Inc., 1966.

Farmer, David H. *The Oxford Dictionary of Saints*. New York: Oxford University Press, 1987.

Ferguson, George W. *Signs and Symbols in Christian Art*. New York: Oxford University Press, 1990.

Flanagan, Laurence. *A Chronicle of Irish Saints*. Pennsylvania: A. Sutton Publishers, 1990.

Goodwin, Malcolm. *Angels—An Endangered Species*. New York: Simon & Schuster, 1990.

Hoever, Hugo. *Lives of the Saints*. New York: Catholic Book Publishers, 1977.

James, Edwin Oliver. *Seasonal Feasts and Festivals*. New York: Oxford University Press, 1961.

Kleinz, John P. *The Who's Who of Heaven*. Maryland: Christian Classics, 1987.

McGinley, Phyllis. *Saint Watching*. New York: Crossroad, 1969.

Metford, J.C.J. *Dictionary of Christian Lore and Legend*. New York: Thames & Hudson, 1983.

O'Connell, J. B. (ed.). *The Roman Martyrology*. London: Wm. Clowes & Sons, Ltd., 1956.

Parbury, Kathleen. *Women of Grace*. Boston: Routledge, Chapman & Hall, 1985.

Pierrard, Pierre. *Larousse de Prenoms et des Saints*. Paris: French & European Press, 1966.

St. Augustine's Abbey Benedictine Monks. *The Book of Saints*. New York: Morehouse, 1966.

Stevens, Clifford. *The One Year Book of Saints*. Indiana: Our Sunday Visitor, 1989.

Tabor, Margaret E. *The Saints in Art*. Detroit: Gordon Press, 1969.

Tchou (ed.). *Dictionnaire des Saints Bretons*. Paris: French & European Press, 1979.

Thurston, H., and D. Attwater (eds.). *Butler's Lives of the Saints* (4 volumes). New York: Harper & Row, 1956.

Urlin, Ethel L.H. *Festivals, Holy Days and Saint Days*. London: Simpkin, Marshall, Hamilton, Kent & Co., 1915.

Waddell, Helen. *Beasts and Saints*. New York: Greenwood, 1934.

Walsh, Maurice (ed.). *Butler's Lives of the Patron Saints*. New York: Harper & Row, 1990.

Weinstein, D., and R. M. Bell. *Saints and Society*. Chicago: University of Chicago Press, 1982.

Weiser, Francis X. *Handbook of Christian Feasts and Customs*. New York: Harcourt, Brace & Jovanovich, 1958.

Williamson, G. A. (ed.). *Foxes Book of Martyrs*. Boston: Baker Books, 1965.

Wilson, Stephen (ed.). *Saints and Their Cults*. London: Cambridge University Press, 1986.

Woodward, Kenneth. *Making Saints*. New York: Simon & Schuster, 1990.

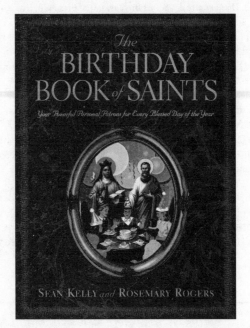